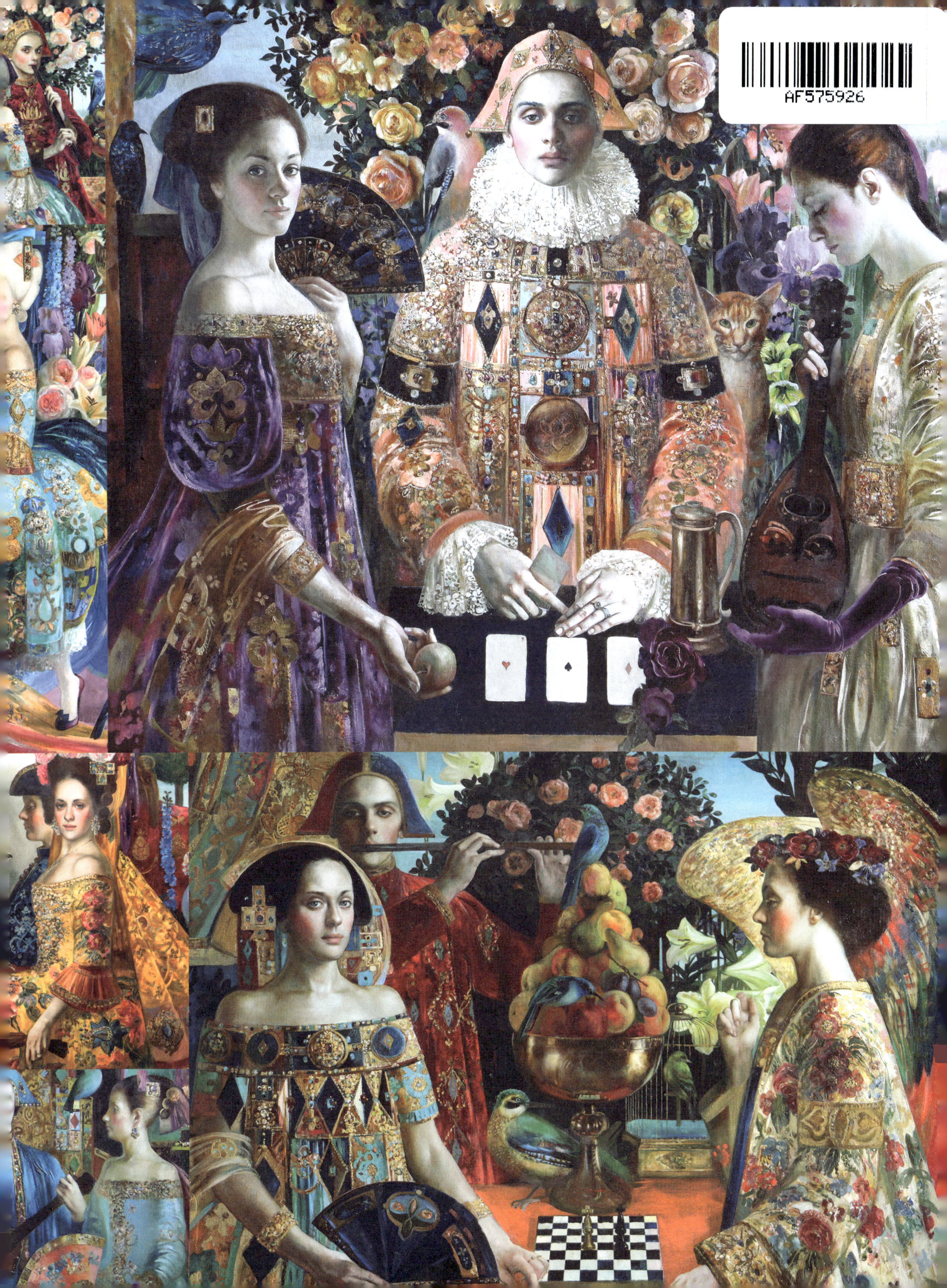
AF575926

RENAISSANCE REALM

The Art of Olga Suvorova

by Michael Fishel

Edited by Nigel Suckling

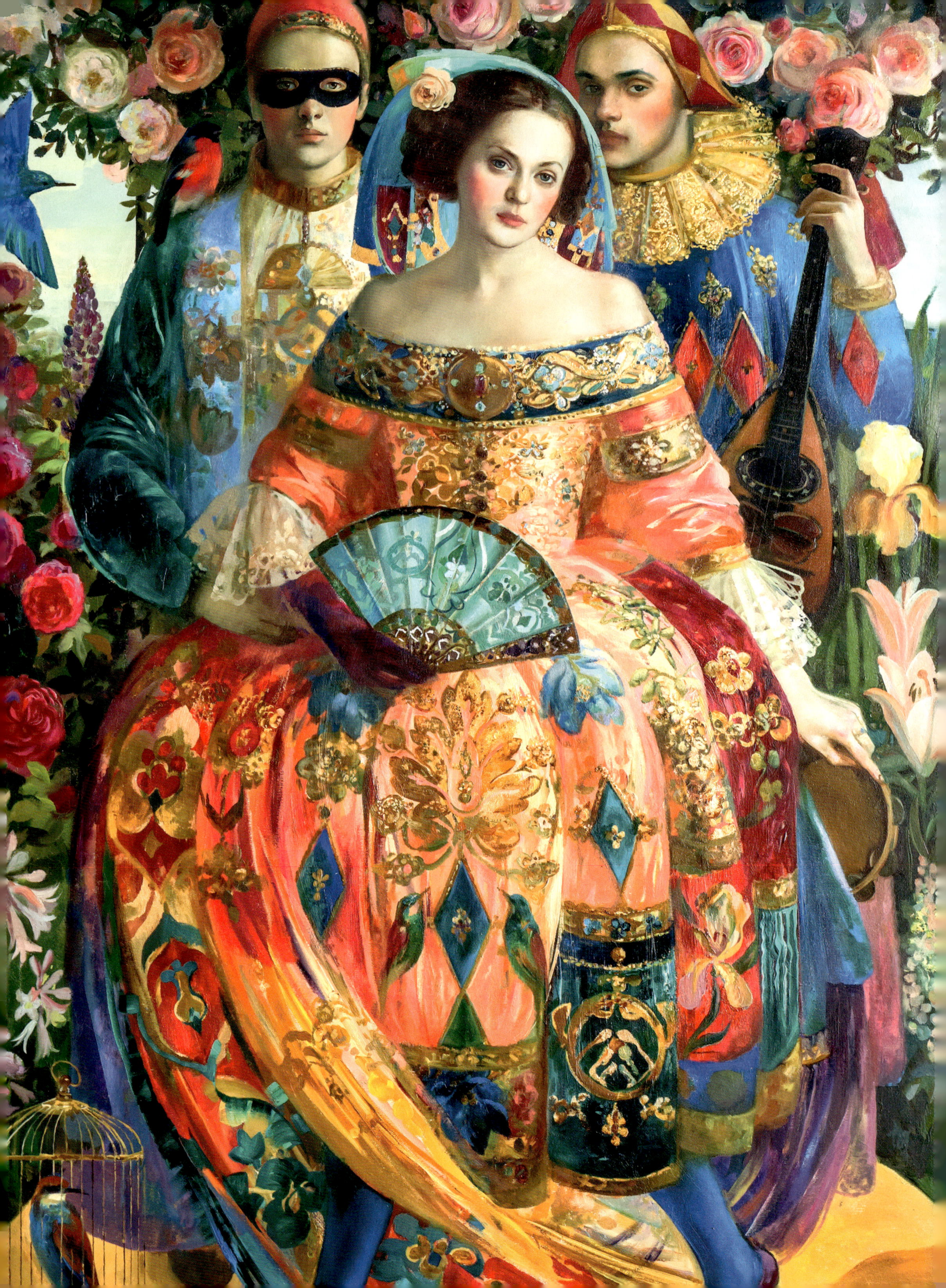

by Michael Fishel

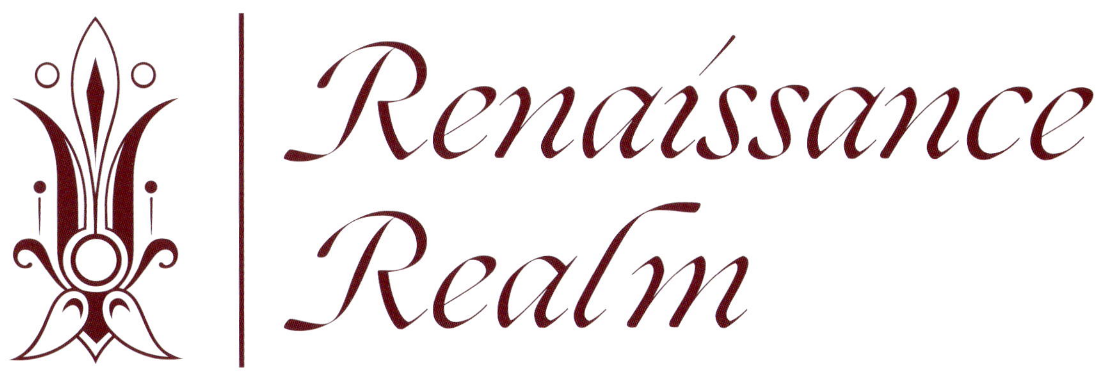

Renaissance Realm

The Art of Olga Suvorova

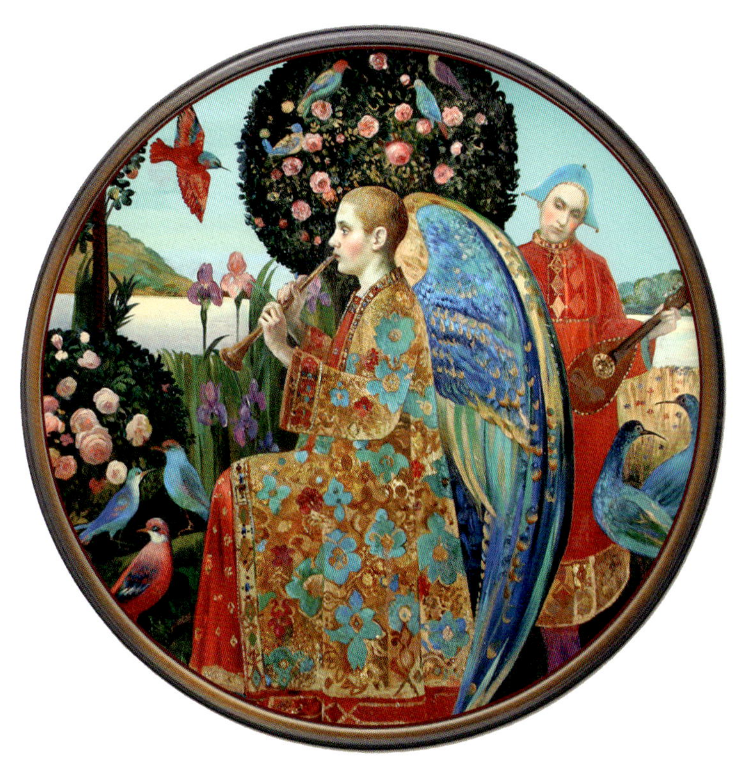

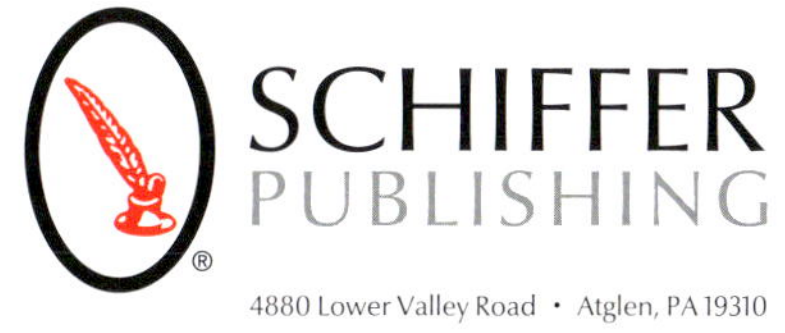

4880 Lower Valley Road • Atglen, PA 19310

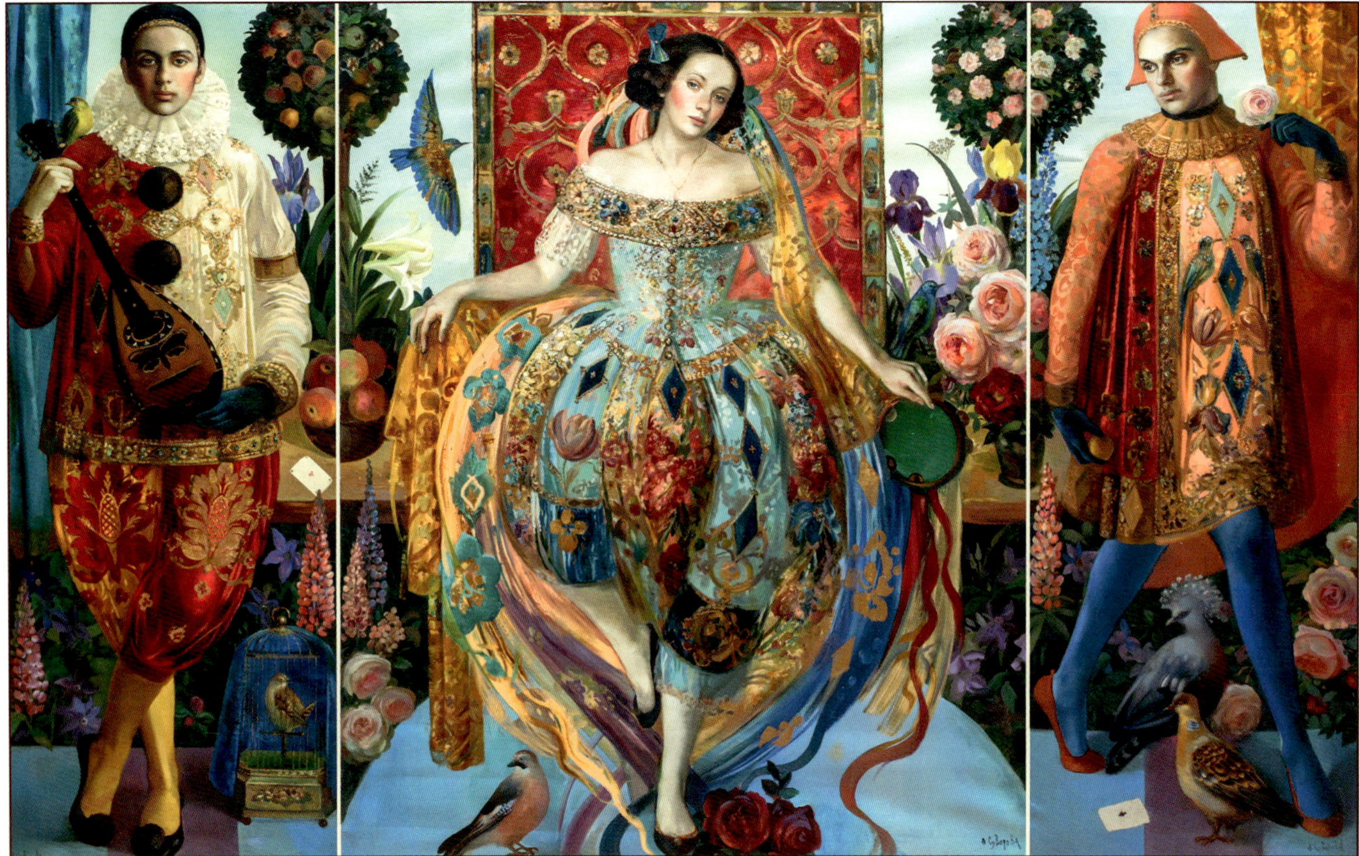

Dancer II, by Olga Suvorova, triptych, oil on canvas, 98 × 160 cm (2015)

Library of Congress Control Number: 2020930941

Edited by Nigel Suckling
Designed by Danielle D. Farmer; art by Olga Suvarova
Cover design by Ashley Millhouse; art by Olga Suvarova

Type set in Ogg TRIAL/Zen New

ISBN: 978-0-7643-6082-4
Printed in China

Published by Schiffer Publishing, Ltd.
4880 Lower Valley Road
Atglen, PA 19310
Phone: (610) 593-1777; Fax: (610) 593-2002
E-mail: Info@schifferbooks.com
Web: www.schifferbooks.com

For our complete selection of fine books on this and related subjects, please visit our website at www.schifferbooks.com. You may also write for a free catalog.

Schiffer Publishing's titles are available at special discounts for bulk purchases for sales promotions or premiums. Special editions, including personalized covers, corporate imprints, and excerpts, can be created in large quantities for special needs. For more information, contact the publisher.

We are always looking for people to write books on new and related subjects. If you have an idea for a book, please contact us at proposals@ schifferbooks.com.

Contents

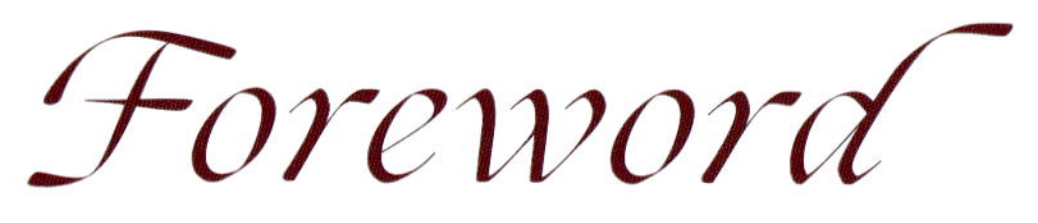

Foreword

by Alexandra Balash

Among the changing series of paintings on display in Olga Suvorova's studio, one in particular remains hanging steadfastly on the wall. It has been there for a very long time, differing in color, picturesque manner, and in its methods of modeling from other works that appear in the workshop. White and shades of dark blue, purple, and violet crumble in laces and shimmer in deceptive sequins on the costumes of the three characters depicted. Columbine—doll, actress—and her two constant companions, Harlequin and Pierrot, are images that became the myth of a retrospective St. Petersburg culture in the early twentieth century. Now they have suddenly returned, anticipating the twenty-first century in the form of new characters of artistic Bohemia. Artistry, together with the unsophistication of this composition, leave an active and direct impression on the memory. Perhaps this work has endured in Suvorova's studio because it was her first to depict this theme, which then became central in her works.

It is interesting to follow the theme's further developments, with large-scale characters in stylized, shaded gold costumes. They are almost always depicted in the foreground of the picture in a continuous, silent dialogue with each other and their viewers. The trajectories of intersecting and breaking gestures and looks create a rich extensional and meaningful structure in each work. Moreover, it is the actual trajectory—mental continuation of movements and gestures, which are restrained and do not go beyond the boundaries of personal space of the characters and their objects—that achieves this. This also concerns the looks—downcast, sweeping away, and only in exceptional cases directed toward a particular person inside the picture. At the same time, there must be one or more characters who looks directly at the viewer, reaching out and waiting for a counter-view in reply. Therefore, the viewers round out the action onto themselves—becoming its full participant, restoring broken ties, updating and enriching the meaning of the depicted event with their own personal experiences.

In search of solid and expressive solutions, this artist consistently turns to the art of the past: surfacing visual metaphors are expressive and associative, as in a poetic text. Plastic movements, the character's gestures, and, of course, their costumes—the texture of the fabric and the significant silhouette, accessories, hairstyles, and makeup—all represent the author's interpretation of the baroque style. At the same time, the appearance of the people shown—the indicative, expressive modern types of their faces, the nervousness in the their hand movements contrasting with the archaic plasticity of their clothes—inherit the creative experience of the English Pre-Raphaelite artists.

A significant event in Suvorova's art is the uprising of new characters and the associated development of the main thematic course of her works—variations and enrichment of their plastic language. For example, the image of a young girl with a floral wreath in her hair becomes the embodiment of clear, constant beauty. Of course, its root can be found in Rembrandt's Saskia as Flora and other works of the great Dutch master.

A completely new meaning in the artist's work is introduced by the later image of Mary in the Byzantine Dalmatian, surrounded by glorifying angels, which reveals a paradoxical and at the same time obvious similarity with the Mother of God of Loreto in Italy. The artist gives her own features to Mary's face, which indicates a new level of her spiritual and creative life, increasingly distinct reflections on the nature of her gift and purpose. The seriousness of such reflections is emphasized by the Byzantine style of these works, in which the paint flares up like precious jewels and gems, similar to a real mosaic.

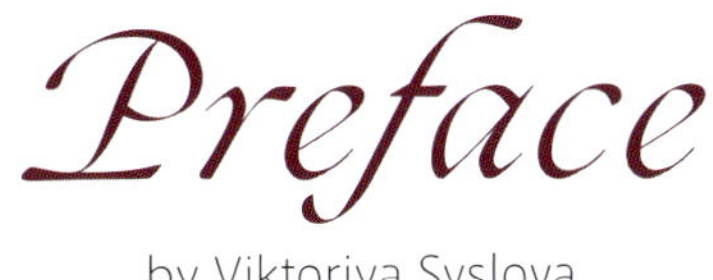

Preface

by Viktoriya Syslova

Where there is no love of art, there is no criticism. Do you want to become familiar with art? Try to love the artist, look for the beauty in his creations.

—Aleksandr Sergeyevich Pushkin, Russian poet

The twentieth century is over. At the threshold of the new millennium we are trying to understand the outgoing century in which we lived, worked, rejoiced, and were disappointed—trying to comprehend the truth. The eternal struggle between good and evil, primary and secondary, the blurring of ideas about the value of human life, the meaning of natural disasters, the denial and acquisition of God—all this is for the twenty-first century.

Perhaps in this it is not so different from other centuries, but this is our time, our joy, and our pain.

After all, the meaning and possibilities of artists can seem almost insignificant in the apocalyptic modern world, where the concepts of the beautiful and ugly are mixed, where denial, decay, and self-expression are considered advantages in art. When one analyzes all the art created by people, one notices that some works disappear quickly while others live forever and are passed on from generation to generation. It is difficult to remain faithful to the chosen path without getting deluded and lost in the intricate labyrinths of modern art, in labyrinths where true values are often replaced by imaginary ones, where one can easily lose the high purpose of art in which a person is looking for empathy for his feelings.

This is what the true artist seeks in his or her work, glorifying morality, beauty, and harmony, always trying to defeat evil.

Olga Suvorova has a bright, truly recognizable style. Once having seen these works, there is no doubt as to their creator, even to a viewer who is far from art. I admire this joyful exultation of colors. It fills your soul with vital energy and warming sun, overwhelms with variety and a rave of colors. You get a strong feeling of unbelievable surrealism and festive atmosphere from her works. Looking at the pictures, you can feel that they are filled with inner light and warmth, even if they are painted in cold, severe colors. Bright ultramarine is associated with the legendary bluebird of happiness. Ocher, with home comfort. That golden glow of decor, with thoroughness and fidelity.

The pictures are not only beautiful, but also remind us of both the cheerful carnival of the Renaissance and its philosophical mood. At the same time, the story lines of the paintings are amazingly modern in their exquisite theatricality. Despite the characters' extravagant costumes, the angel or bird wings some of them have, the often-detached, thoughtful faces, they still seem to live among us in their parallel world, and this talented artist allows us to see them. The figures are unexpectedly dynamic in their static poses. They dance, play cards or musical instruments, flirt, or are lost in their reveries. They are recognizable, and when you notice their familiar images in this artist's new paintings, it seems as if you are meeting good old friends.

In addition to people, animals are also often present. They are absolutely real—mysterious cats with their languid grace, reliable and faithful dogs, ravishing birds and, of

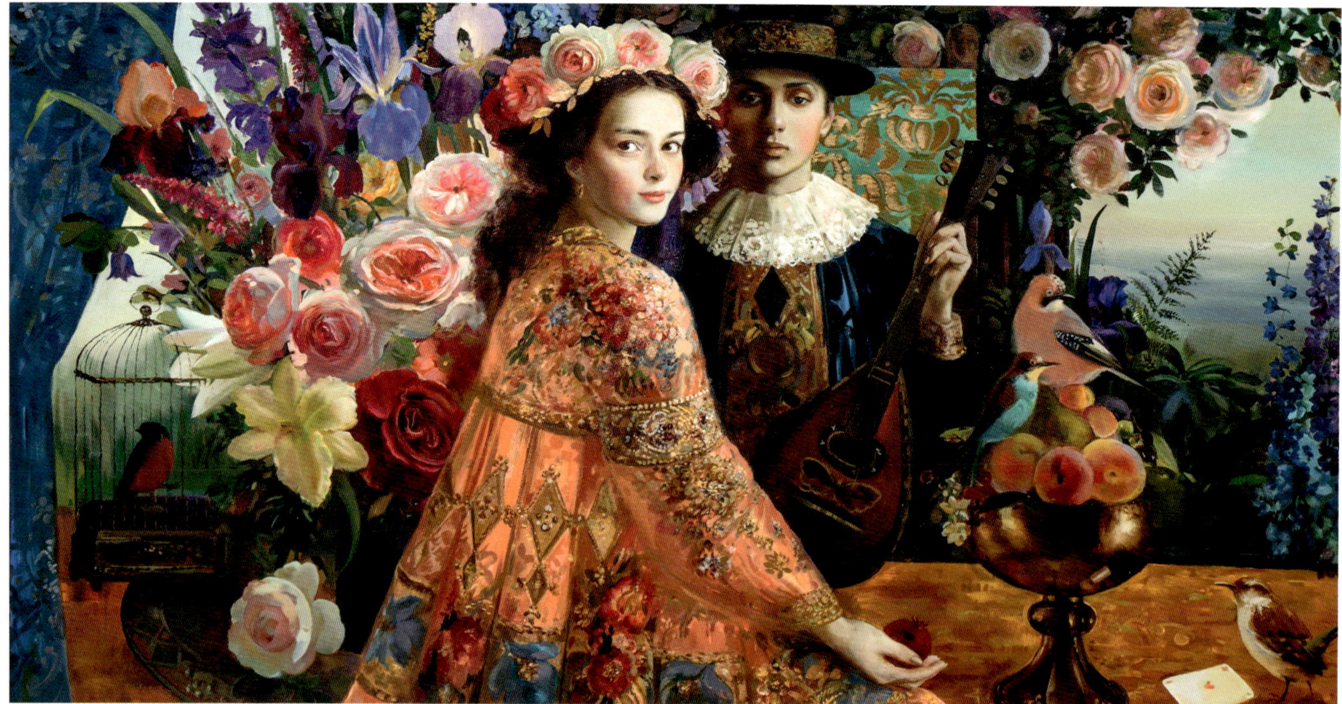

Music VI, by Olga Suvorova, oil on canvas, 70 × 120 cm (2018)

course, the most beautiful flowers: peonies, roses, lilies and many, many others. A revel of life, light, colors, and the energy of the sun overwhelms in a wonderland filled with the heroes of Suvorova's pictures! A special surprise is the fact that such beauty is born on the shores of the harsh Neva River, in a city with a serious lack of sunlight, where cold rains occur too often and a low, pearl-gray sky dominates the beautiful scenery. Perhaps that is the reason why we have the desire to admire these works over and over again. They warm the cockles of the heart.

You may like or not like these paintings, but they can never go unnoticed.

There is a parable about an angel: A man asked his angel, "Why, when I feel good, are there two sets of footprints in the sand—mine and yours? And when I feel bad, you leave me and there's only one set of footprints in the sand?" And the angel responded: "When you were sick, I carried you in my arms."

Introduction

by Michael Fishel

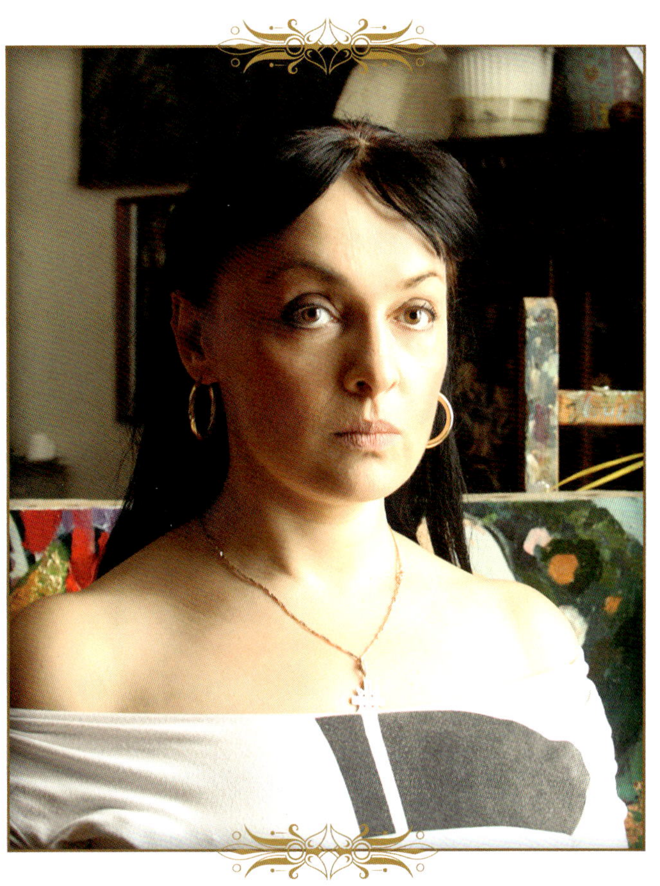

Olga Suvorova, photo courtesy of Olga Suvorova (2002)

Olga Suvorova was born in St. Petersburg, Russia, in 1966. She studied monumental composition at the famous St. Petersburg Academy of Fine Arts. Her career has been greatly influenced by her parents, both highly praised artists in St. Petersburg.

In 1989 Suvarova graduated from the I. E. Repin's Institute for Painting, Sculpture and Architecture (Mylnikov's studio) at the St. Petersburg Art Academy in Russia and was awarded with a gold medal. In 1993 she was honored with a first prize from Russian president Boris Yeltsin from a competition among more than 3,000 artists.

It is for her stirring portraits that Olga first gained her reputation in Russia and then abroad. These paintings have a startling vitality. Filled with warmth and harmony, the paintings inspire a like kindness and compassion in Olga's viewers. In her paintings, Suvarova sometimes uses silk fabrics for costume details. She exhibits often in Paris and London, and has also had shows in Italy, Germany, Sweden, Finland, France, Britain, Ireland, China, and the US. Her work is highly regarded and acquired by galleries and serious art collectors around the globe.

Following is Suvarova's story in her own words.

Childhood

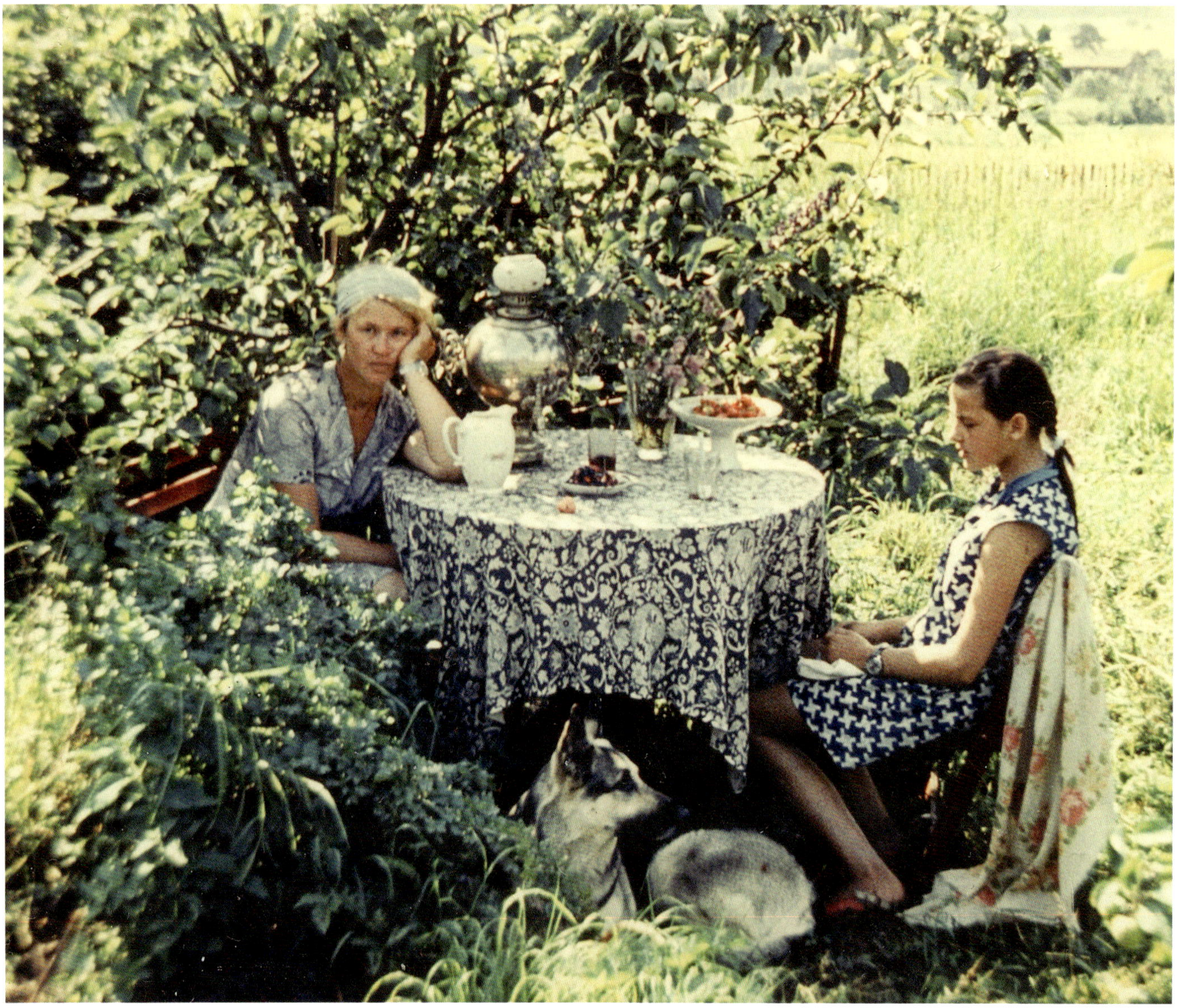

Suvorova and mother, Natalia Suvorova, photo courtesy of Olga Suvorova (1978)

I was born in Leningrad in 1966, now known by its historical name, St. Petersburg. The city was founded in 1703 by Tsar Peter I and the site was not well chosen—it was almost a swamp. Despite this, it is one of the most beautiful cities in the world and is called the Northern Venice because of the abundance of bridges and canals. Unfortunately, the climate here is harsh, with long winters and short summers. Situated in the latitude of Alaska and Greenland, there are polar nights that last from May 12 to July 31 in which darkness never falls. During this time you lose sleep and want to walk around the city instead, looking at the bridges being split for the ships to pass. I love my city and its royal architecture, despite the ever-rainy weather and frequent flooding. The bridges, more than 800 of them, are individual and each is a masterpiece.

One could write entire books about the cultural life of St. Petersburg. No wonder it is called the cultural capital of Russia. St. Petersburg used to be the political capital of Russia too, but after the Revolution of 1917, the new Soviet government moved the capital to Moscow. However, St. Petersburg has a special creative atmosphere. All sorts of arts have flourished here, from the time of Peter the Great to the present day. Such famous authors and musicians as Alexander Pushkin, Fyodor Dostoevsky, Lev Tolstoy, Pyotr Tchaikovsky, Mikhail Glinka, and Rimsky-Korsakov, and artists Il'ya Vefimovich Repin, Viktor Vasnetsov, and Mikhail Vrubel lived and worked in my city. It is impossible to list them all.

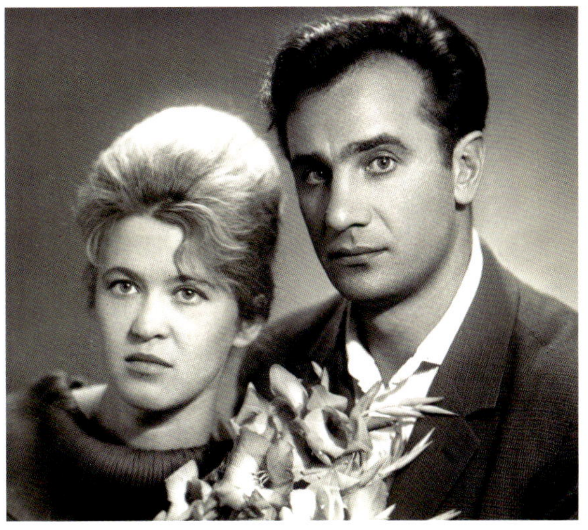

Suvorova's parents, Igor and Natalia Suvorova, photo courtesy of Olga Suvorova (1965)

St. Petersburg's main characteristic is that it is open to new ideas. As such, it is richly diverse, with opposing styles and trends coexisting in enviable harmony—from traditional classics to cutting-edge art. Generally, Petersburg to Russia is as London is to the world—the "trendiest" city. Here you can meet people who write strange music and complex and sad poems, who give avant-garde performances, who design amazing clothes, and who organize unusual and paradoxical performances, and it all becomes a cult.

The city's founder, Tsar Peter I, was a cruel ruler but played a big role in the formation of the National Art School. The city needed its own architects, sculptors, and painters to decorate palaces and build beautiful houses. From that came a project to create an academy of three notable arts, which eventually became the true center of artistic life in Russia. I was to study at that academy, but let us not run ahead.

I was lucky to be born into a creative family; my parents were professional artists. My father, Igor Suvorova, is an Honored Artist of Russia. He works in the cityscape genre. Many of his paintings are devoted to the lost monuments of architecture—churches destroyed during the Soviet period. Another creative theme became his landscapes, dedicated to Northern Karelia. His work is housed in the State Russian Museum, St. Petersburg. My mother works

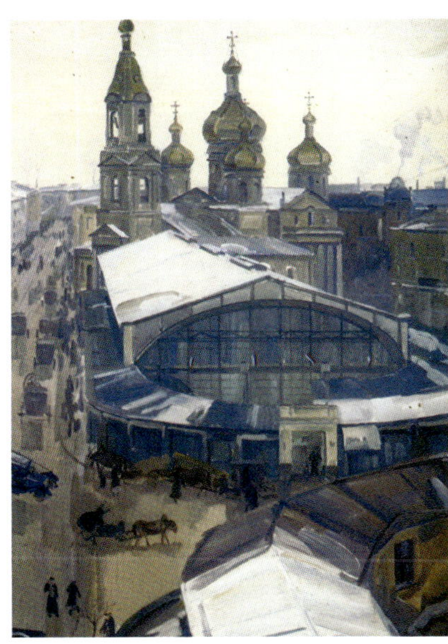

Church of the Assumption of the Blessed Virgin Mary, by Olga Suvorova, oil on canvas, 103 × 127 cm (1987)

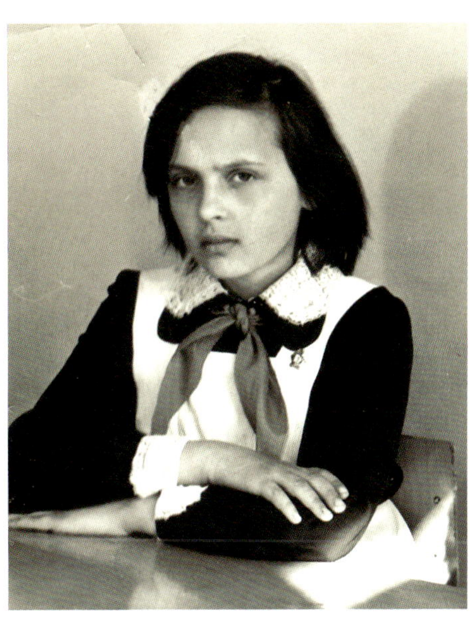

Suvorova at grade school, photo courtesy of Olga Suvorova (1976)

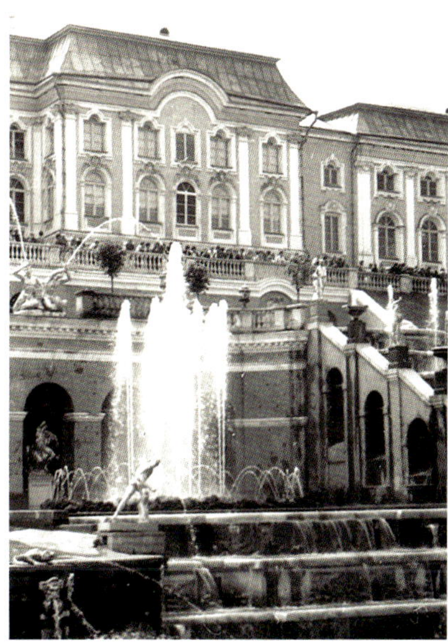

Leningrad, USSR, photographer unknown (1966)

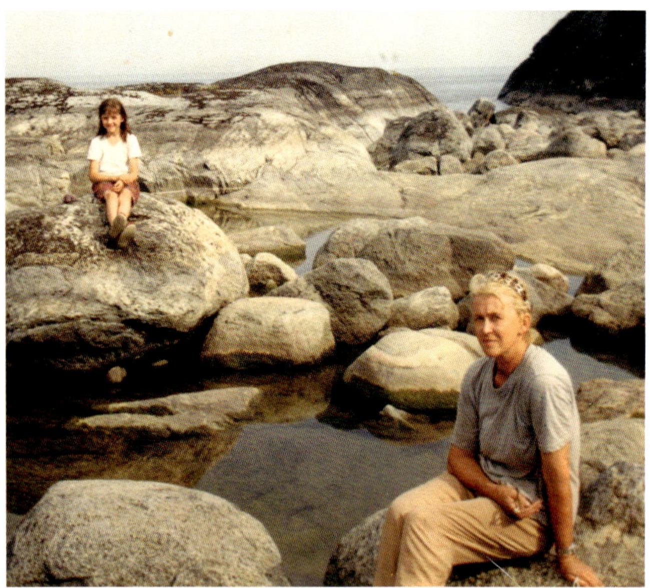

Suvorova and mother Natalia at Ladoga, photo courtesy of Olga Suvorova (1998)

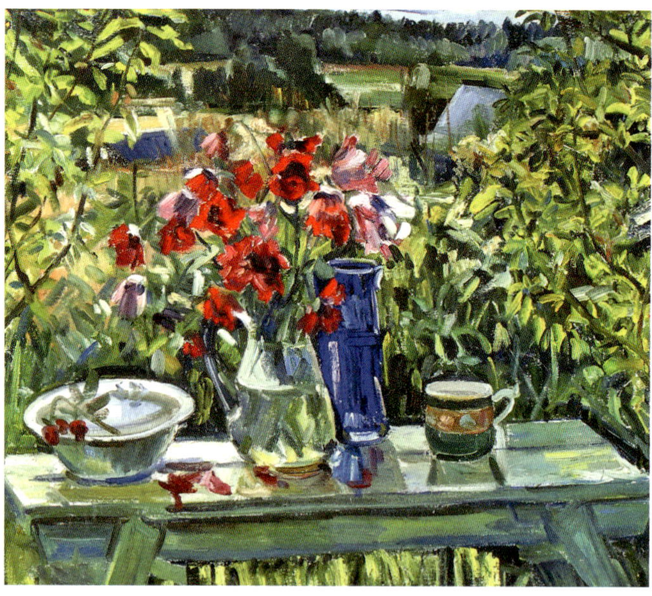

Summer Day, by Olga Suvorova, oil on canvas, 93 × 100 cm (1998)

in the genre of still life paintings. Her many colorful and decorative paintings are the exact opposite of my father's. I always wondered: how could the two masters live more than half a century together? In fact, the answer is simple—people find in each other their strengths and weaknesses and together they form a whole. It is rare in the creative world. They went through the Leningrad blockade during World War II, which lasted 900 days, without losing their optimism. To this day they have kept the desire to create, to make masterpieces with their own hands. Bright flowers, fruits, and samovars are remembered for a long time. It is a special joy to look at my mother's still lifes in winter, when there are severe frosts outside the window and everything is white.

My grandfathers and great-grandfathers worked far from the creative professions and carried the Temnomerov surname. Several generations were engaged in religious activities and were theologians, archpriests, and leaders of the Russian Orthodox Church. After the 1917 revolution, the family broke up. Some emigrated to the United States and France; some were shot. I am in search of their descendants, but unfortunately this surname no longer exists in Russia.

From early childhood, as far as I can remember, I spent all my time in my parents' workshop, because my mother could not afford a nanny. I enjoyed watching my mother drawing fruit. After a picture was finished, I was allowed to eat something from the luxurious still life. To keep me from bothering my parents, I was usually given a roll of wallpaper. Turning to the reverse, I drew pictures from children's fairy tales. Tubes of paint, brushes, colored paper, and many props kept me entertained. I was especially interested in the objects that still lifes were made from—a large number of different Russian samovars and all kinds of colored glass vases. Blue glass in particular looks beautiful in the sun—the shadows and highlights it casts on the the table are amazing. I wanted to try using oil paint, but my parents did not allow it, explaining that I was too little; but the truth is, it was a big problem to wash paint off a child!

From the age of six I traveled on my own to a children's art class. Sometimes I did not want to go, preferring to be with my friends, riding bicycles and playing for hours in the yard. In these cases, my mother explained to me: "When you grow up and become an artist, you will not need to wake up early in the morning and go to work." It worked every time. I was too young to understand that sometimes it's better to go to work every day and get a guaranteed salary once a month, than to paint pictures in a workshop that are not always successful and cannot find a buyer. This is the so-called throes of art, when you can rework a picture several times in one day to achieve a desirable result.

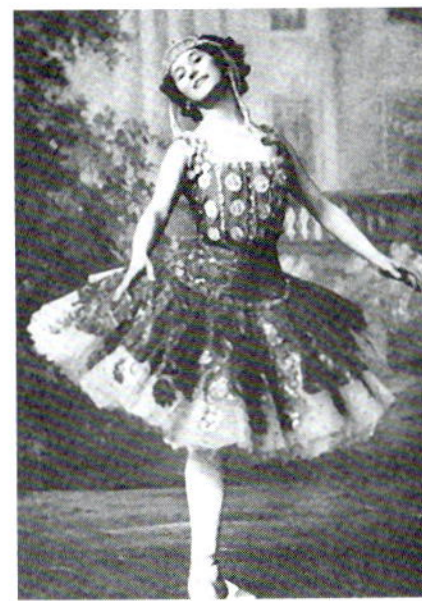

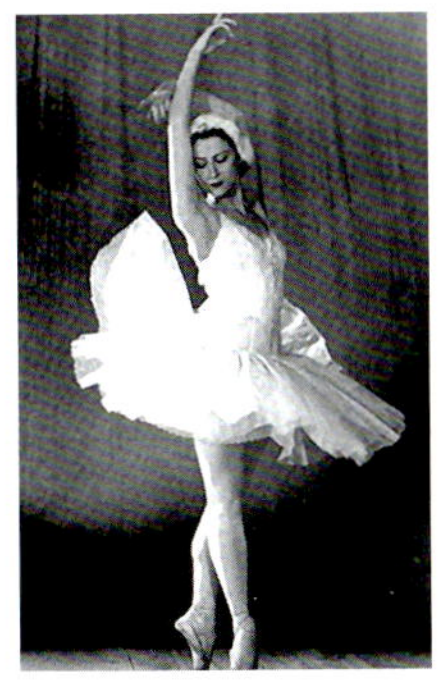

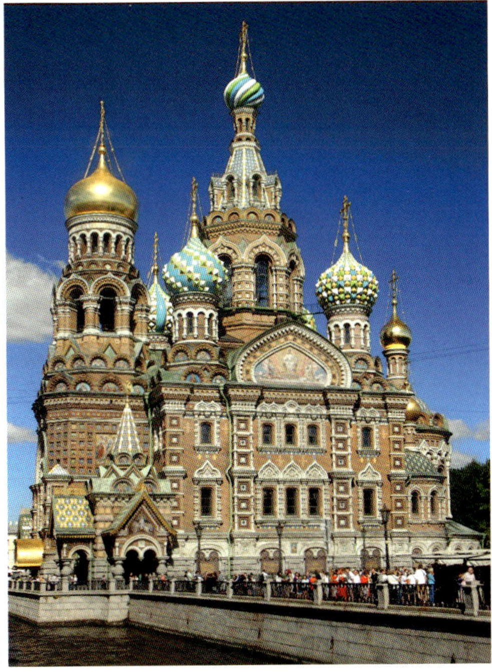

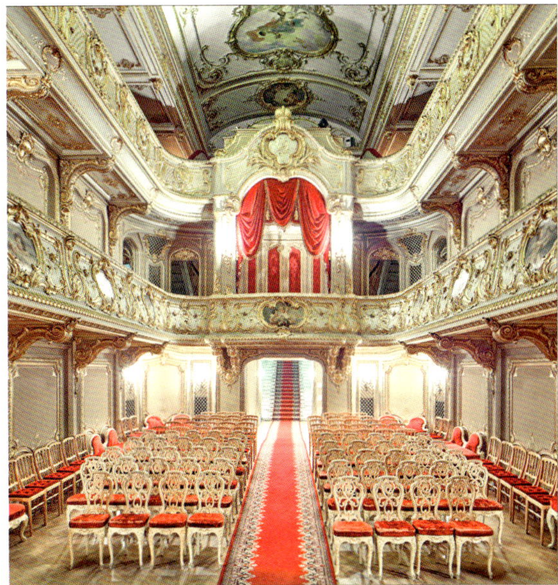

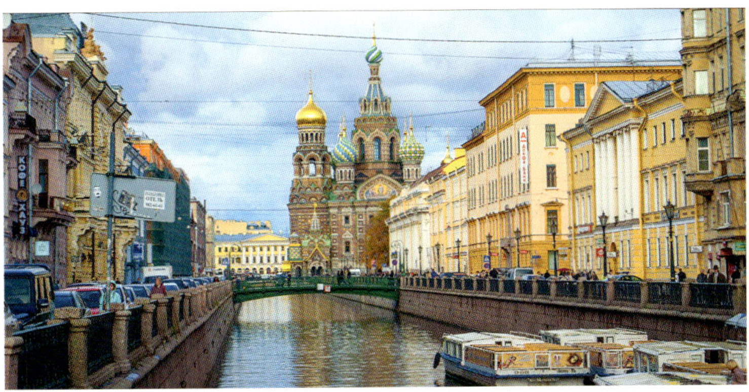

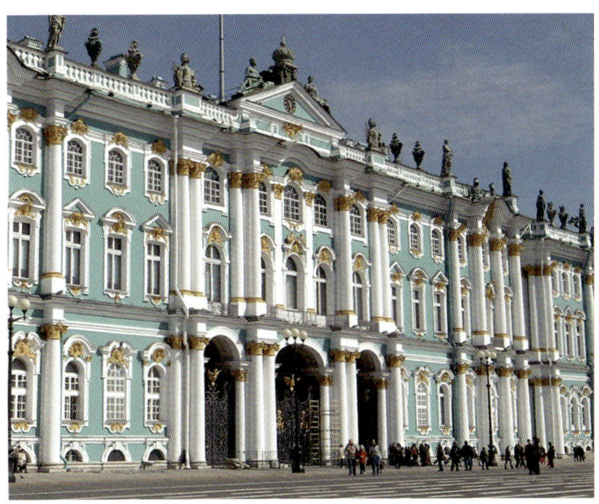

Time passed quickly, and I went to study at a secondary art school at the Academy of Fine Arts, where I entered the painting department. The school also had sculpture, graphics, and architecture classes. Here it was possible to combine art and science. Our school had well-equipped drawing classes, where plaster casts of antique heads, hands, feet, skulls, and human skeletons stood on glass shelves. Large manuals hung on the walls to teach the basics of drawing, and instead of school desks, there were easels. My school day consisted of eight lessons. In the morning I had three lessons of drawing or painting, then composition, and after that physics or mathematics. Unfortunately, I did not take to mathematics as I was not interested in the algebraic formulae.

Also, I could not understand why a future artist might need mathematics and physics. I can change a light bulb without knowing

Russian Ballerina I, date and photographer unknown

Russian Ballerina II, date and photographer unknown

Church of the Savior on Blood, St. Petersburg, Russia, photographer unknown

Yusopf Theatre, St. Petersburg, Russia, photographer unknown

View of a canal, St. Petersburg, Russia, photographer unknown

State Hermitage Museum, St. Petersburg, Russia, photographer unknown

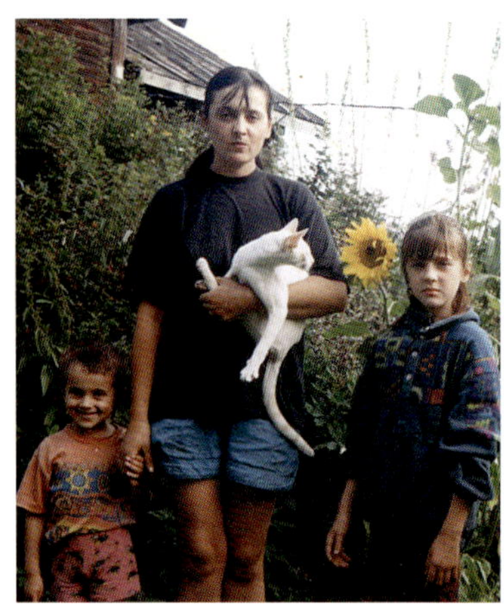

Suvorova and her children in the country, photo courtesy Olga Suvorova (1997)

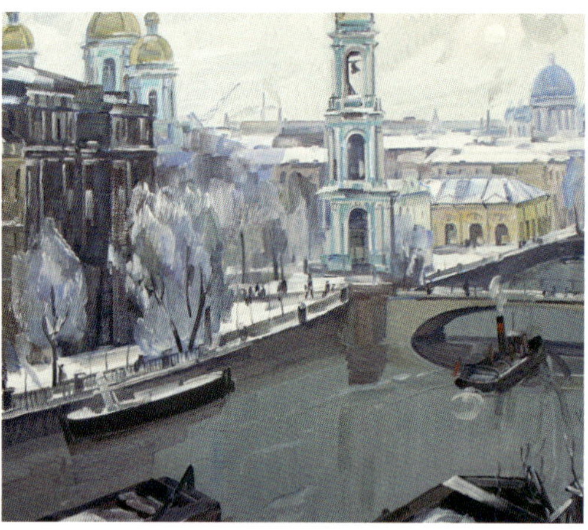

Krukov Channel (detail), by Olga Suvorova, oil on canvas, 87 × 117 cm (2010)

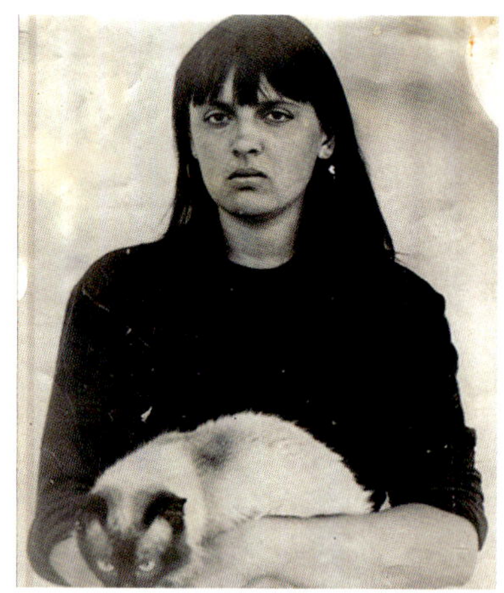

Suvorova and her cat, photo courtesy Olga Suvorova (1990)

physics. It felt a waste of time to study something I would not need in the future. Much more interesting for me were painting lessons, where my first teacher, G. Rysina, taught us interesting things. For example, if you look at a red square for a long time, at the edges of red your eyes will see a green color appearing; that happens because red causes green. A woman needs a perfect complexion to wear a bright-red dress, otherwise her face will have a greenish tint. Blue causes a yellow tint, and if you want to look tanned, you need to wear a blue blouse. These principles are often used by stylists. She also taught us that you could see the weak points of your work if you take a black glass and catch the reflection of your painting in it. It helps in parsing the tonal difference.

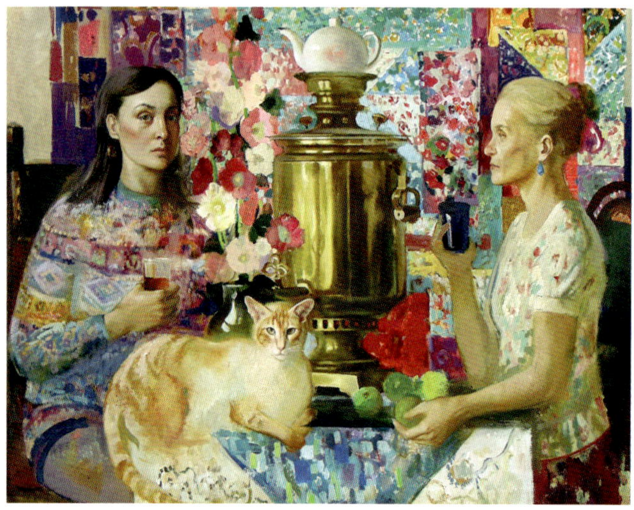

Tea Party, by Ekaterina Bogomolova, oil on canvas, 90 × 70 cm (2012)

Composition lessons were especially interesting. Composition is the most difficult part of painting: how to arrange the figures and where the light sources come from, as well as the laws of perspective, not to mention the color scheme. It is far more difficult than any mathematical problem. Our teacher often said, "You can teach even a monkey to draw in pencil, but not everyone can beautifully blend the colors." We were also taught to draw pictures on a given topic—this is another rule for a professional artist. Some time passed before I realized that neither parents nor teachers can teach art. It is impossible, and if it were easy, there would be a lot more brilliant artists, musicians, and writers. Nobody knows where geniuses come from; there are very few of them.

In junior school we worked only with colors that can be diluted with water. Drawings were made in pencil, we were not allowed to use red chalk or charcoal. I used to soak the eraser in kerosene—the so-called "white spirit" effect. This made it soft and doubled its size, so it was easier to erase unsuccessful drawings. We were often given antique sculptures to draw—for example, the plaster head of Homer. We had to draw in pencil and it seemed boring, but we could not do without it because on the next step we had a live model posing for us. Anatomy was an obligatory discipline; we were taught how to draw human bones and studied the names of all parts of the skeleton.

Finally, in high school, I began to paint in oil. After watercolor, where if something did not work out it was difficult to correct the mistake, oil painting seemed much simpler —if it did not work out, you could just repaint it. But that was

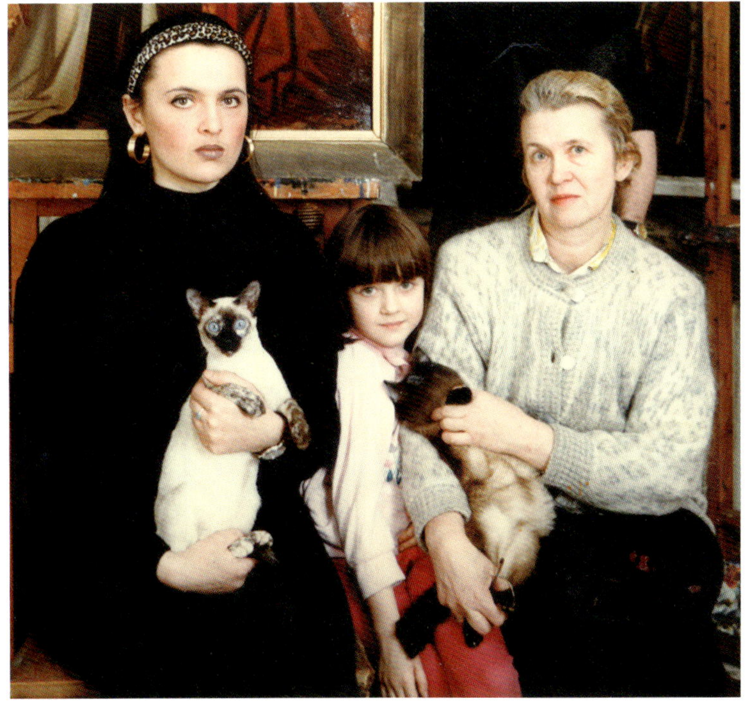

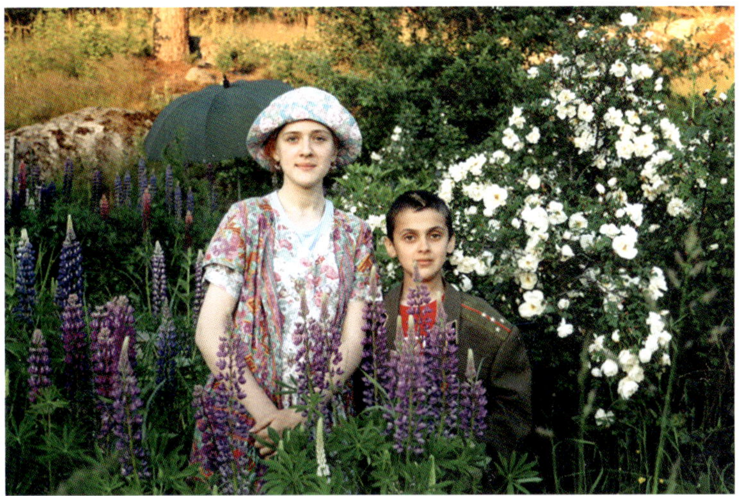

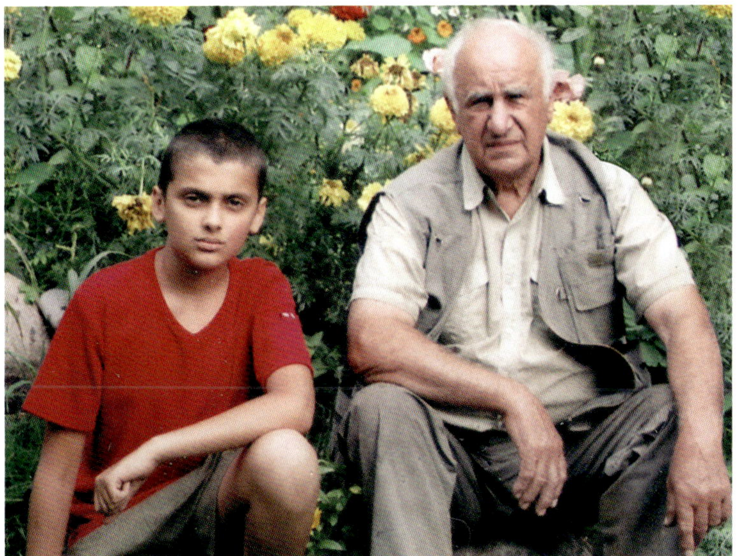

only the first impression. It turned out that oil had many technical subtleties of its own. Later on, at the university, we heard lectures on painting technology, where we were taught ways to mix paints and what varnishes to use. A lot of time was spent on preparing the canvas. You need to stretch the linen fabric, dilute special glue and glue the fabric, then prime it with a special primer, and only then tighten the canvas onto the frame. Of course, you can buy a finished canvas in the art store, but the quality will be much poorer. It was a time-consuming process, but it taught me to be attentive to the future picture.

During preparation of the canvas I often thought that the great artists, such as Michelangelo and Leonardo, always had students or apprentices to rub colorful pigments, prepare canvases, wash brushes, clean the palette of colors, and do all the hard chores. But we modern creators have to do everything ourselves. Therefore, I thoroughly plot the picture, doing preparatory sketches and choosing colors. I cannot afford to leave the picture unpainted. Even if something goes wrong, I will rework the painting many times until the result suits me. Any picture needs to be finished, because otherwise it is a useless waste of time, canvas, and paints. Sometimes, teachers asked us to copy from a great master's work. I chose Albrecht Dürer—he has magnificent drawings and engravings. Copying helps you to draw better; it trains the hand so your strokes become more accurate and professional.

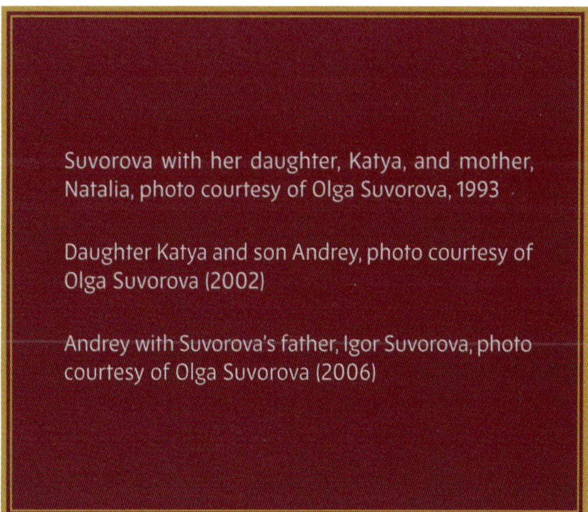

Suvorova with her daughter, Katya, and mother, Natalia, photo courtesy of Olga Suvorova, 1993

Daughter Katya and son Andrey, photo courtesy of Olga Suvorova (2002)

Andrey with Suvorova's father, Igor Suvorova, photo courtesy of Olga Suvorova (2006)

The first time I went on field practice with the art school it was to Revda city in the Ural region, more than 2,000 km (1,242 miles) from St. Petersburg. We traveled by train for two and a half days, but the long train trip with guitar songs was entertaining and time passed quickly. Fifteen years old, I felt independent for the first time and understood that practice should be done on a 100% basis. Once we arrived at the city, we stopped at a local school. The next day, my friend and I went sketching. We were in a small Ural village with old huts scattered over the hills, and it felt like we were in the nineteenth century. Time had stopped here, although it was the 1980s. People lived their own way of life. For the first time I came across the Old Believers. These people are wary and unfriendly to visitors, but I treated them with respect. They live by the old rules and follow ancient traditions. They have strong family values and many are farmers. They do not drink or smoke, and they keep religious fasts.

Once, when my friend and I were painting a landscape, she lit a cigarette and one of the local Old Believers came up, snatched the cigarette out of her hands, and ground it out on her chin. I was shocked. After that, we worked in groups; it was safer, as we understood that our visit aroused great interest among the locals. It was understandable, since there is no entertainment in the small village and life is monotonous. Everyone knows each other, and here came artists from St. Petersburg. We felt like clowns in a circus, as locals followed our every step. After drawing landscapes, we were taken to a steel rolling plant for more sketching. For the first time I saw huge factory workshops where workers smelted metal. The temperature in the workshop was like that in a sauna, about 60 degrees C (140 degrees F). The workers were constantly using the drinking-water machines. I do not know

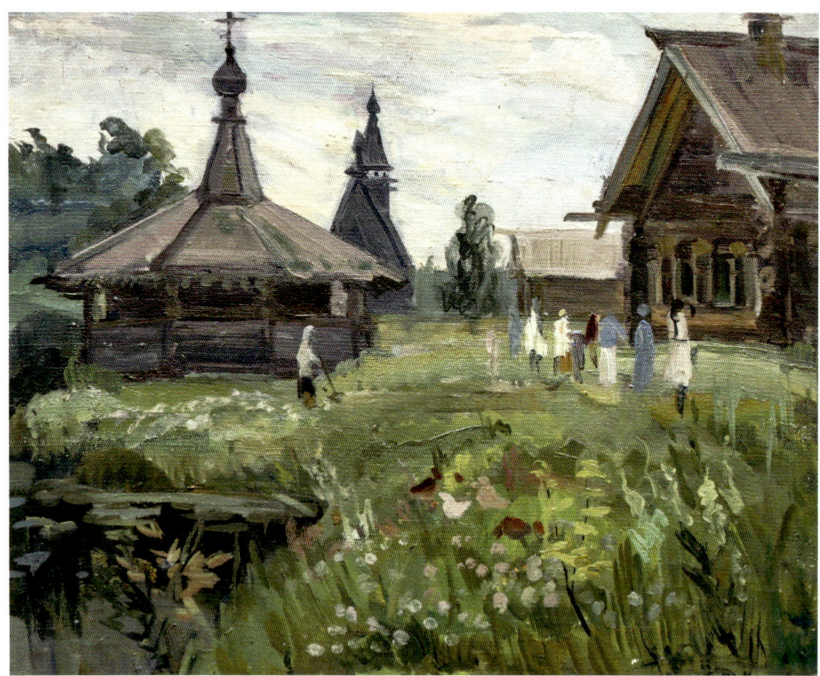

Kostroma, by Olga Suvorova, oil on canvas, 40 × 50 cm (1982)

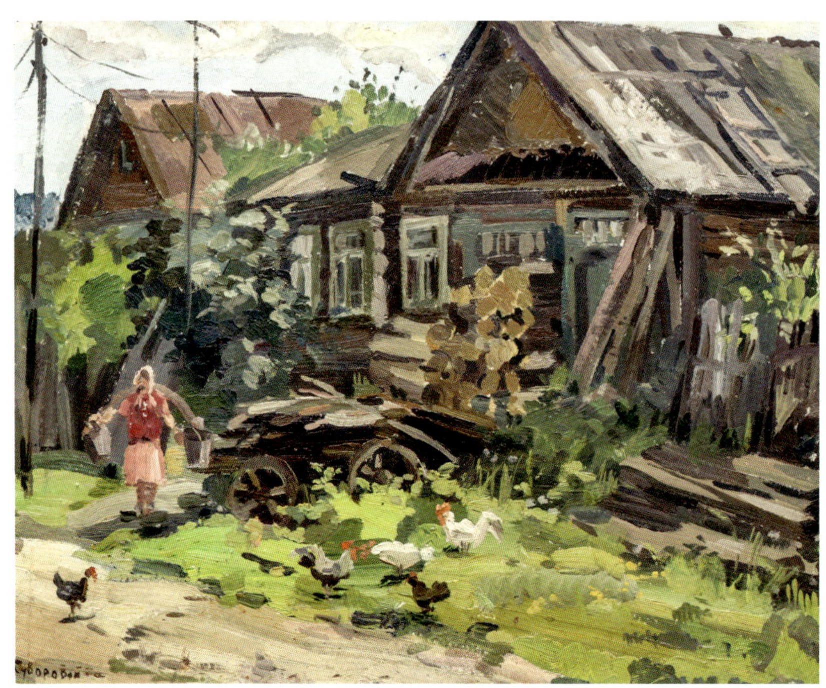

Ural, by Olga Suvorova, oil on cardboard, 40 × 50 cm (1981)

how people work in such hard physical conditions in such heat. Probably it is a habit and you need to be very healthy. Only half an hour later I was sweating, and my eyes were tired from looking at the hot metal. It reminded me of a volcanic eruption, except that you didn't have to run and hide. I drew only one small sketch; I could not do more.

It was beautiful outside on the street—nature, the Ural Mountains, the Chusovaya River. There was a temple on the riverbank, and worship was in progress. I quietly walked over and looked in the open window, from which came the sounds of chanting. I was struck by the voices. The singers were ordinary old women, but the sound was so clear and the notes were so high that I had shivers running up and down my spine. I had the feeling of time travel, as if I'd been transported from the 1980s to a century earlier. The day before we had visited a modern factory, and suddenly I was listening to religious chanting.

The study practice passed quickly and I arrived home, my parents meeting me at the station. My work now seemed childish, timid, and boring. My father used to say, "Study and complete all tasks, and the quantity will change to quality, and you will find your own unique style." The next school year flew by. We began preparing for admission to the competitive Academy of Arts. Everyone knew that a limited number of students would be admitted, most of them well-trained, thirty-year-old adults with great experience. They came from different parts of the Soviet Union and did not want to go back home empty-handed.

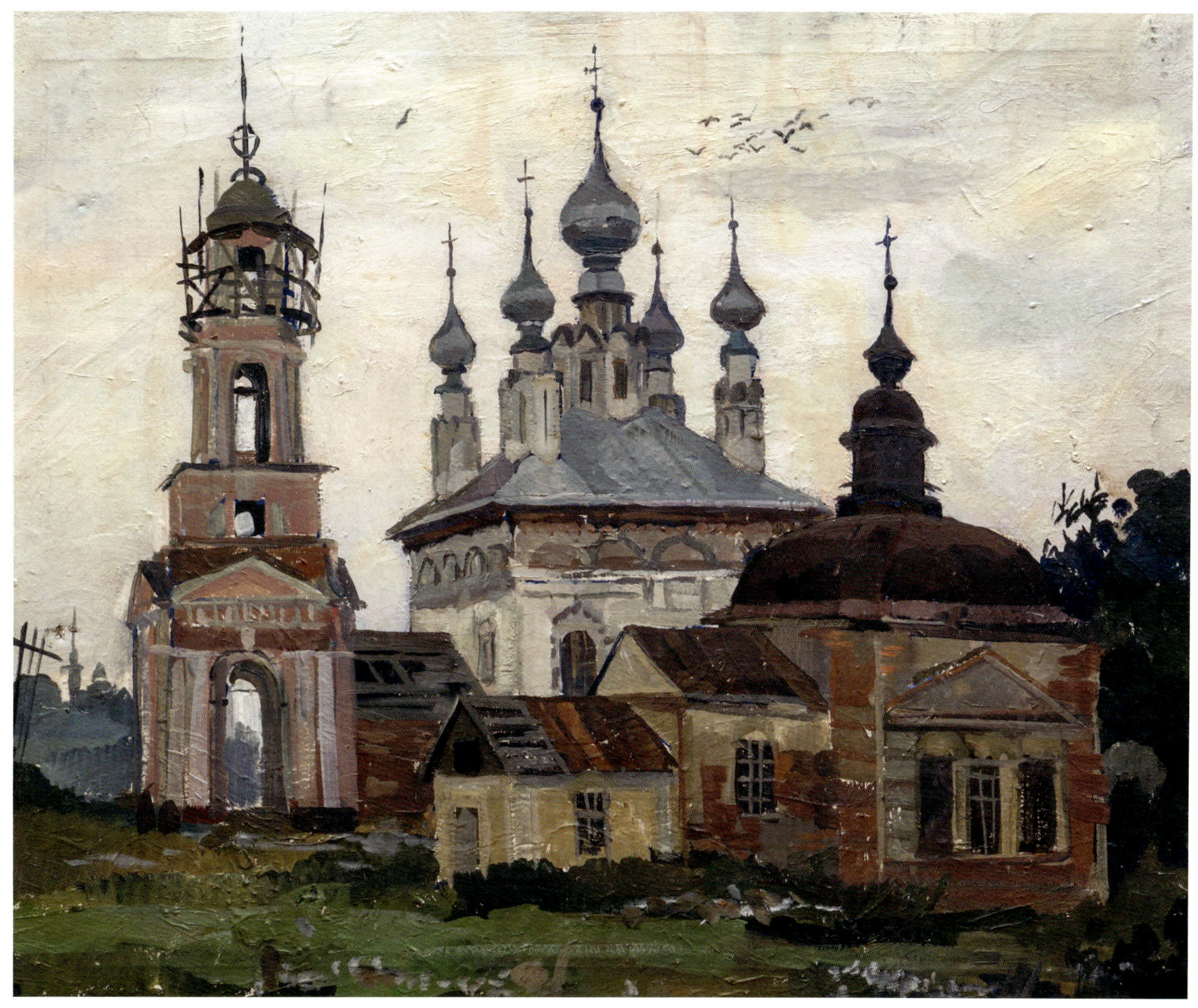

Church on the Volga, by Olga Suvorova, oil on canvas, 50 × 60 cm (1982)

But I am running ahead. Meanwhile, I had field practice again, and this time we traveled along the so-called Golden Ring of Russia to the city of Kostroma. Many artists dreamed of going there. Kostroma is on the great Russian Volga River in the center of European Russia. Many of its houses are decorated with wooden carvings and there are churches and monasteries. All this inspired us, and we wanted to get to work immediately. Many Russians artists have also visited Ples, near Kostroma on the Volga River. Russian landscape painter Isaac Levitan lived and worked in Ples; so did the brilliant Russian singer Fedor Shalyapin, who bought a country house there. These small towns on the Volga River had a creative atmosphere, and I wanted to draw every church. The local population is diverse. We came across nomadic women in their colorful skirts and wanted to capture all this on paints and canvas. Unfortunately, we had not brought enough art materials, so first the white paint came to an end, and then the canvases. I had to go to the hardware store and buy white paint made for painting window frames. Of course, it was awkward to work with.

Once, as I stood painting an ancient, half-ruined church, a stooped grandmother in a headscarf approached and asked me to draw a portrait of her late husband. She gave me an old, faded photo in which a man's face could barely

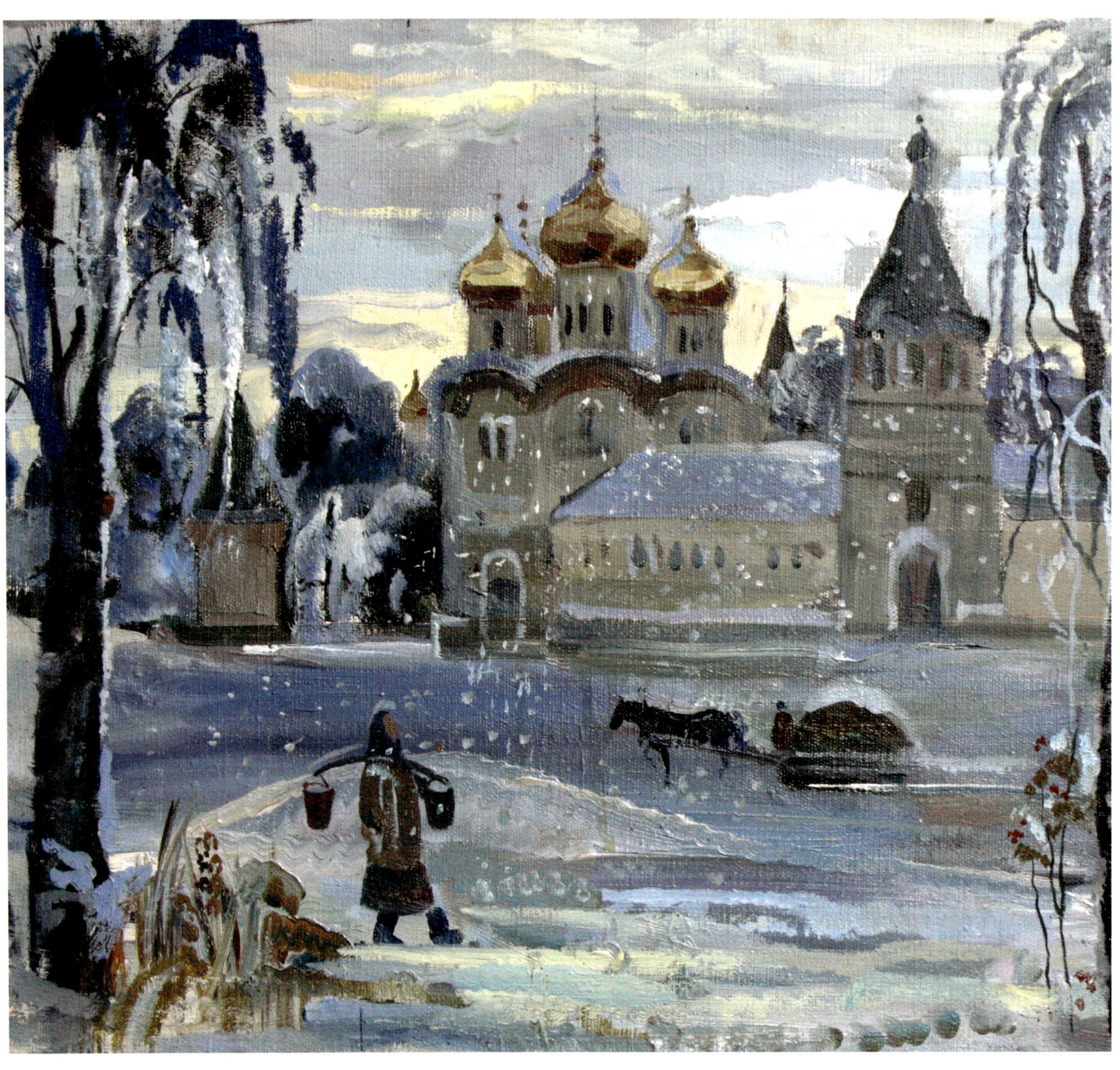

Kostroma Winter, by Olga Suvorova, oil on canvas, 40 × 60 cm (1983)

My father used to say, "Study and complete all tasks, and the quantity will change to quality, and you will find your own unique style."

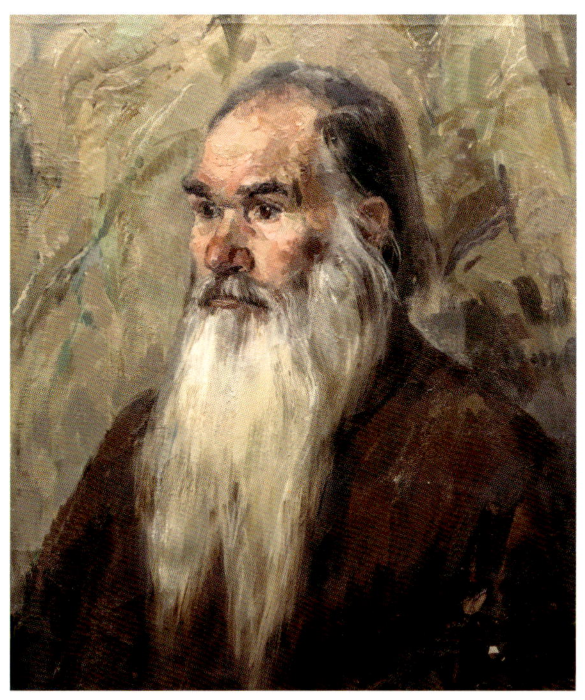

be seen. For several days I worked on this portrait, and in the end the goal was achieved. It turned out to be a good picture. Grandma was pleased and wanted to thank me. She brought me to her house and opened a huge chest with wrought iron handles. She pulled out a white lace tablecloth; it was over a hundred years old, she said, and was heavy and beautiful. I thanked the granny for such a precious gift. This tablecloth still attracts great attention. My mother uses it in her still lifes as a prop.

Portrait of a Sitter, by Olga Suvorova, oil on canvas, 60 × 50 cm (1985)

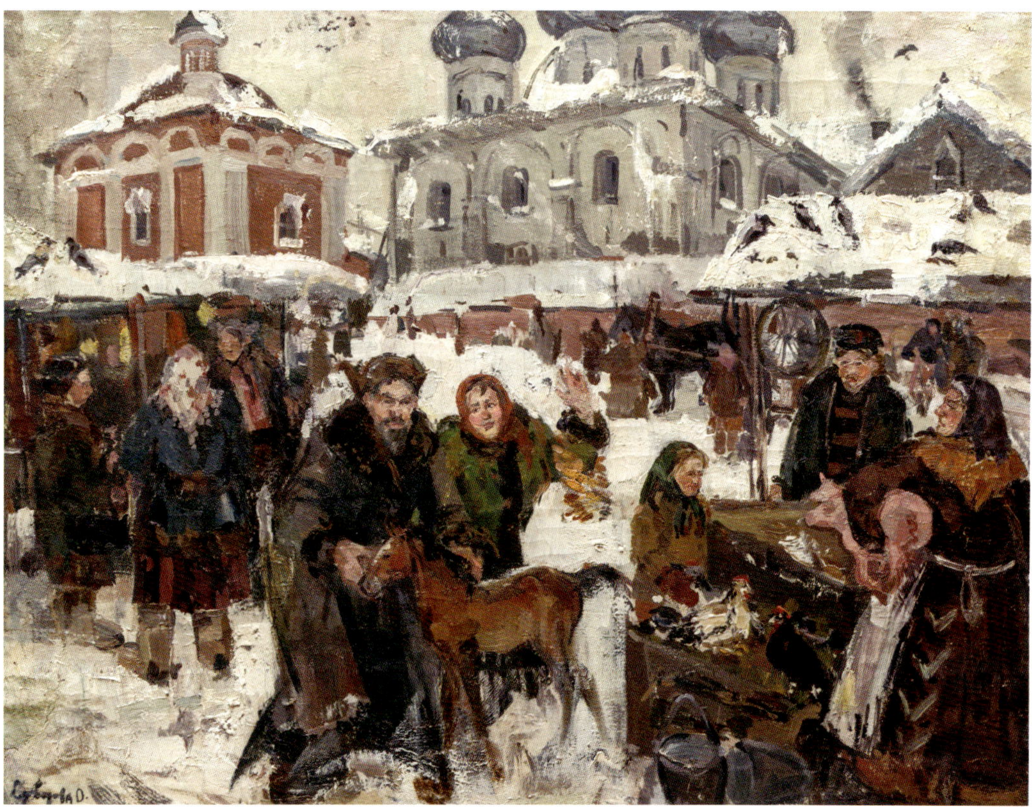

Bazaar, by Olga Suvorova, oil on canvas, 100 × 110 cm (1984)

Student Years

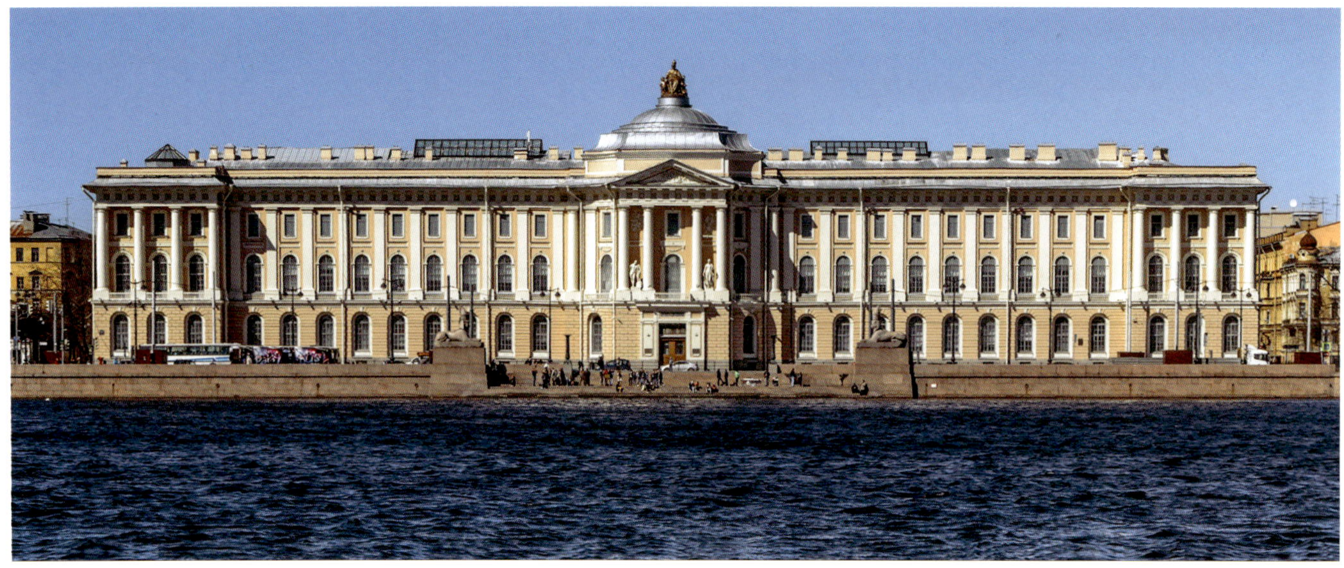

Academy of Art, St. Petersburg, Russia, photographer unknown

After graduation, I took exams at the Academy of Arts. Students came from all parts of the Soviet Union, some of them trying for the seventh or eighth time. The exams had standard assignments: head drawing, painting, naked model, oil portrait painting, and composition on a given topic.

I did not get lucky with the nude model, as I drew a seat on the side of the catwalk, where the model could not be clearly seen. In addition, she was extremely tanned. Artists who have painted nude models are well aware that it's hard to capture a tanned body. It is too yellow, and therefore hard to convey the beauty and shades of the human skin. I was terribly nervous and afraid that the time allotted would not be enough. The work turned out badly, but I entered it anyway. Many students could not deal with the stress, left their work unfinished, and left the exam. That seemed silly to me, because you need to keep things together and not give up, go all the way to your goal. By leaving, you give way to others.

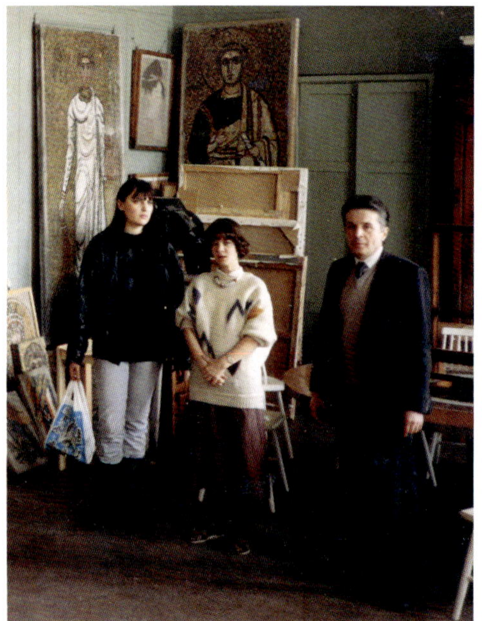

Suvorova at the Academy of Art workshop, photo courtesy of Olga Suvorova (1987).

The academy had many different faculties and departments, and I entered the department of painting. I was the youngest in the group, and the only female. The team was international, and each classmate brought variety to our student life. My companions consisted of adults who had finished school long ago. Many had families and small children. They studied and worked after school. In fact, there is some benefit in having people of different ages, religions, and professional backgrounds in the same group to learn from each other. At first it was difficult, as I was not good at drawing, but I tried hard and went to the academic library to copy drawings of old masters.

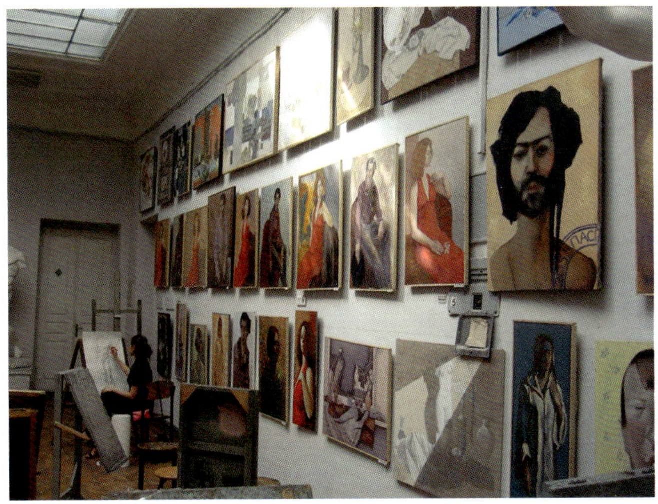

Academy of Art studio, St. Petersburg, Russia, photographer unknown

After the second course we had another field practice, and this time went to the Crimea, to the city of Alupka. Famous Yalta is nearby; so is the small city of Gurzuf, where Anton Chekhov lived and worked. I didn't enjoy the southern climate of Crimea, as I prefer the frigid climate of northern Russia. Crimea is beautiful in its own way, but the crowds of tourists were a hindrance. We had to climb high into the mountains with our sketchbooks and heavy wooden boxes filled with paints, which was difficult in the heat. But once you get up there, you see a magnificent, panoramic view of a boundless blue sea and fabulous mountains, and you stand there, not knowing what landscape to choose for the study. There was a beautiful view in any direction. There were no people there, and only the occasional hang glider interrupted the idyllic scene.

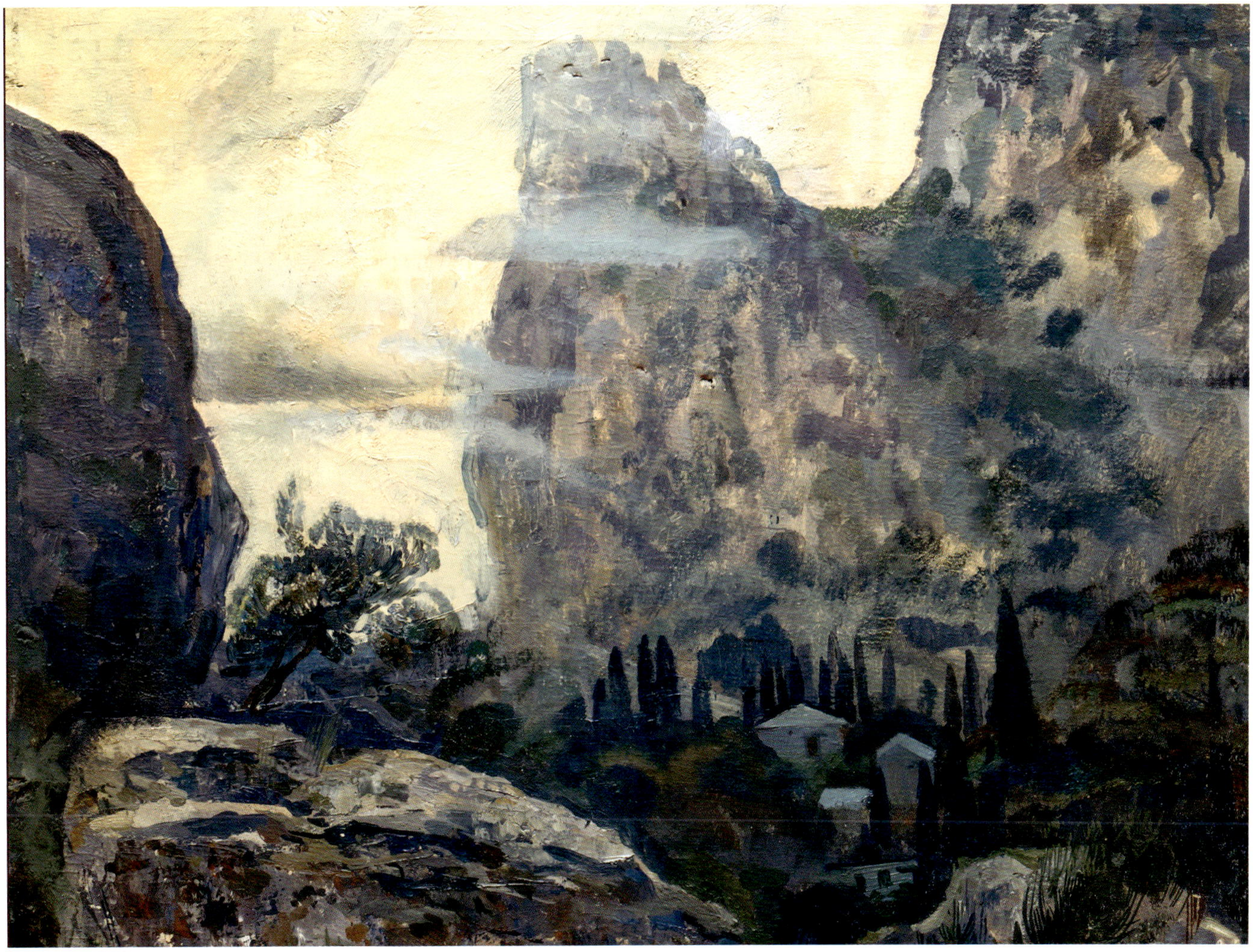

The Crimea Alupka, by Olga Suvorova, oil on canvas, 55 × 60 cm (1986)

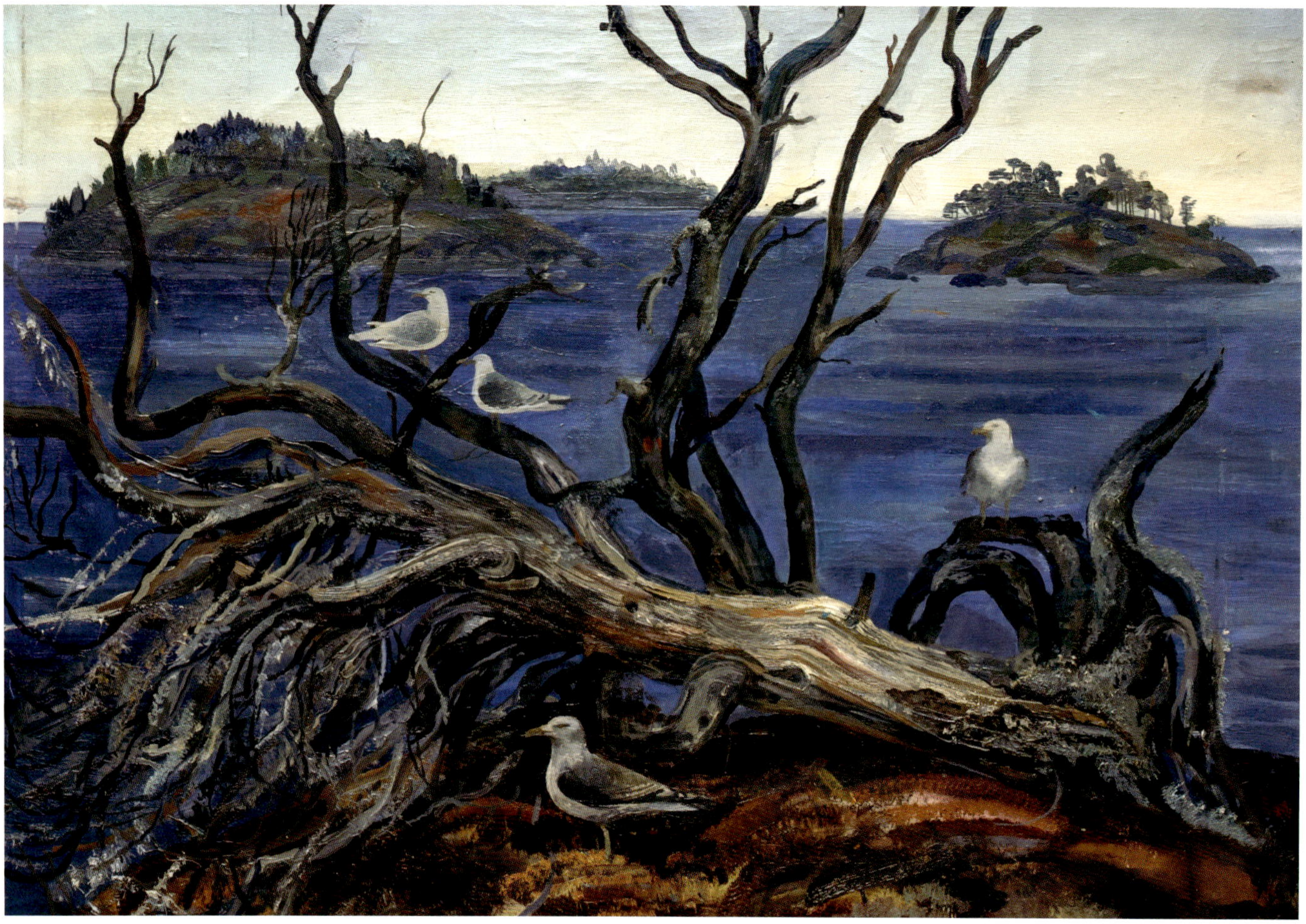

Dry Tree, by Olga Suvorova, oil on canvas, 95 × 110 cm (1988)

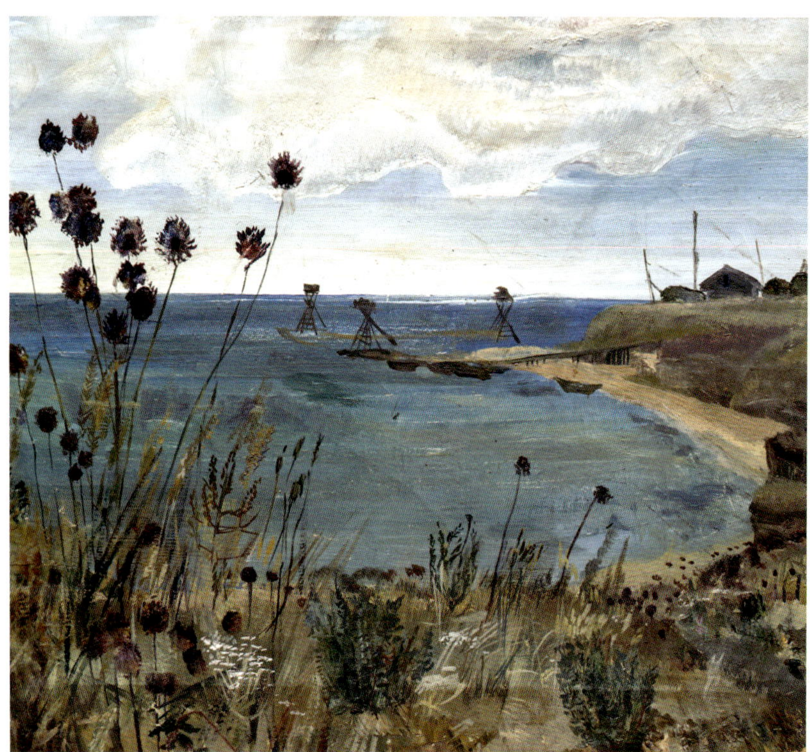

Crimea Kerch, by Olga Suvorova, oil on canvas, 45 × 55 cm (1986)

We went fishing in the evening after work, and the next morning we drew a model for three hours, then went sketching again. It was almost impossible to work on the street, as crowds of holidaymakers, tired of lying on the beach, would gather behind my back. They loudly discussed my work, gave advice, and asked me to draw their portraits. Over time, I got used to working in crowded places; I developed patience and concentration. While Europeans are restrained and will never interfere with your work, Russians are the opposite; they are used to speaking their mind.

The study practice flew by. After returning to St. Petersburg, I immediately went north to Karelia, on the Lake Ladoga shore, where my parents had a country house, or *dacha*. I helped my parents with the household,

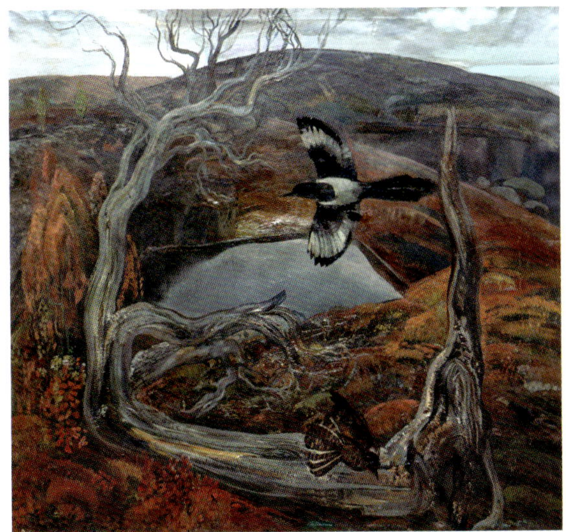

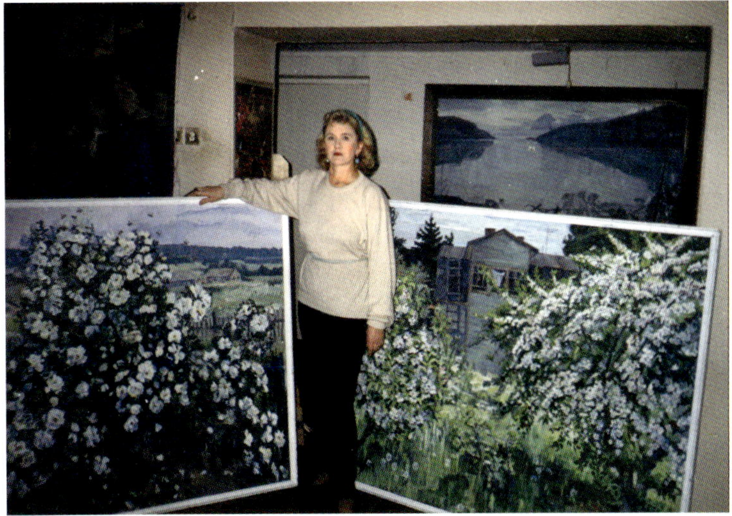

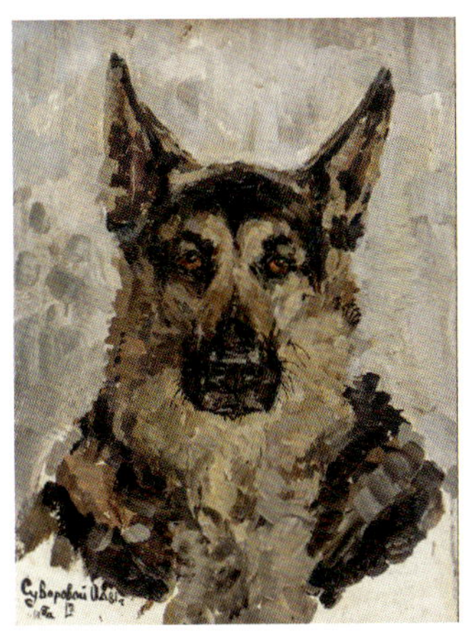

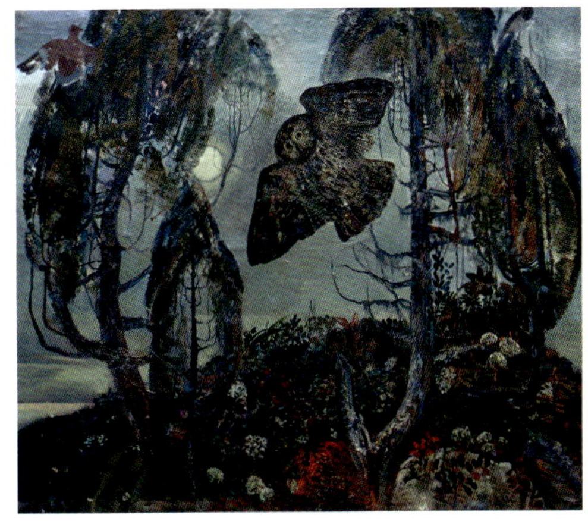

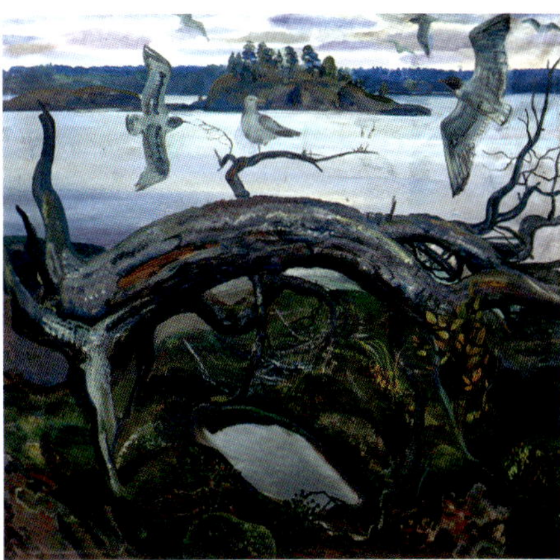

and they painted their pictures. My mother posed her still lifes under flowering apple trees, and my father painted landscapes of a northern nature. Studying at the academy, I tried to complete the tasks of my teachers and did not part from the canons of painting in the socialist realism style. But in summer I had a chance to experiment, and even then I liked the decorative approach. I wanted to paint landscapes with birds and other animals, because I can compare nature to a city that is occupied by its inhabitants, and even a common magpie or owl are incredibly beautiful in flight.

My father used to take me on his painting excursions. It happened like this: Together we climbed into a boat and took at least two canvases, one long and the other square. This was needed to be able to choose the appropriate shape for a particular view. A big artist's umbrella was needed in case of rain and for protection from the bright sun. Despite the fact that Karelia is in the far north, the sun shines brightly, especially when it is reflecting off the water. The suntan you get there is not yellow but brown-gray and lasts much longer than the southern tan. So without an umbrella you can quickly get sunburnt. We took our favorite shepherd dog with us in the boat—I have never met a smarter dog in my life. Then we started the engine and drove around Ladoga at full speed. It was the best time, when I could enjoy nature and at the same

Ladoga Landscape, by Olga Suvorova, oil on canvas, 120 × 135 cm (1987)

Natalia Suvorova, photo courtesy of Olga Suvorova (2000)

My Dog, by Olga Suvorova, oil on cardboard, 50 × 40 cm (1981)

Owl, by Olga Suvorova, oil on canvas, 110 × 115 cm (1989)

Ladoga I, by Olga Suvorova, oil on canvas, 85 × 110 cm (1985)

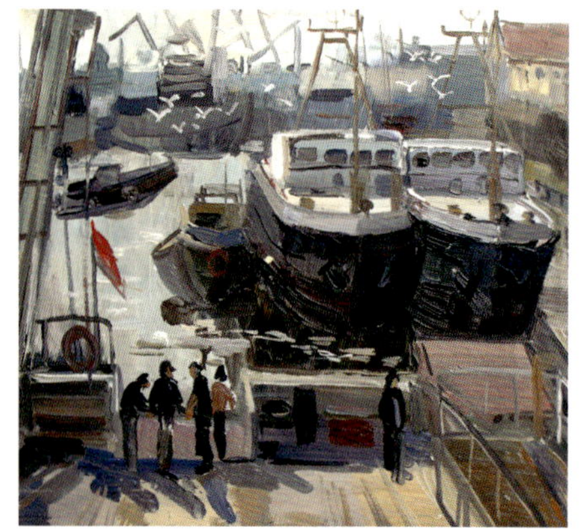

Leningrad Ships, by Olga Suvorova, oil on canvas, 50 × 60 cm (1983)

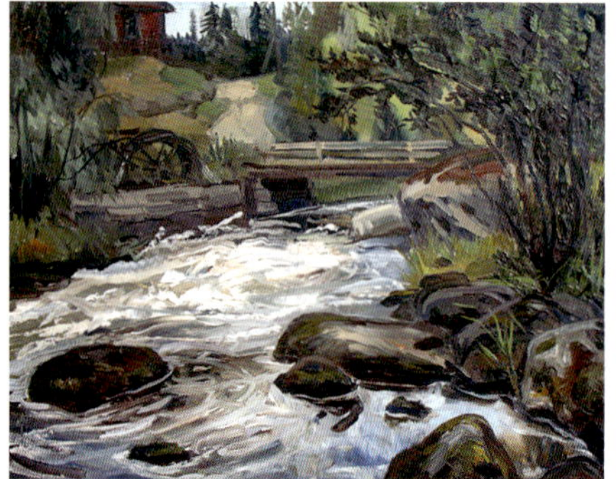

Karelia I, by Olga Suvorova, oil on canvas, 50 × 60 cm (1985)

time draw it, choosing any place I liked. At that wonderful time I did not have to think about students or teachers or grades. I just portrayed the beloved North.

Karelia is a small area with a huge number of lakes and rivers. Lake Ladoga is one of the largest in Europe, with a depth of more than 230 meters (754 feet). The huge number of islands amazes; they are incredibly beautiful and diverse. The weather changes quickly, especially in the fall. We often had to stay on an island overnight and wait for the wind to calm down, and for the huge waves to stop swamping our boat. Many fishermen rest at the bottom of this unpredictable lake. Some might say the North is nothing special, but I spent much of my childhood, youth, and adult life here, and for me this lake is the most beautiful place in the world. Every person has a special place they return to over and over, and for me it is Lake Ladoga.

We traveled swiftly on the boat, my father masterfully avoiding dangerous areas, because if you sink there, you may not survive a swim to the shore because the water is so cold. Once we chose the island we liked, we got to work. Trying not to disturb my father, I went far away along the rocky shore, set up a sketchbook, and started to draw. I wanted to do independent work, not like my father's. I felt like drawing a variety of mosses that covered the rocks; they looked like pieces of green velvet with silvery incisions. Especially magical were the old trees with storm-twisted roots. Water and sun had weathered them for many decades,

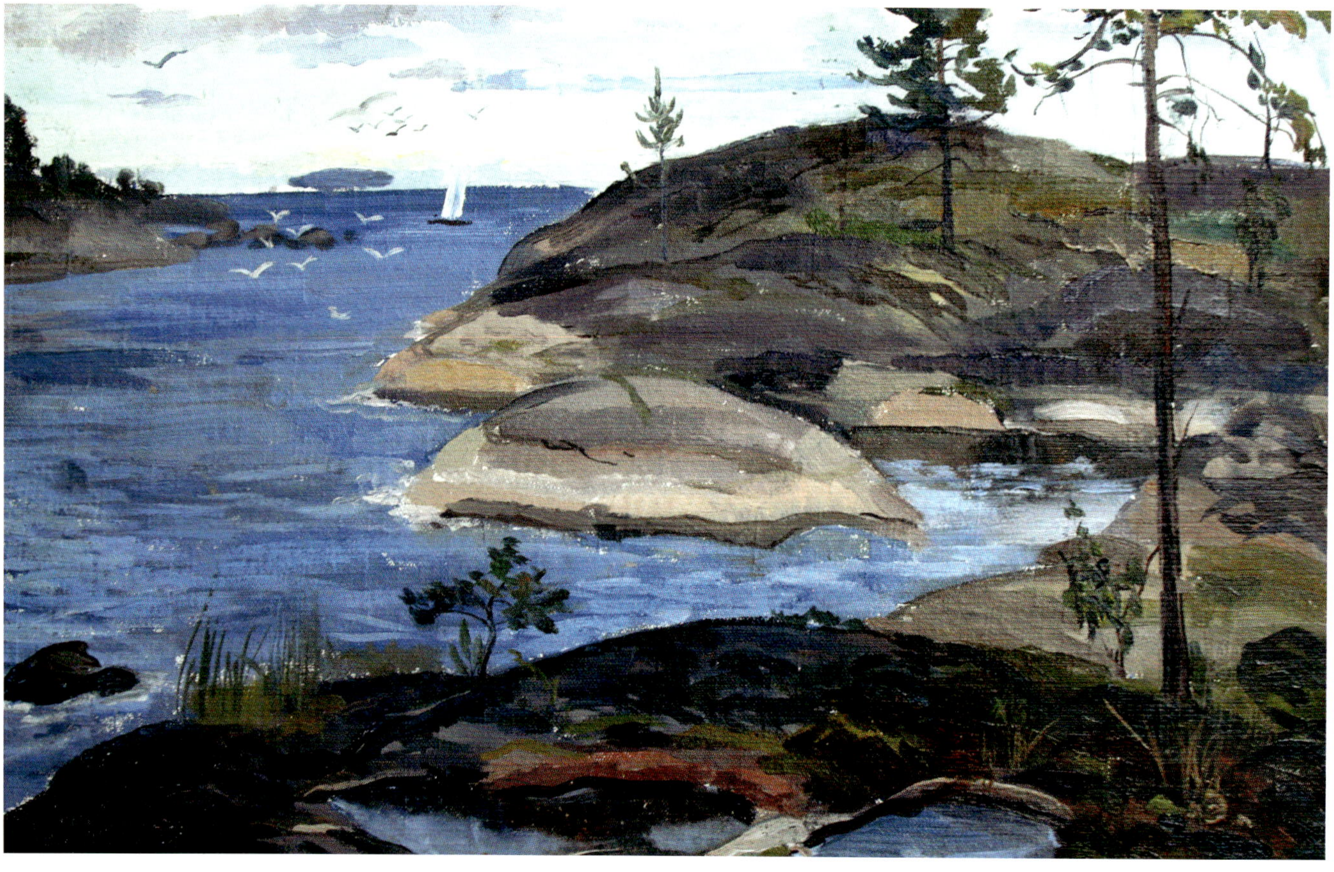

Ladoga II, by Olga Suvorova, oil on canvas, 45 × 60 cm (1986)

and they looked like fairytale creatures. Many gulls accompanied passing fish shoals, now and then swooping into the water for their prey. I was surrounded by huge granite rocks covered with twisted pines, flowering heather, thickets of blueberries and cowberries. In some places, the gulls' nests were right on the ground, and you needed to walk carefully to avoid stepping on the chicks. The older ones scattered in different directions, hiding in stone crevices.

I wanted to express my feelings about this environment in my landscapes. I think the North is minimalistic, harsh; you feel its power and strength. Unfortunately, neither a painting nor a good camera can truly capture the scale and splendor of undisturbed nature. Occasionally a seal swam by. It would look curiously at me, then hurriedly swim away. My dog would watch, understanding that there was no way to chase the seal. The sun was setting, the day was over, and we had to wash our brushes and clean the palette. That was the most annoying chore, but we could not escape it; otherwise they would dry out and it would be difficult to clean them later.

Once we arrived home in the evening, my father would put my landscape next to his and analyze the work. We argued a lot, because not all people have a talent for teaching. You need to be able to explain what is wrong and, most important, how to fix it. The next day I joined my mother; she was drawing a still life from a samovar. She had a greasy touch and worked with stiff tassels made of pig bristles. You could move a few steps away from her picture and see a beautiful, bright, expressive canvas, somewhat similar to the French Impressionists. But when I looked at the picture closely, I saw a bright color mosaic. Her works are always filled with positive energy, expressed in the intensity of the light, despite the fact that they depict a short northern summer. I was not personally drawn to still lifes, preferring landscapes and compositions with people.

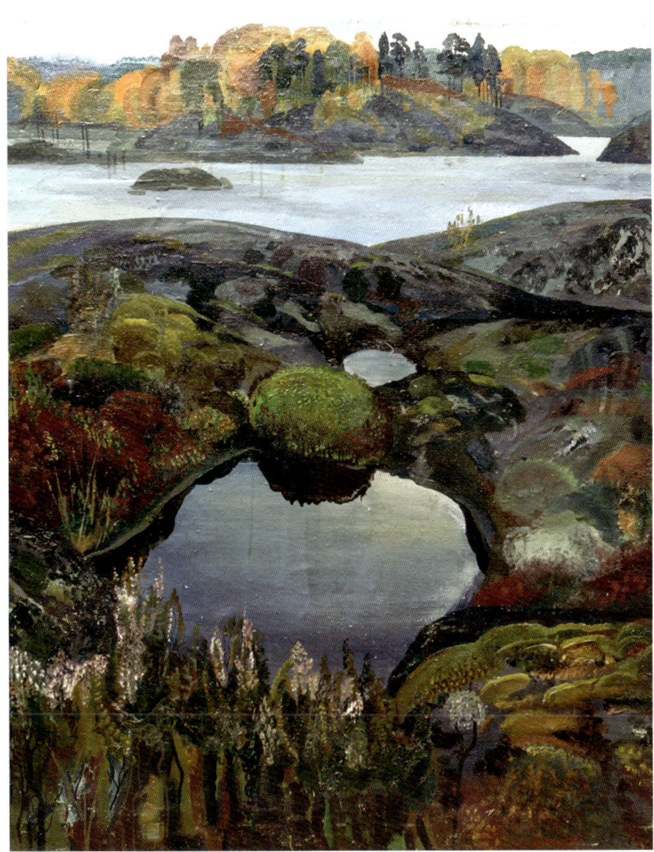

Northern Mosses, by Olga Suvorova, oil on canvas, 95 × 100 cm (1988)

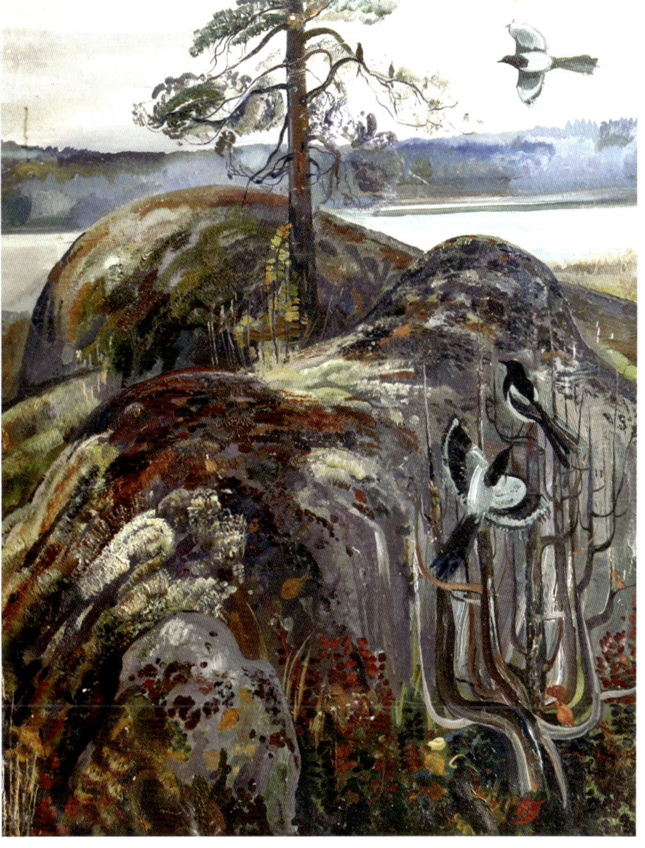

Karelia II, by Olga Suvorova, oil on canvas, 90 × 100 cm (1989)

Early Works

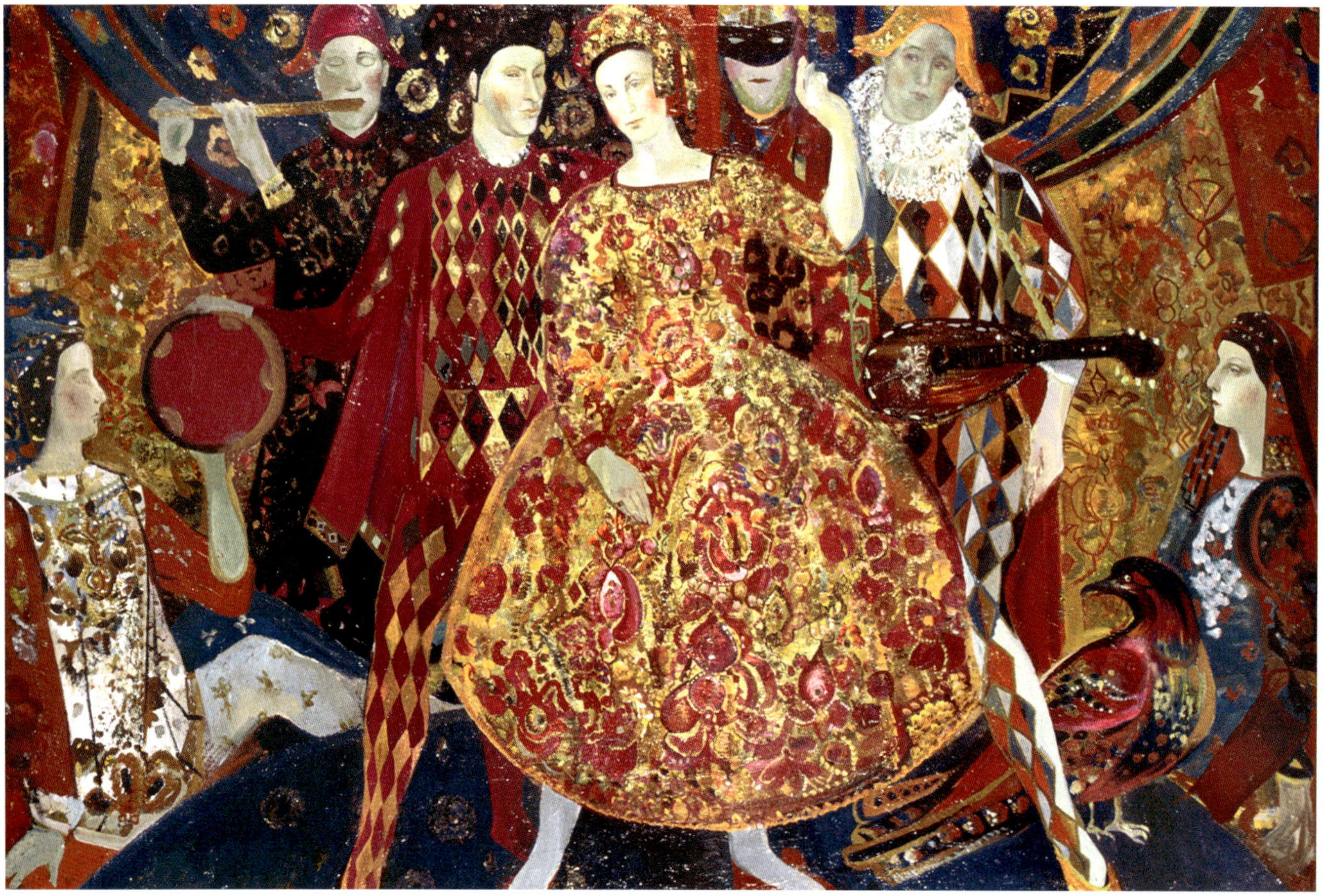

Carnival, by Olga Suvorova, oil on canvas, 95 × 145 cm (1992)

In the third year, students were sent to the workshops of famous masters. I got into the studio of monumental painting under Professor Andrei Mylnikov's guidance. It was difficult to enter, as many students wanted to learn from this master. Monumental painting is when an artist can work with architecture—paint walls and ceilings, and make stained glass windows, frescoes, and mosaics.

Outstanding works of monumental art were produced in ancient Rome, ancient Egypt, and Byzantium. From early antiquity to the late Renaissance, monumental painting and sculpture were among the main methods for decorating stone, brick, and concrete buildings. They were widely used in temple and burial complexes. Stained glass techniques were a breakthrough

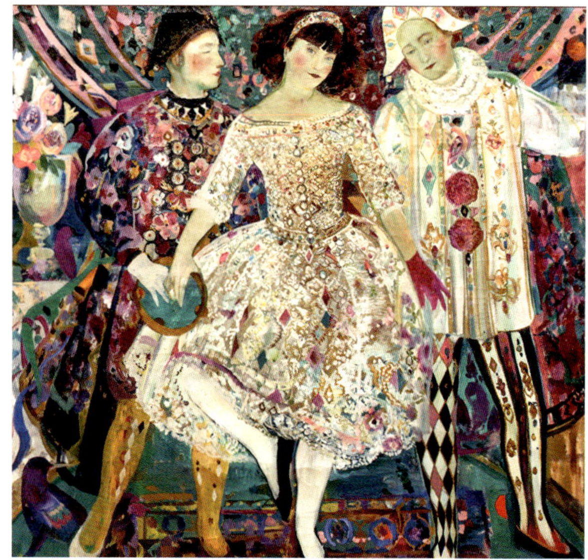

White Columbine, by Olga Suvorova, oil on canvas, 140 × 159 cm (1992)

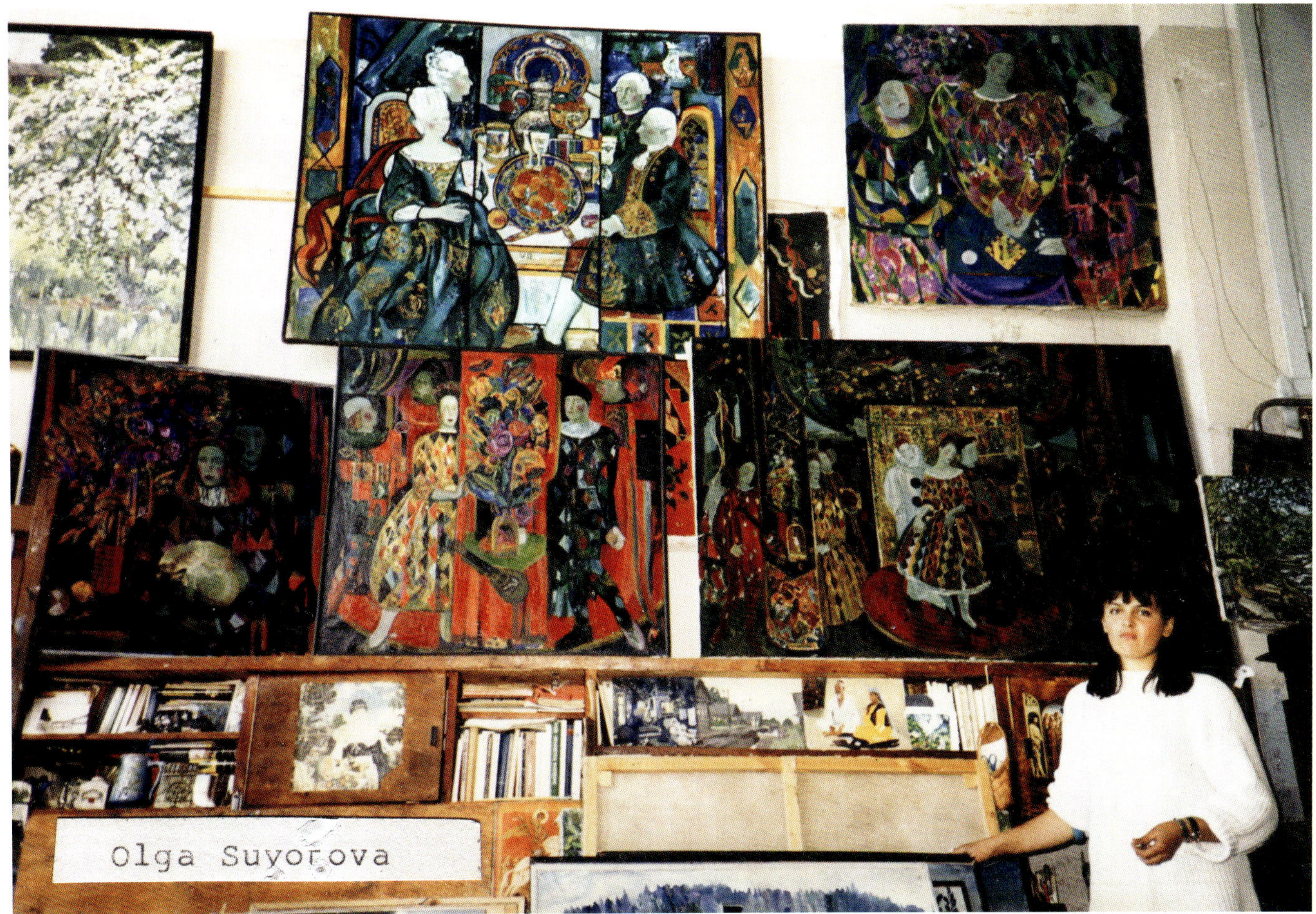

Olga in her studio, photo courtesy of Olga Suvorova (1992)

development in medieval art. The leading Renaissance masters created many frescoes that were grand in scope and execution. I wanted to master all the techniques. In our workshop we made large-scale practice drawings, about 2 meters (6.5 feet) tall, so that we could later draw freely on large walls. We studied mosaic technique, which is interesting and also quite laborious. For this we had to break a large amount of multicolored glass with a special hammer and lay it out in pieces, in a certain order.

As an exercise, I copied the head of St. Dimitry of Solun from the male Mikhailovsky Monastery in Kiev. From the mosaic technique point of view, the icon represented a sample of the highest level of skill of the Old Russian and Byzantine mosaics. When I finally laid out the mosaic, my fingers were taped with medical plaster. The fact is that when you crack a mosaic glass, called smalt, you unwittingly cut your fingertips. The result of the work was worth it, because it is a beautiful art, and most importantly—eternal. Compared to oil paintings, mosaics can withstand outside environmental conditions, so many ancient Greek masterpieces have survived to our times. I also studied mural, a painting technique on wet plaster. But most of all I liked ceramics; you can mold a bas-relief from clay, color it with special paints, and bake it in a high-temperature furnace. After baking, the colors spread and become glossy and bright, and the effect is unpredictable. Still, painting remained the most important study for me.

I worked hard all summer and autumn, and the teachers offered me an exhibition at the Academy of Arts. It was an honor to put my paintings on public display. Soon I got married and had a daughter, which meant balancing my studies and childcare. I did not want to take a sabbatical.

Unfortunately, five years later we divorced. I think student marriages are a mistake, especially in the creative world. It is common in Russia for girls to go to college to get a diploma and also a husband. In my opinion, this is wrong, because individuals are not fully formed at a young age. Conflict often results when one of the spouses develops creatively, while the other remains at the same level.

I graduated from college with excellent marks, but I did not want to study in graduate school. I wanted to work abundantly and be free from reporting to teachers. This was a time of complete freedom. After I joined the Leningrad Union of Artists, I could participate in all major exhibitions. But then in the 1980s, perestroika broke out. The Soviet Union soon collapsed, and for many people it was a very difficult time. Perestroika also influenced the artists' union, where the old, well-established system was broken and nothing new was created in its place. Under the communists, artists had had a regular salary and worked on government orders, creating pieces for public organizations. Having studied at art school for six years and spent six years at the institute, I suddenly realized that we, the people of art, were no longer needed by our country.

Thanks to perestroika, the borders opened and it became possible to fly even to the moon, but where to get money for the trip? A lot of people were left unemployed, and not only in the creative professions. Once I hired a plumber, who turned out to be a former violinist. On another occasion, I called a car to transport some furniture, and the porters were musicians. People, especially older generations, found it hard to adapt to the new life. The government helped young and novice artists for a while, and I was awarded a Boris Yeltsin prize (the then-president of Russia), a scholarship to support young, talented artists. But it was only a little money, and paints, brushes, and canvases were very expensive. I did not want to live at the expense of my parents, especially since they were artists too; so I had to do additional work—paint blitz portraits sitting on the street, make copies of famous old masters, and so on.

At that time, paintings were not selling in Russia. People were too busy looking for jobs. Canny art dealers bought paintings cheaply from artists and resold them for a higher price in Europe. It was very profitable to buy a picture in the socialist realism genre and then, for big money, put it up in some gallery in London or Paris. But time passed and I

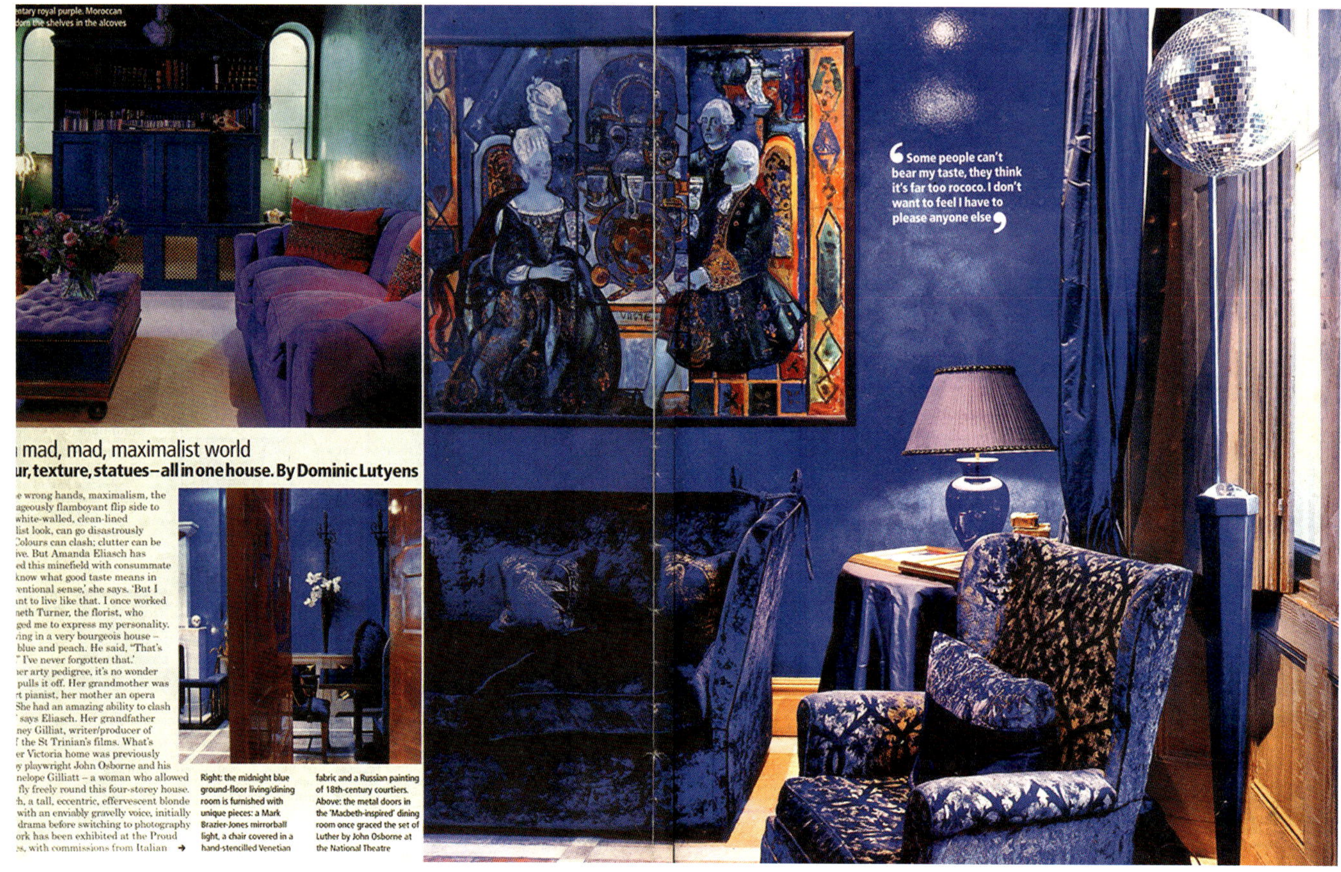

mad, mad, maximalist world

ur, texture, statues–all in one house. By Dominic Lutyens

e wrong hands, maximalism, the ageously flamboyant flip side to white-walled, clean-lined list look, can go disastrously Colours can clash; clutter can be ive. But Amanda Eliasch has ed this minefield with consummate know what good taste means in entional sense,' she says. 'But I int to live like that. I once worked neth Turner, the florist, who ged me to express my personality. ing in a very bourgeois house – blue and peach. He said, "That's " I've never forgotten that.' er arty pedigree, it's no wonder pulls it off. Her grandmother was t pianist, her mother an opera She had an amazing ability to clash ' says Eliasch. Her grandfather ney Gilliat, writer/producer of the St Trinian's films. What's er Victoria home was previously y playwright John Osborne and his nelope Gilliatt – a woman who allowed fly freely round this four-storey house. h, a tall, eccentric, effervescent blonde with an enviably gravelly voice, initially drama before switching to photography ork has been exhibited at the Proud s, with commissions from Italian →

Right: the midnight blue ground-floor living/dining room is furnished with unique pieces: a Mark Brazier-Jones mirrorball light, a chair covered in a hand-stencilled Venetian fabric and a Russian painting of 18th-century courtiers. Above: the metal doors in the 'Macbeth-inspired' dining room once graced the set of Luther by John Osborne at the National Theatre

'Some people can't bear my taste, they think it's far too rococo. I don't want to feel I have to please anyone else'

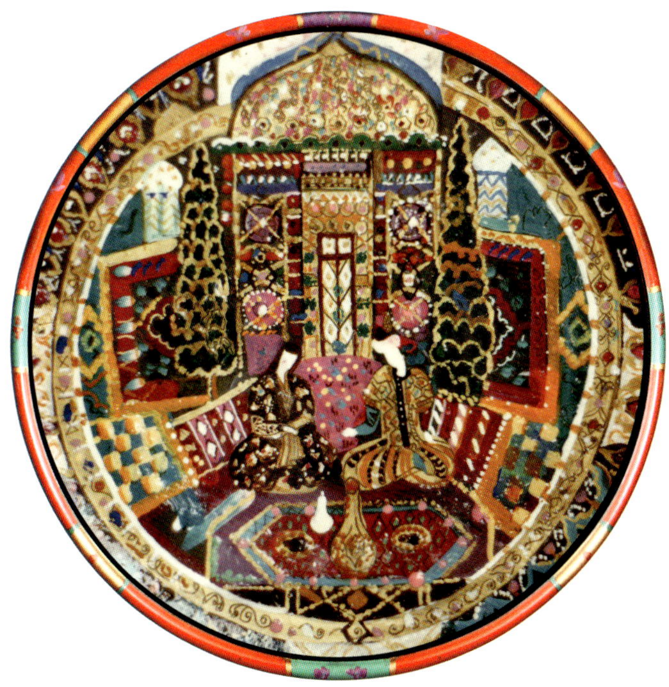

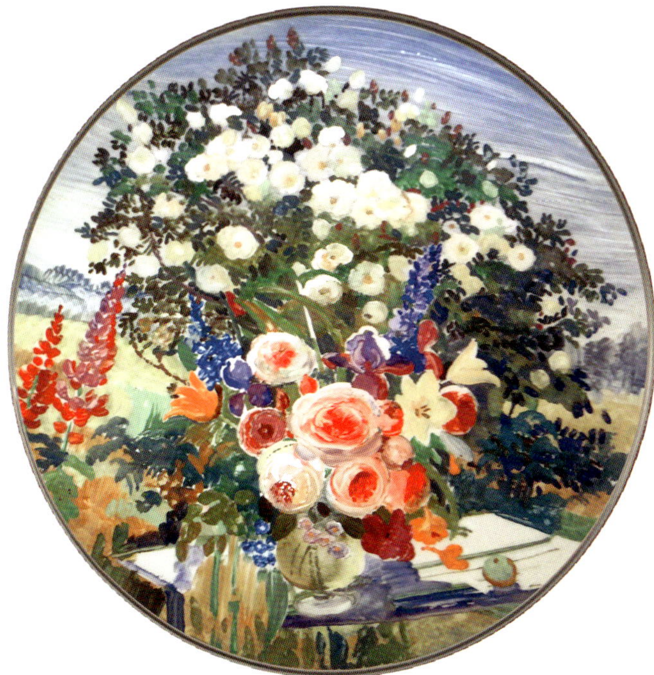

continued to work in a decorative style. I liked participating in exhibitions. You can gauge how professional your work turned out to be and observe how many people stop and seriously consider your work.

Exhibitions are also good places to make connections. At one exhibition, I met an English architect who had a small gallery in central London. He was a hobbyist, not a professional art dealer. He liked Russian art and organized artist exhibitions with great enthusiasm. Also, his gallery took part in annual exhibitions throughout England. As a result of that encounter, I traveled to England for fifteen years and sold my paintings there. He was an intelligent, well-educated person who understood Russian art. He sold Russian paintings with great respect, not like many gallery owners who sell them like potatoes on the market. He knew about the styles and trends of painting of that time. Any exhibition in London was of great interest to me as well; here I could absorb new ideas and see things that were extraordinary and expressive.

Decorative ceramic dish, by Olga Suvorova, diameter 40 cm (1994)
Decorative ceramic plate, by Olga Suvorova, diameter 40 cm (1994)

OPPOSITE

Photo of the painting ***Green Banquet***, English Interior, ES magazine, photo courtesy of Olga Suvorova (2002)

For a long time, artists of the Soviet Union worked in the genre of socialist realism. Paintings depicting soldiers, steelworkers, and milkmaids, as well as portraits of Lenin and his entourage, were starting to annoy me. Of course, this was a high-quality Soviet school, and now very few people work in a similar way. The social realism manner demanded a knowledge of human anatomy and the ability to assemble large, multifigured works. However, I felt that the verve had been lost. I wanted to see something new, and the London exhibitions provided that opportunity. In England, I began to paint portraits on commission. I tried to draw from life, to sit the customers in front of me and for several hours try to depict their face, hands, character, and personality. It is especially difficult to draw beautiful female faces, as you need to try to make them uniform and without flaws, and it does not always work out. Sometimes you have to redraw a face several times.

I often had to draw children, and this is difficult since a child is constantly in motion. It is difficult for a child to sit in one place. My daughter was an exception. From an early age, she posed for me with her favorite cats in the garden. She spent many hours, with small interruptions, trying to sit still. Children have their own world that an adult cannot really enter. When I draw a child, I feel this brief moment—right here, right now. Children grow up quickly. Today a six-year-old child is sitting in front of me, and tomorrow he is a teenager with his own character, habits, and experiences.

Animals, too, appear in my portraits and paintings, as my whole life I have been surrounded by my favorite pets: cats, dogs, parrots, and fish. My parents instilled a love for pets. I really love cats for their independence and ability to feel the mood of the owner, and their sincere love not just for Whiskas. Animals bring diversity to our lives and teach our children to be more humane and to take responsibility for them from an

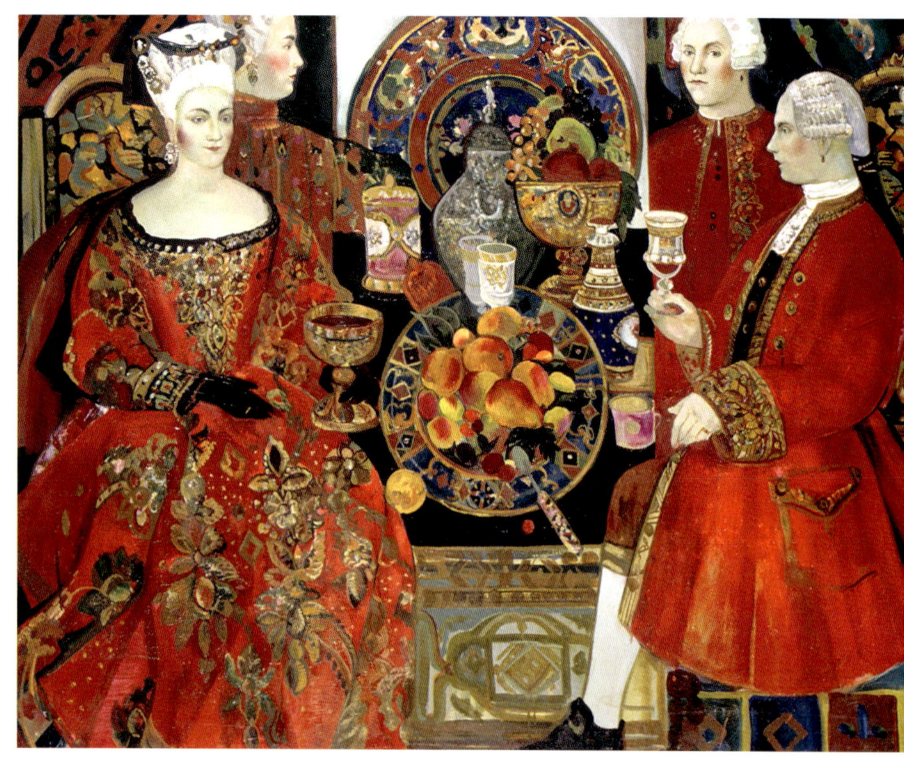

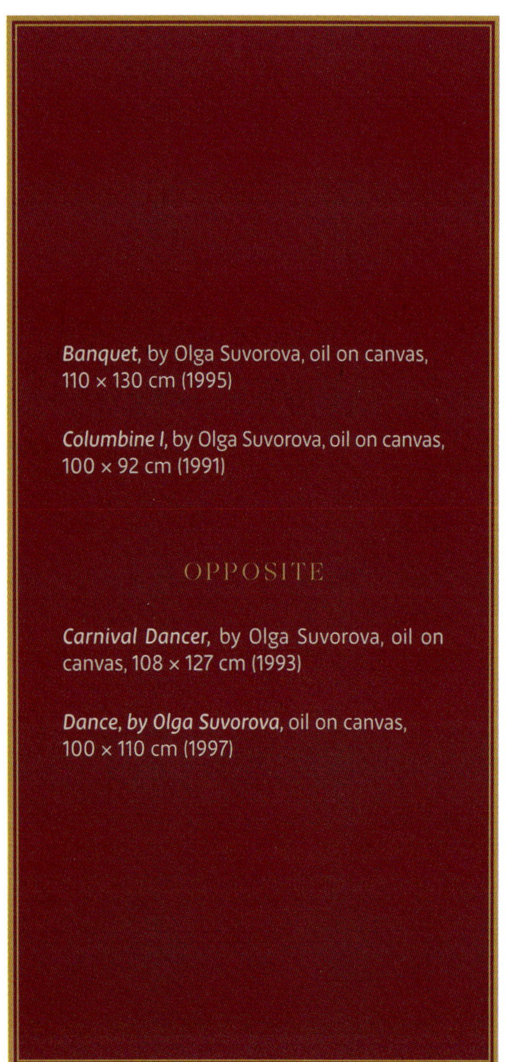

Banquet, by Olga Suvorova, oil on canvas, 110 × 130 cm (1995)

Columbine I, by Olga Suvorova, oil on canvas, 100 × 92 cm (1991)

OPPOSITE

Carnival Dancer, by Olga Suvorova, oil on canvas, 108 × 127 cm (1993)

Dance, by Olga Suvorova, oil on canvas, 100 × 110 cm (1997)

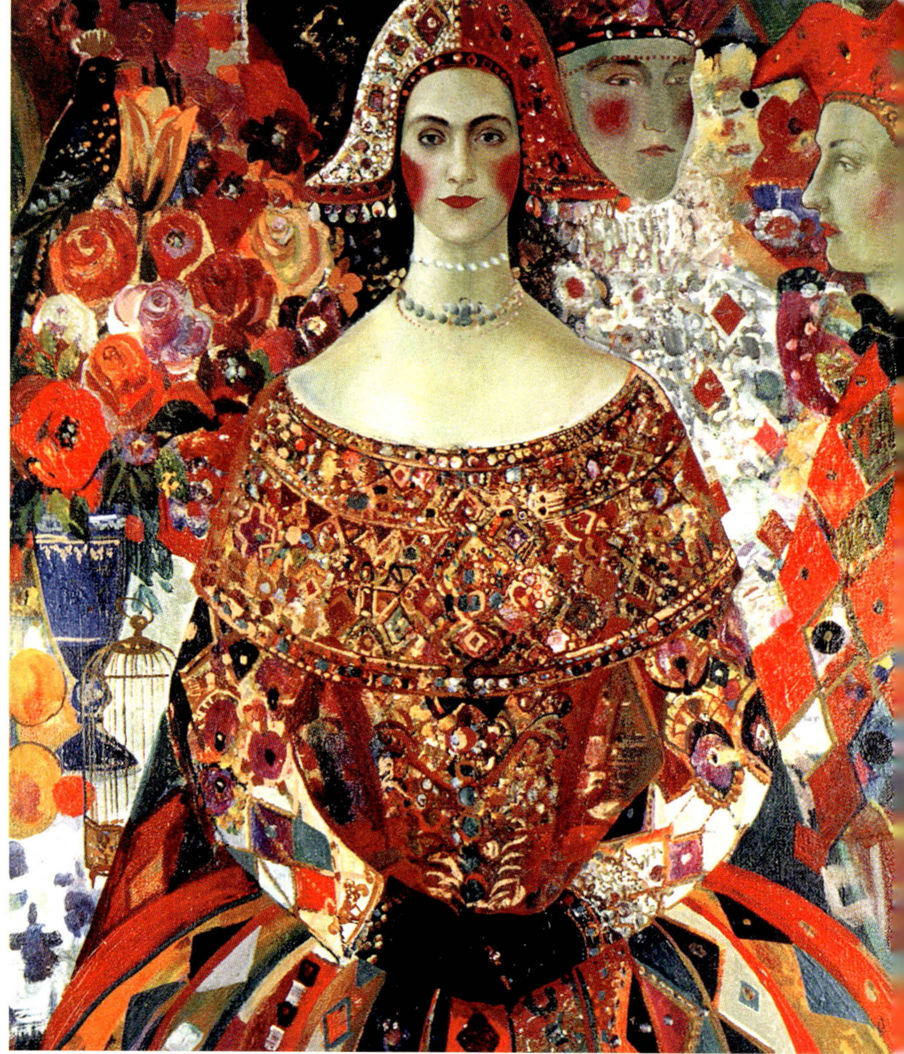

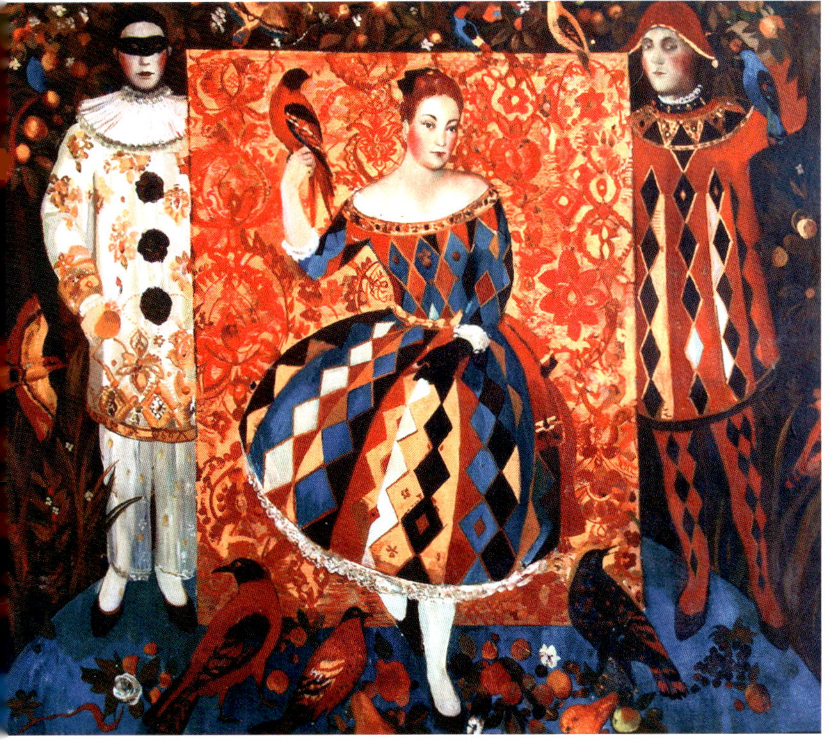

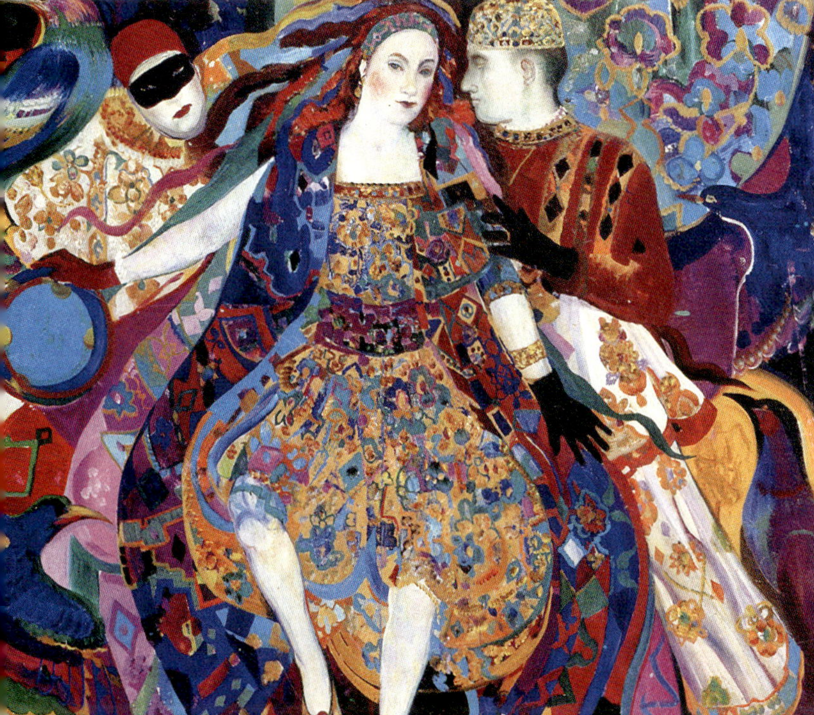

early age. It seems to me that a child who grows up with a cat or dog in the house will not turn out to be a cruel person.

Many portrait artists use just a photograph of a customer's face. It can help, but it's better to see people live—communicate with them, and watch how they act. We try to look better in photos than we are in real life, and in the end the picture does not always look natural. People often come to me with a request to paint a portrait in some antique dress, and I understand that. Everything around us is modern; everyone has the same phones, cars, and clothes, devoid of individuality. I am glad that my hobby is painting and that it is also my favorite work. My profession allows me to communicate with different people and their life stories, which are not always funny and sometimes even tragic.

Visiting museums in London, I was struck by the Pre-Raphaelites. I had studied this period in art history, of course, but to see a picture first-hand in a museum is very different. Their style and the scenes of their paintings had a great influence on me. I liked that the artists often invited their friends and relatives to be models. At first, Pre-Raphaelites preferred Gospel subjects but avoided the classical canons of church painting in their pictures. They interpreted biblical characters and stories symbolically rather than literally. This was close to my perception of religion. In my paintings on this serious topic, I have tried to express a modern point of view, portraying not the canonized Mary but almost the real person. I had a lot of ideas on this topic. I tried to approach the Bible as a source of human drama. My paintings are not intended for the decoration of churches; they have a literary, poetic meaning rather than religious one. Many artists from the Pre-Raphaelite fraternity were already known during their lifetime and appreciated by their contemporaries. This is rare among creative people.

I wanted to experiment more, so I began making collages from glued silk. I was wondering how silk, glued to the canvas, might glitter and reflect light in different directions and found that the picture completely

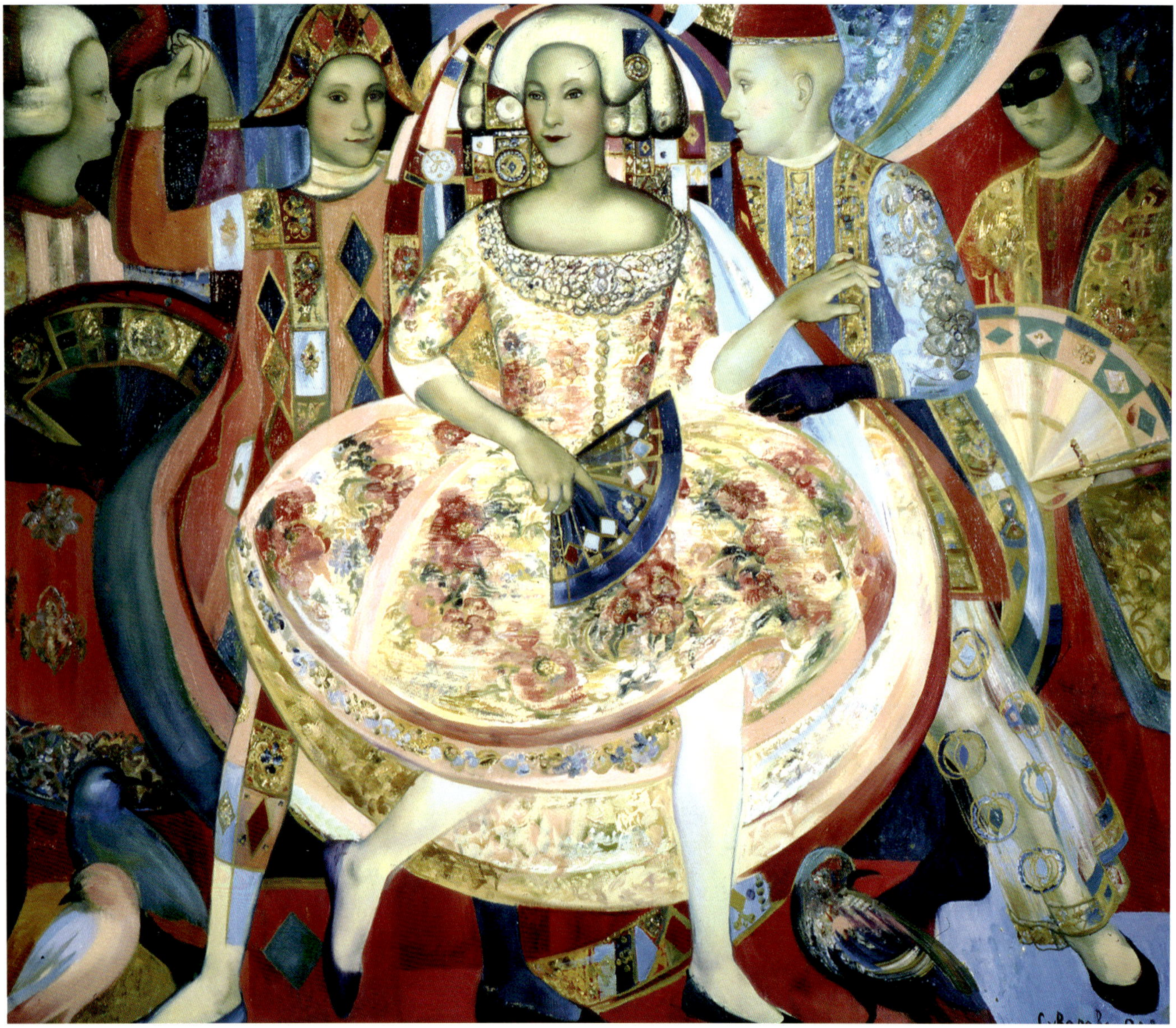

Masquerade I, by Olga Suvorova, oil on canvas, 90 × 115 cm (1998)

changed color when lit by the sun's rays. The combination of bright blue silk and gold leaf reminds me of the feathers of beautiful birds from southern countries. I am constantly looking for different color options and want to achieve the perfect result. It is not always possible, so there are series of paintings with similar themes, but they can have completely different colors.

Sometimes I do not feel like working, I am not in the mood. Then suddenly a randomly watched film or an art album of a famous master pushes me forward. New images crowd into my mind, so I take up the brush.

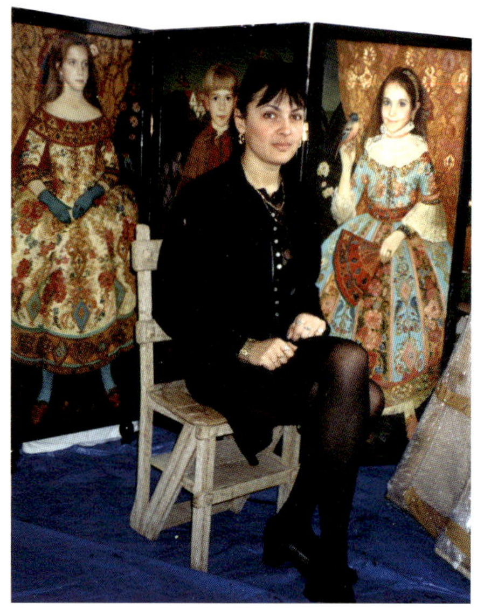

Suvorova before her art exhibition in London, photo courtesy of Olga Suvorova (1998)

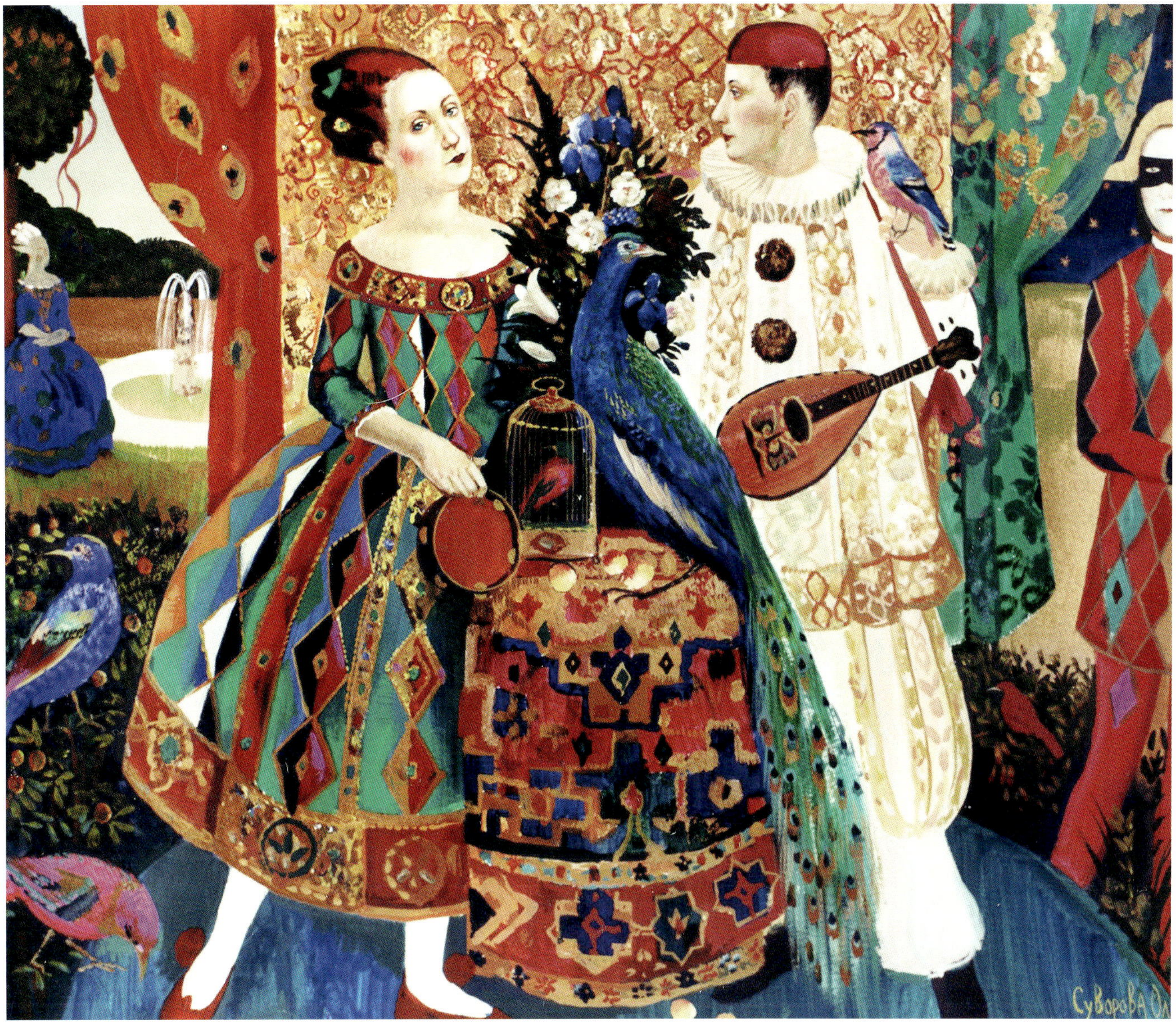

Masquerade I, by Olga Suvorova, oil on canvas, 90 × 115 cm (1998)

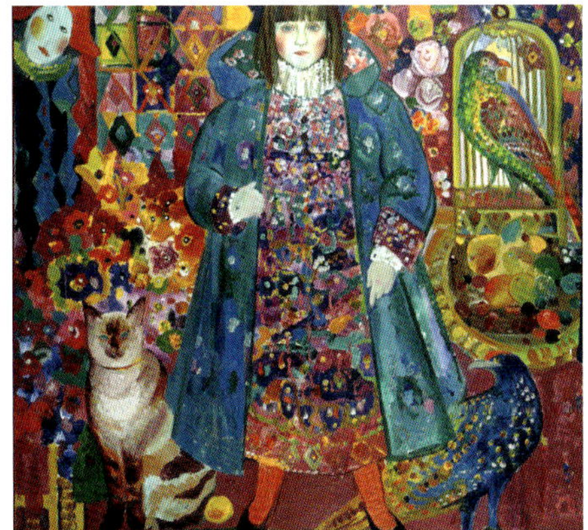

Katya, by Olga Suvorova, oil on canvas, 95 × 100 cm (1993)

For many years I have been inspired by a master of theatrical art, the famous set designer Lev (Leon) Bakst. In Russia, this artist belongs to the masters of the Silver Age. He worked with such famous artists as Somov, Dobuzhinsky, and E. E. Lancere. His theatrical costumes, created for Russian ballet soloists, will amaze even those uninvolved in the theater. The portraits of ballerina Anna Pavlova and Vatslav Nijinsky belong to his brushes. He created amazing fabrics and decorations for the Dygilevsky ballet (Ballet Russe). Even in his lifetime, his theatrical costumes were exhibited in the Louvre. Looking at his work inspires you to paint something really significant.

Cat, by Olga Suvorova, tempera on paper, 50 × 55 cm (1995)
Lady, by Olga Suvorova, oil on canvas, 95 × 100 cm (1995)

OPPOSITE

Marie Antoinette, by Olga Suvorova, screen, front, tree oil, 160 × 55 cm (2018)

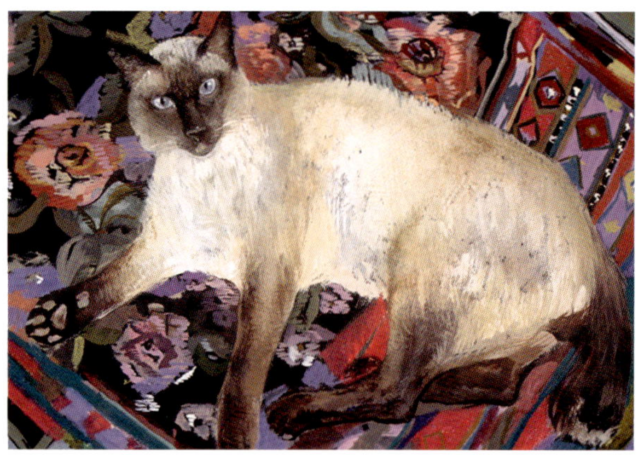

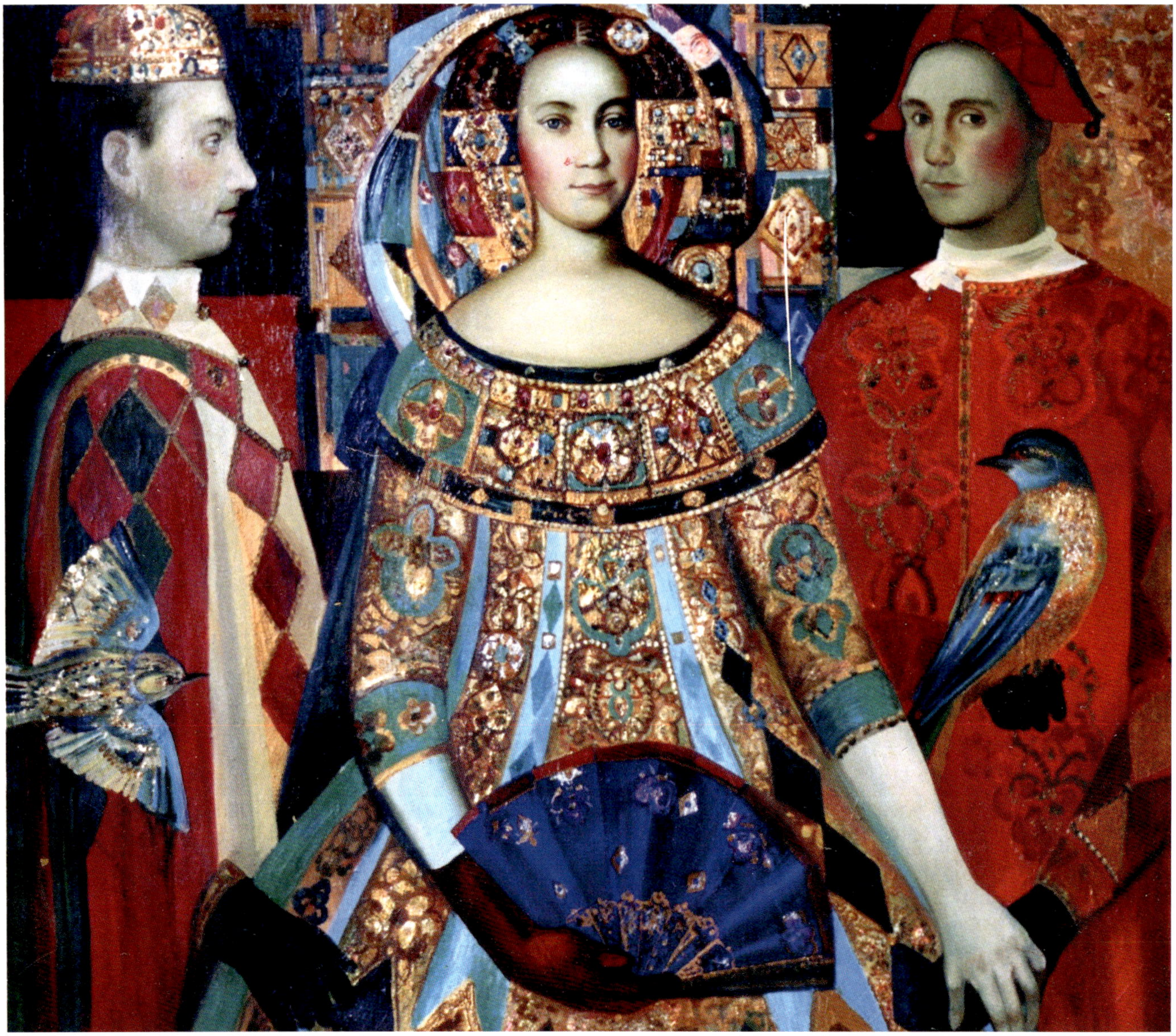

Unfortunately, not all paintings can achieve the same high quality. People in the creative professions always argue about which is more important—talent or craftsmanship? It seems to me that there is no talent without daily work. We need to strive constantly so that each new work is better than the previous one.

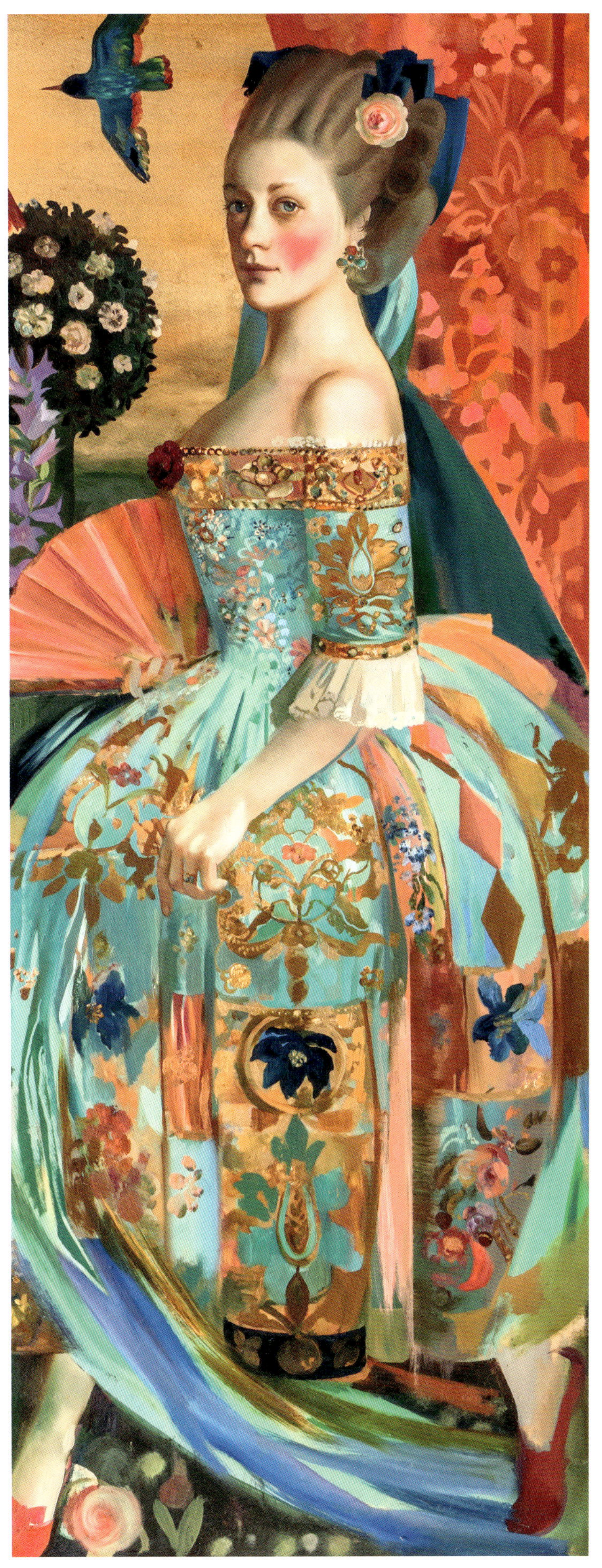

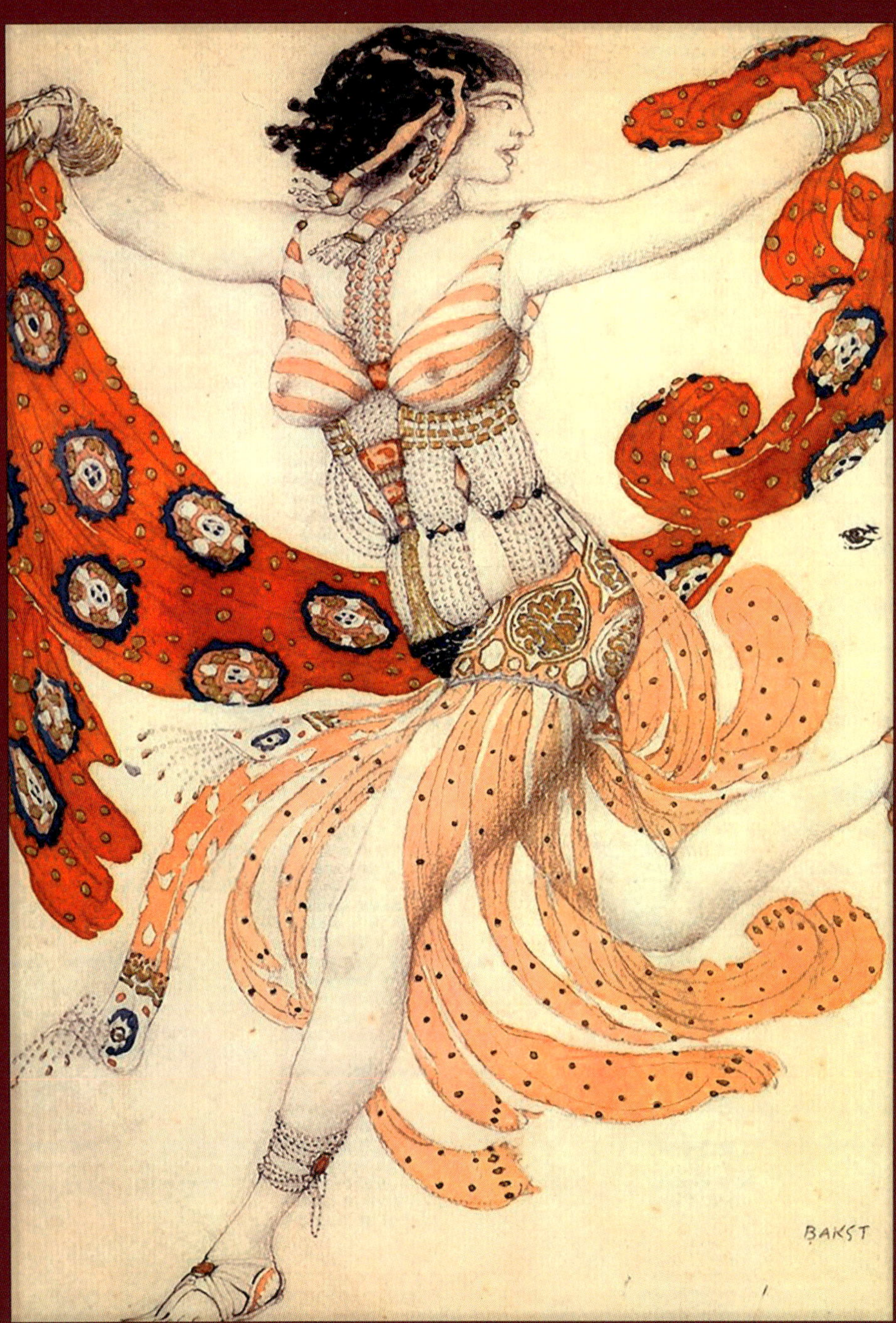

Sketch I, by Leon Bakst, date unknown

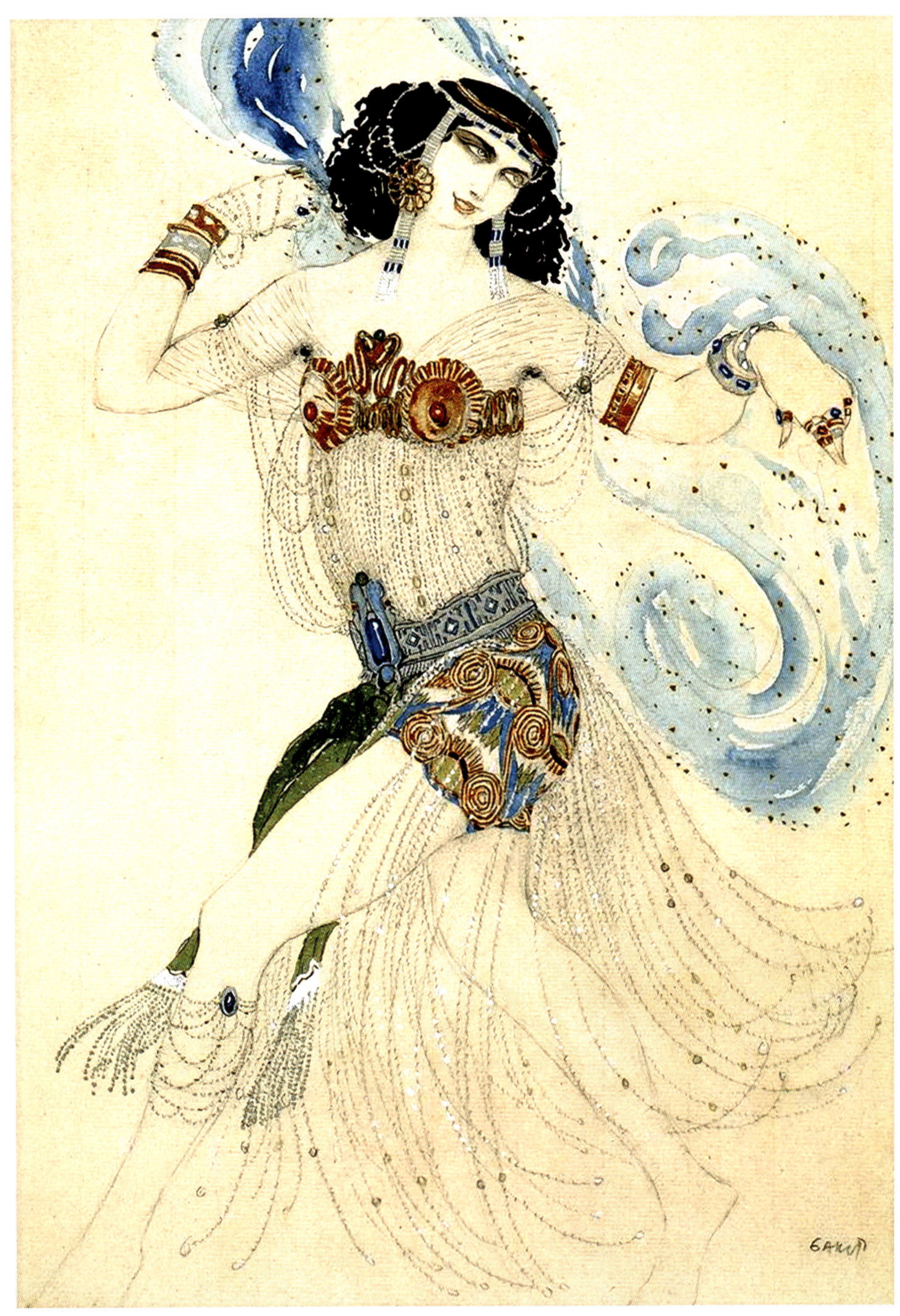

Sketch II, by Leon Bakst, date unknown

Screen Works

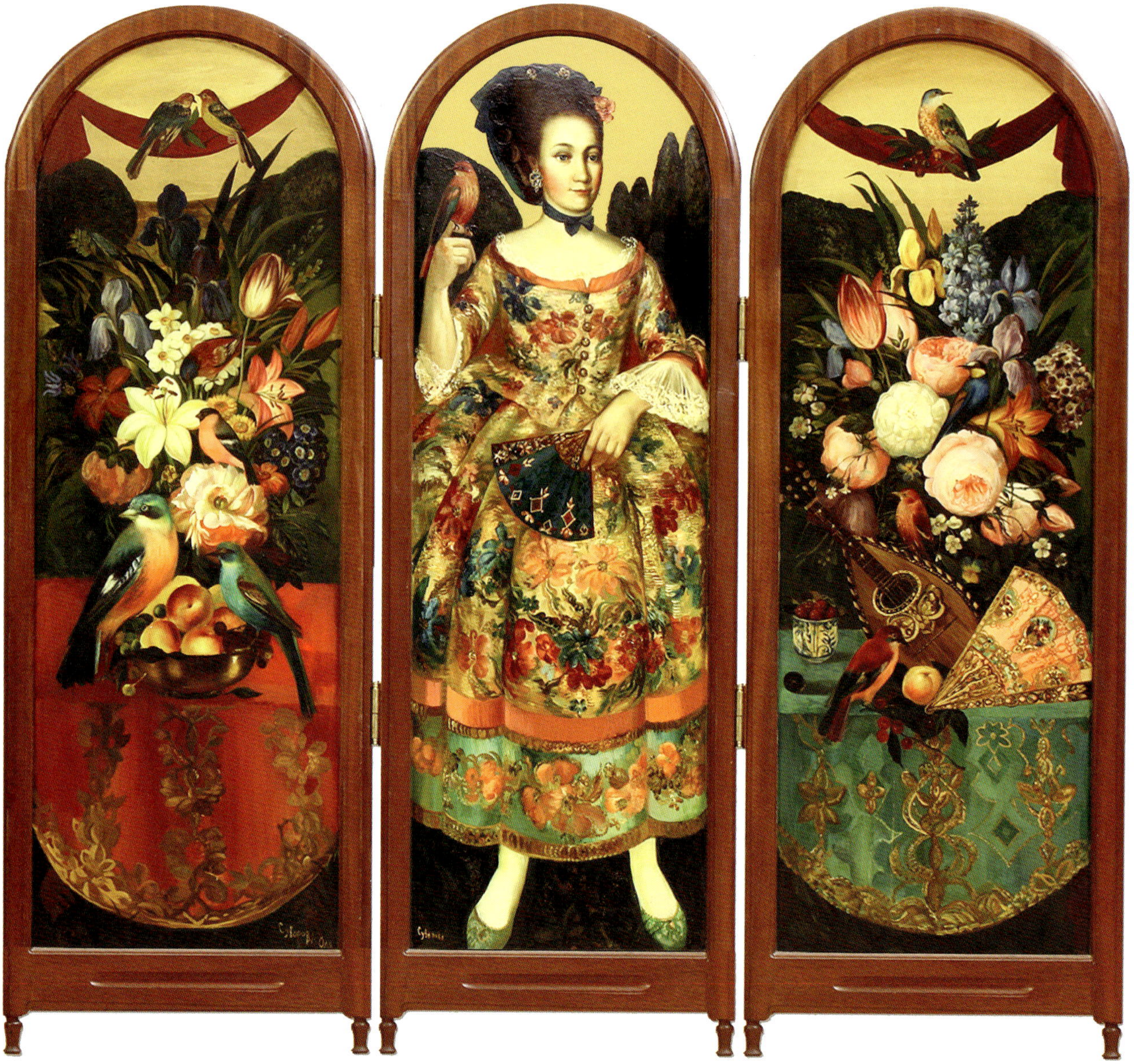

Hunters, by Olga Suvorova, screen, front, wood oil, 150 × 60 cm (2002)

I try to move in several artistic directions, and love decorative art. I am into painting on wood, furniture manufacturing, and interior design, with suitable paintings in different styles. At one point I was interested in the Russian art of Peter the Great's epoch, especially in the portrait painter Vishnyakov. He is not well known to the modern viewer. There is an amazing combination of Russian *parsuna* (nonreligious portraiture) in his works, which have elements of primitivism, but the faces of the characters are quite realistic. This style pushed me to create a series of decorative screens. A famous antiquarian teacher at the Baron Stieglitz Academy, at the Department

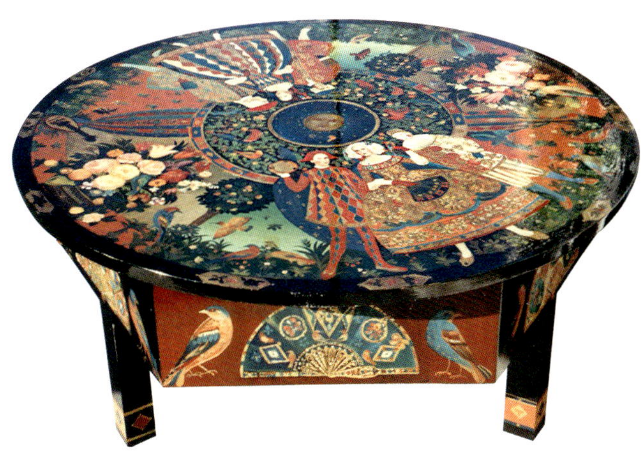

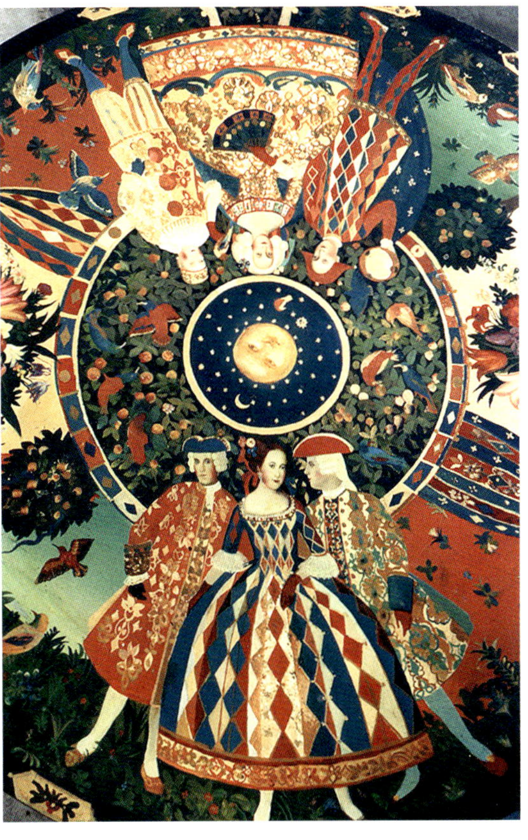

CLOCKWISE

Theatre, by Olga Suvorova, wooden table, tree oil, diameter 120 cm (2000)

Theatre (detail)

Masquerade, by Olga Suvorova, screen, front, wood oil 165 × 80 cm (1998)

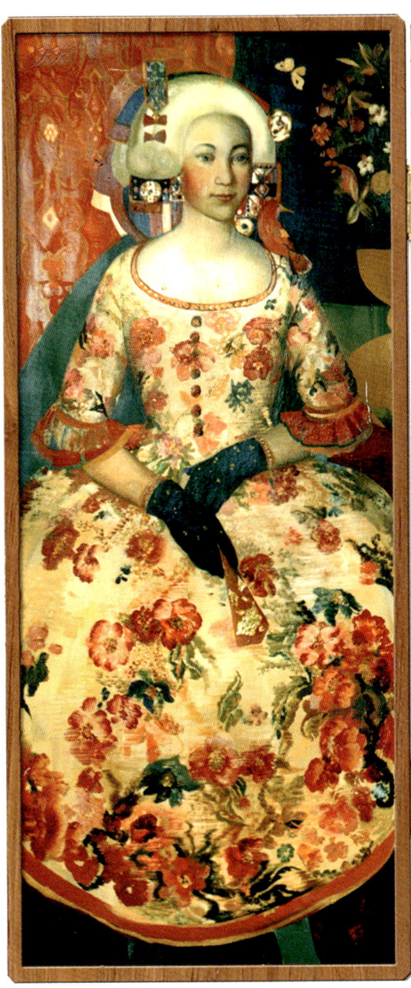

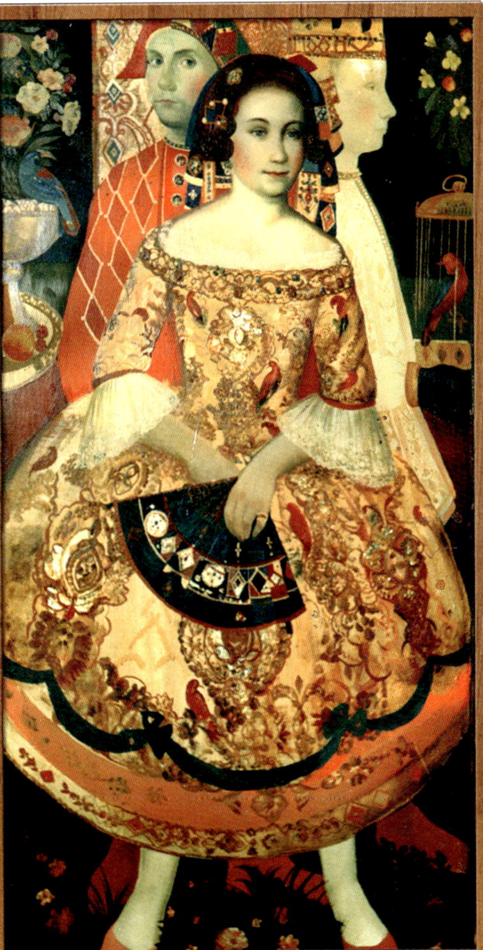

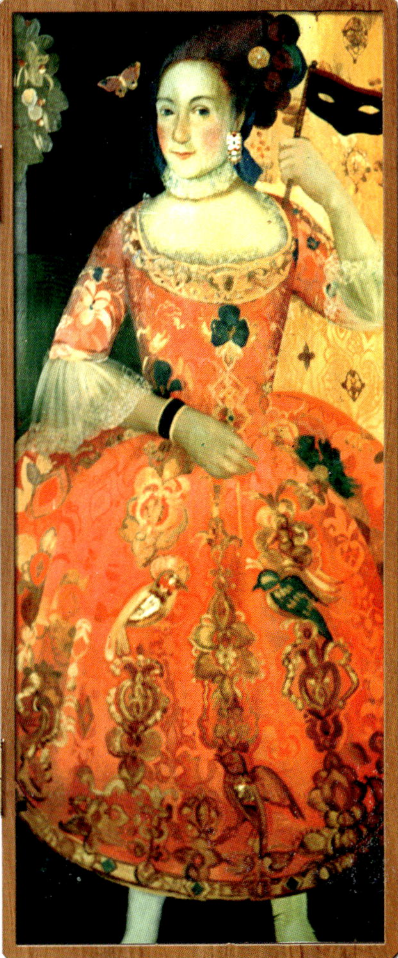

of Furniture, helped me make the screens professionally. Following my sketches, he made complex, ornate frames and legs for the shutters of my screens. Then a wooden base was inserted into this frame, on which the painting was made.

I have always believed that any carpentry product should be both utilitarian and beautiful. So I painted my screens on both sides, as the interior would not look very attractive if only painted on the outside. The painting style was deliberately decorative. Knowing anatomy, I made the figures anatomically incorrect, the poses of noble women static, and their faces almost resembling rummaged dolls. Despite being overloaded with details, each side was different from the other. The height of my screens allowed them to be used practically as intended. Once, I depicted a whole family on the screen. On one side were the parents, and on the other were their three children. The color of their costumes, the landscape, their country house—everything was discussed in advance. Now the children are adults, and they probably have their own children, but I hope my work was not in vain. Perhaps this screen now stands in the house of one of the family members.

Once, when I shipped a screen from St. Petersburg to a London exhibition, the baggage ended up in Italy. The exhibition's grand opening was to take place the next day. Vast nervous energy, effort, and time were spent on phone conversations, and we managed to get the precious cargo there on time.

Imperial, by Olga Suvorova, screen, front, wood oil 165 × 95 cm (1996)

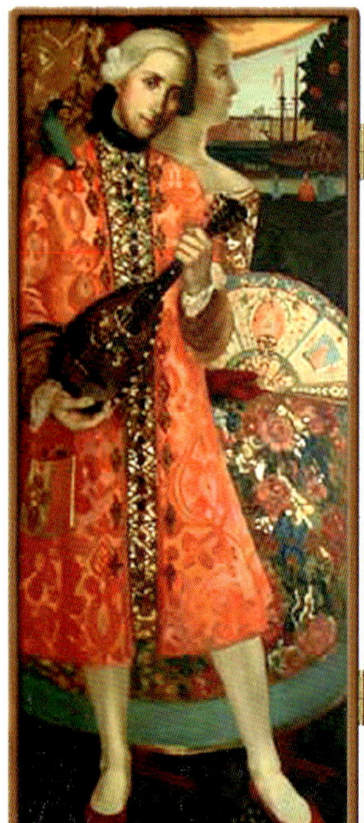
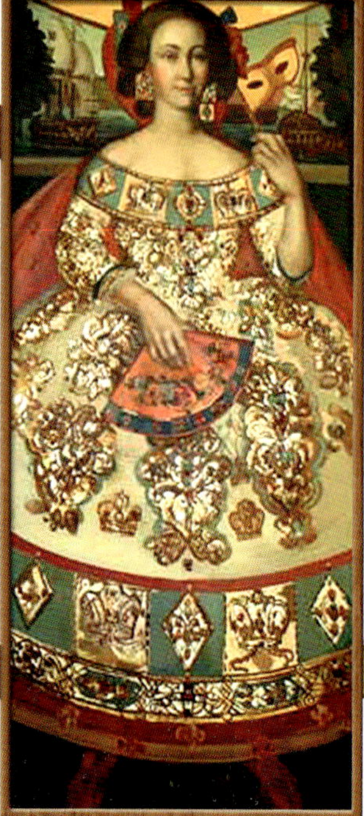
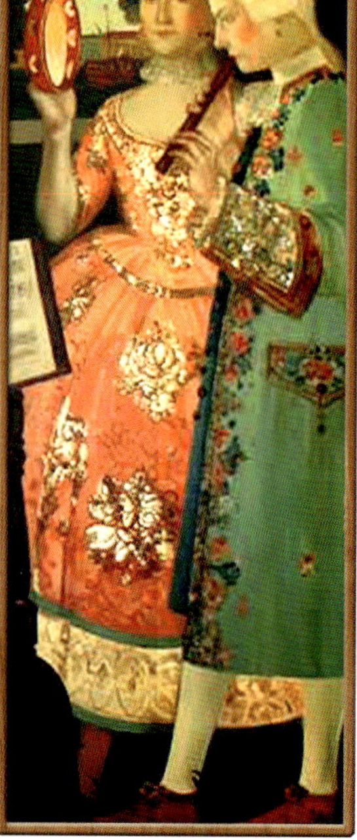

Game I, by Olga Suvorova, screen, front, tree oil, 160 × 65 cm (1995)

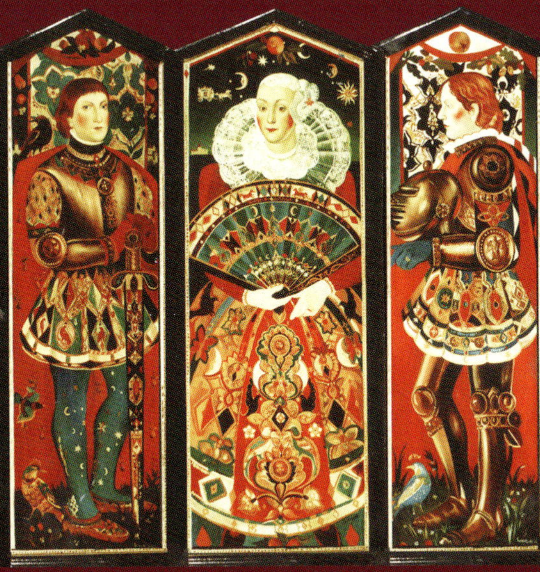

Knights, by Olga Suvorova, screen, front, tree oil,165 × 60 cm (1997)

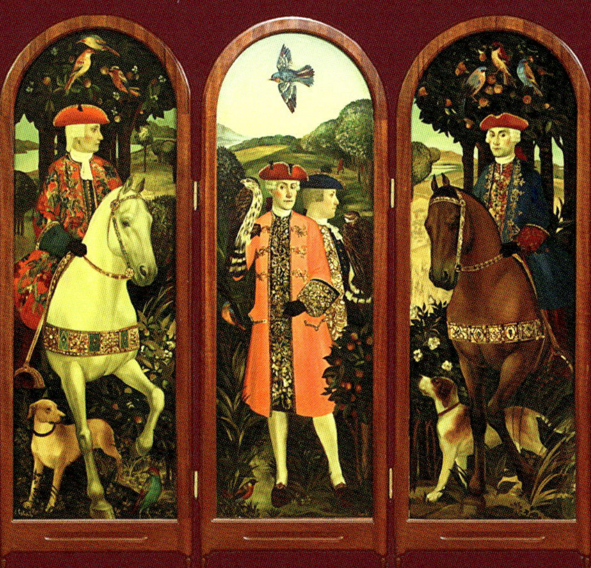

Hunters, by Olga Suvorova, screen, back, wood oil, 150 × 60 cm (2002)

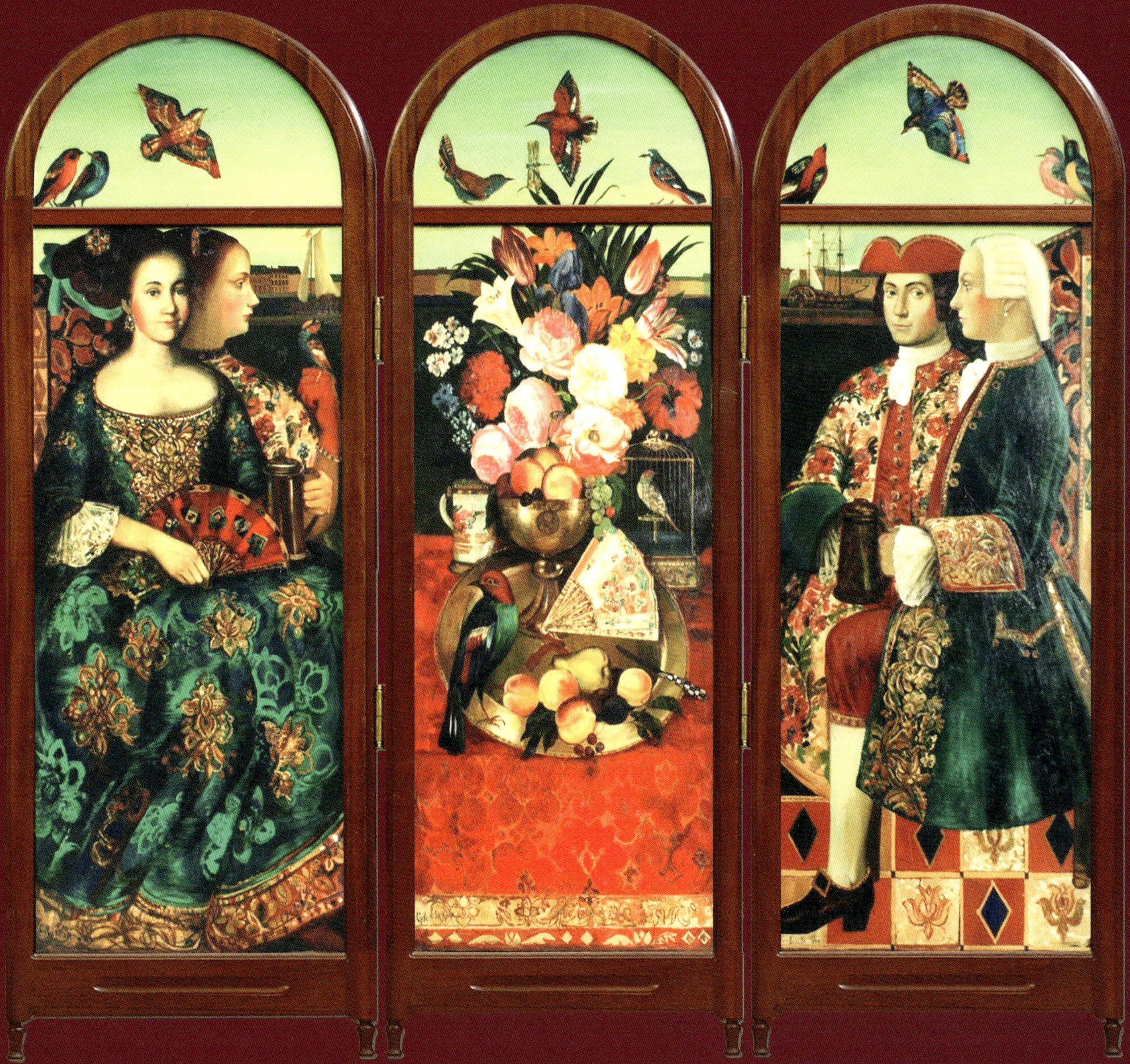

St. Petersburg, by Olga Suvorova, screen, front, tree oil, 165 × 90 cm (1999)

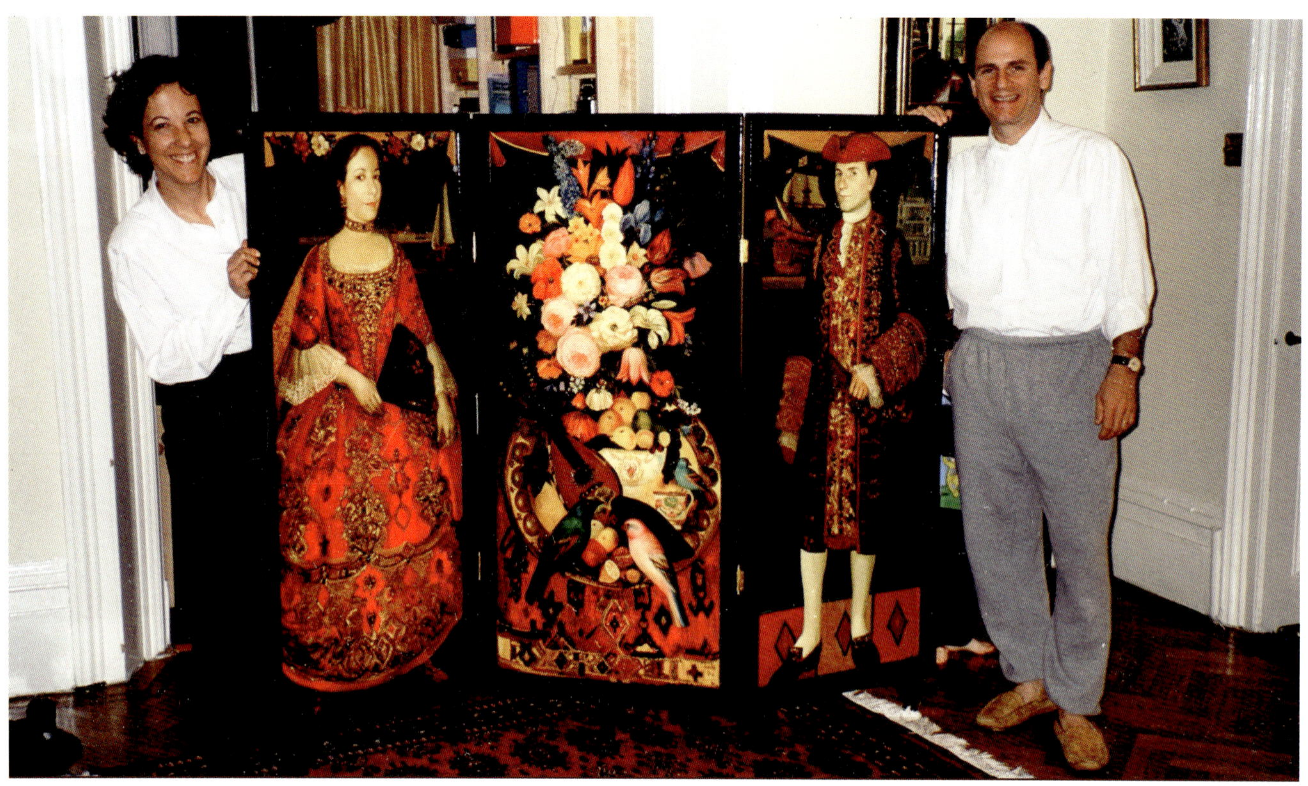

Family from England Portrait, by Olga Suvorova, screen, front, wood oil, 165 × 90 cm (1996)

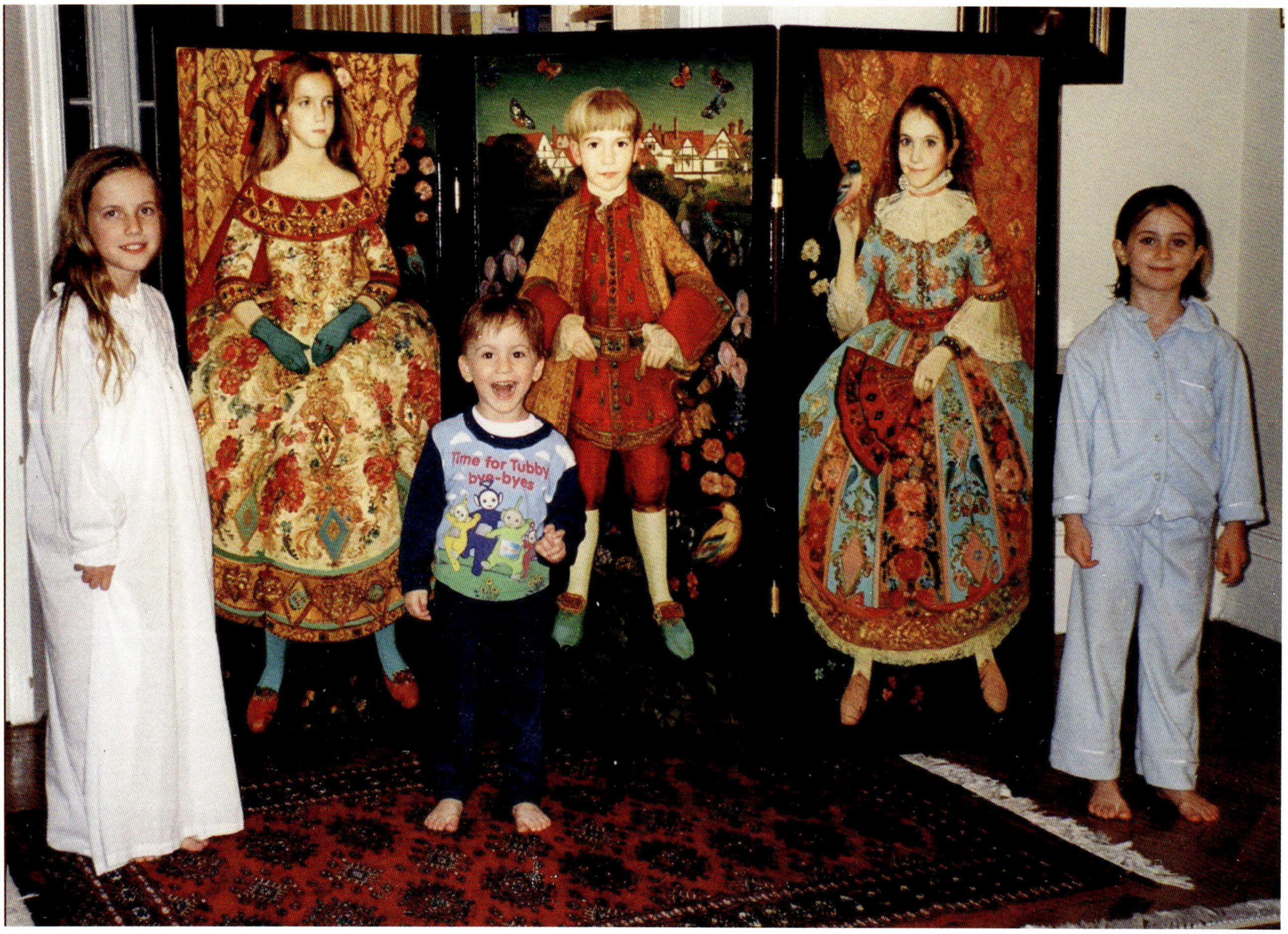

Family from England Portrait, screen, back, photo courtesy of Olga Suvorova, (1996)

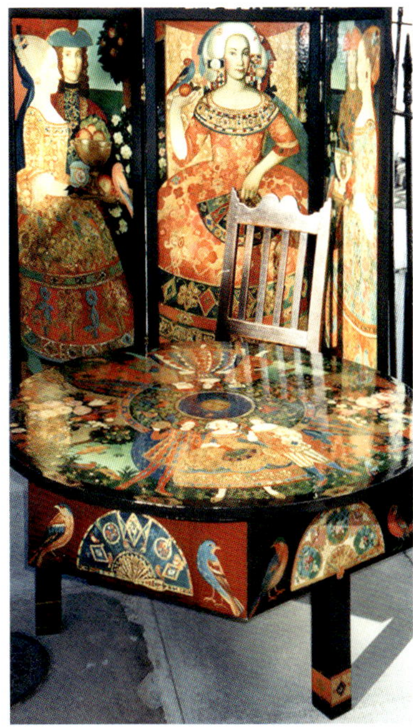

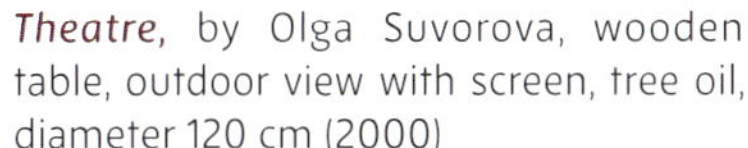

Theatre, by Olga Suvorova, wooden table, outdoor view with screen, tree oil, diameter 120 cm (2000)

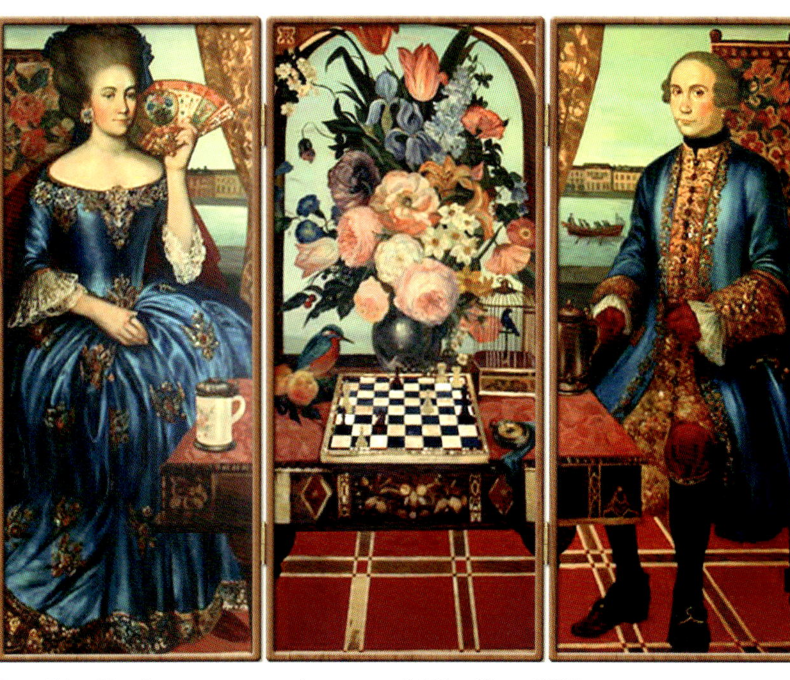

Game II, by Olga Suvorova, screen, front, tree oil, 160 × 65 cm (1995)

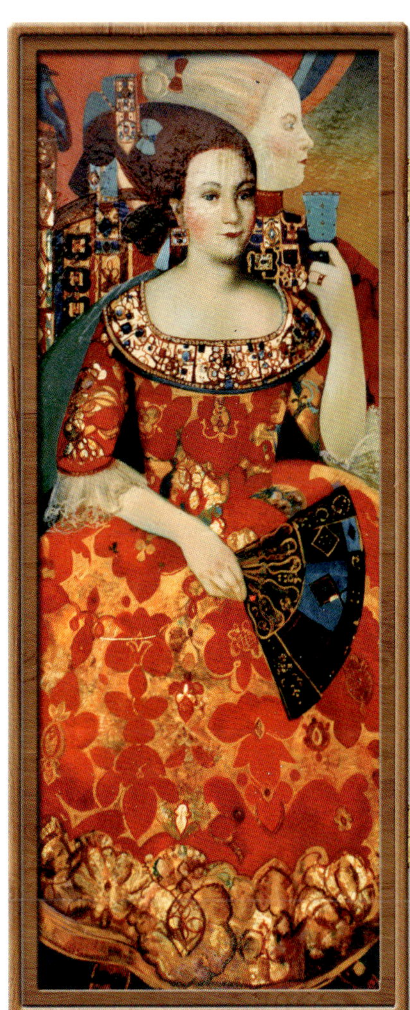

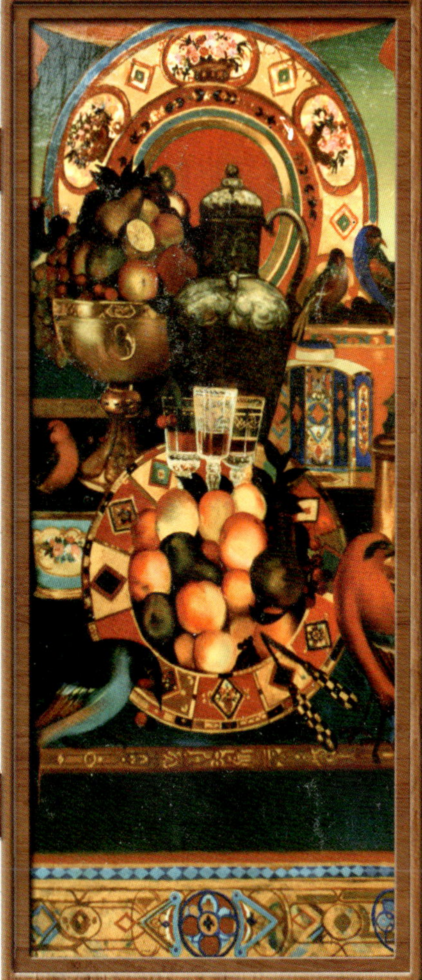

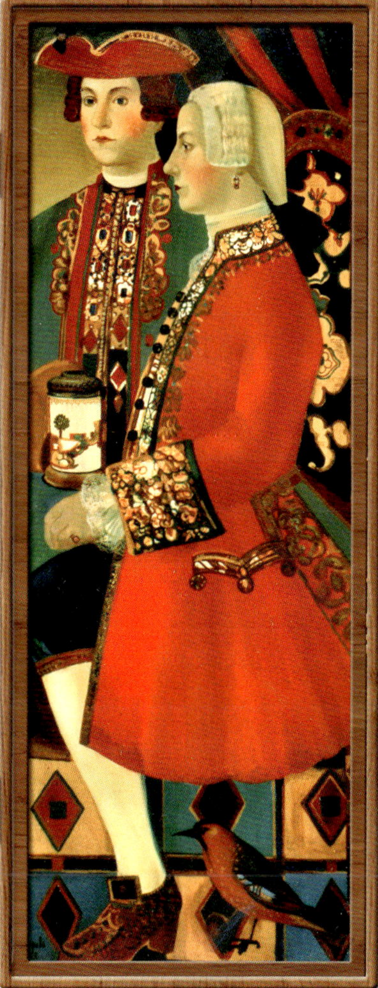

Banquet I, by Olga Suvorova, screen, front, tree oil, 165 × 95 cm (1995)

Plein Air Works

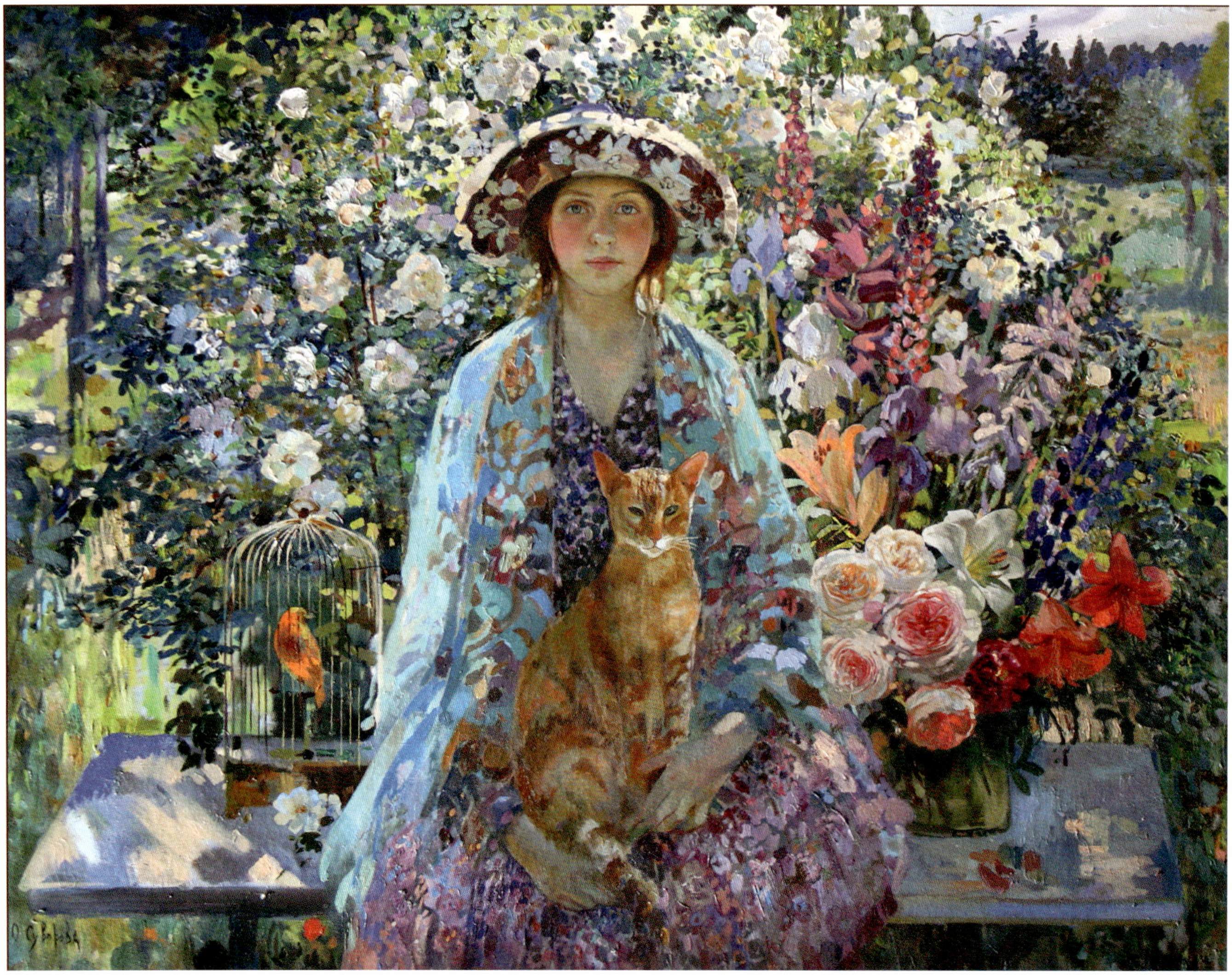

To expand my field of activity, I try to draw in my garden every summer. My daughter is grown, so I use my friends and relatives as models. Plein air painting offers a chance to learn new things. I figured out how to work with the sun, follow its movement in the sky. I watch the shadows changing on the subjects' faces and clothes, and one landscape can look completely different as conditions change. It reminds me of Claude Monet, who created a series of paintings of haystacks at different times of day and under different weather conditions.

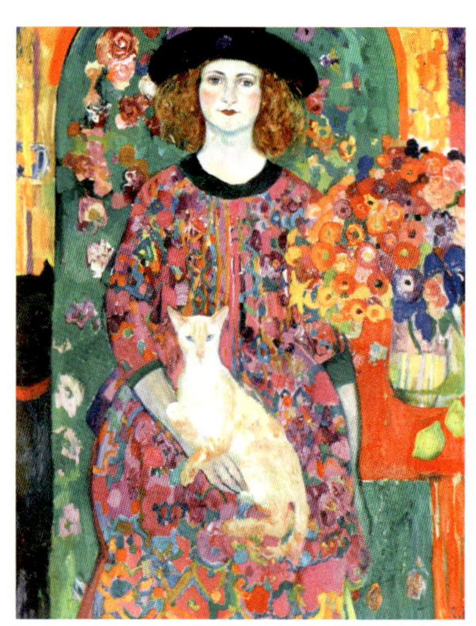

Summer Holidays, by Olga Suvorova, oil on canvas, 103 × 135 cm (2015)
Vika, by Olga Suvorova, oil on canvas, 110 × 85 cm (1998)

Many artists have loved to paint their gardens. Even the genius Gustav Klimt alternated work in his studio with painting études on the street. His magical works *The Sunflower* and *Poppy Field* still inspire me and led me to create several portraits influenced by him. Unfortunately, the abundance of his paintings printed on bags, cups, and T-shirts has made his art seem commonplace. But it is fashionable, and nothing can be done about it.

Suvorova with Katya, photo courtesy of Olga Suvorova (1995).

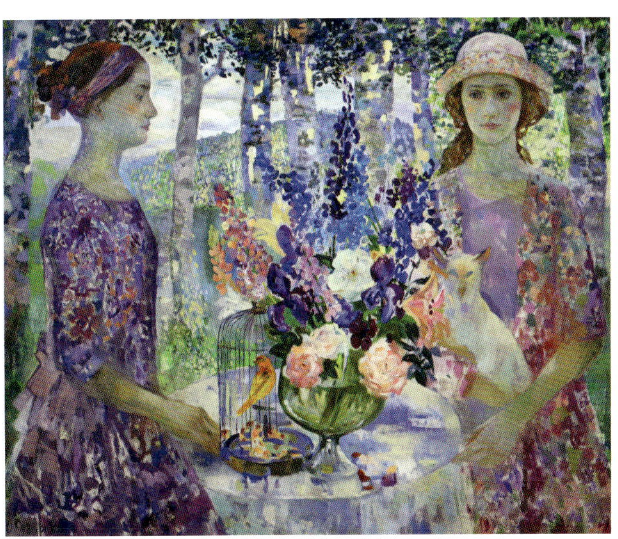

Birch, by Olga Suvorova, oil on canvas, 120 × 135 cm (2011).

Since I live in the North, summer is an extremely important time. I always want time to create as many paintings from nature as possible, but our summer is quite short, and the weather does not always allow you to work in the open. It often happens that I install an easel in the right place, bring a palette, brushes, and all the necessary props—and then it inevitably begins to rain. Or, even worse, a strong wind rises. Even a special artistic umbrella does not help then. It's hard to keep up with the weather. You have to wait for the sun to come out again, and then immediately go back to work, even though you have to start over. I don't like to work in cloudy weather because the green grass, flowers, and model look unnatural, but when the sun comes out, everything comes to life. It is especially beautiful when the model is sitting against the sunlight: her face is covered with sun glow and reflections from the green grass, and her hair becomes like multicolored lace.

When my daughter, Katya, posed for me in the garden. I dressed her in pretty summer dresses, chose the right hats with beautiful ribbons, and sat her on a bench with blooming pink bushes behind her. A model's job is hard work. The body's muscles become "wooden" from sitting still for so long, so you need to stretch from time to time. Sometimes I posed for my daughter, and she did not allow even the slightest movement on my part. I tried to sit still, remembering the Academy of Fine Arts models who stood still on the podium for hours.

My mother also posed for me, always reading a book so it would be easier for her to sit motionless. It is especially difficult to work in hot weather: delicate flower buds bloom quickly, and by evening they wither. I like to work in the evening when the sun is about to set and the shadows become rich blue. When the sun disappears behind the horizon, the colors become muted, and only white lilies gently glow in the darkness, exuding their scent.

I often paint in the garden alongside my mother. She draws a still life with flowers, while I paint a model. I was lucky to be born into a creative family; as in any family, we have our differences, but art reconciles us. I am glad that my daughter has also became an artist. She often confers with me about this or that picture. Thus, the arts have united three generations. We need each other, as working together is always easier.

Russian poet A. Pushkin wrote: "Ah, red summer, I would admire you, if not for the mosquitoes and flies!" That says it well, because the mosquitoes distract from work. They land on your eyes and hair, get into the paint, and stick to the paintings. I try to ignore this.

I want to convey nature's beauty, but it is so colorful and varied that sometimes it's impossible to find the right paint color, especially bright pink or purple shades. The art industry produces many colors, yet some shades are almost impossible to convey. It's like when you print a poster in a printing office: the reds and purples become primitive and flat.

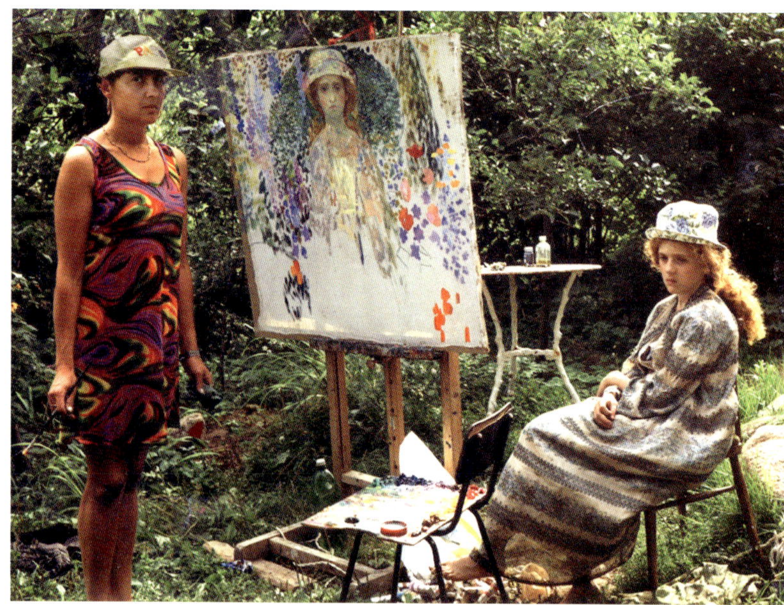

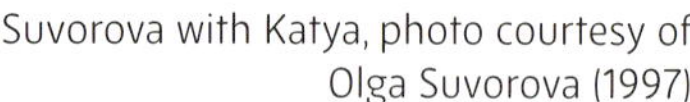

Suvorova with Katya, photo courtesy of Olga Suvorova (1997)

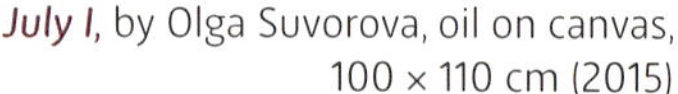

July I, by Olga Suvorova, oil on canvas, 100 × 110 cm (2015)

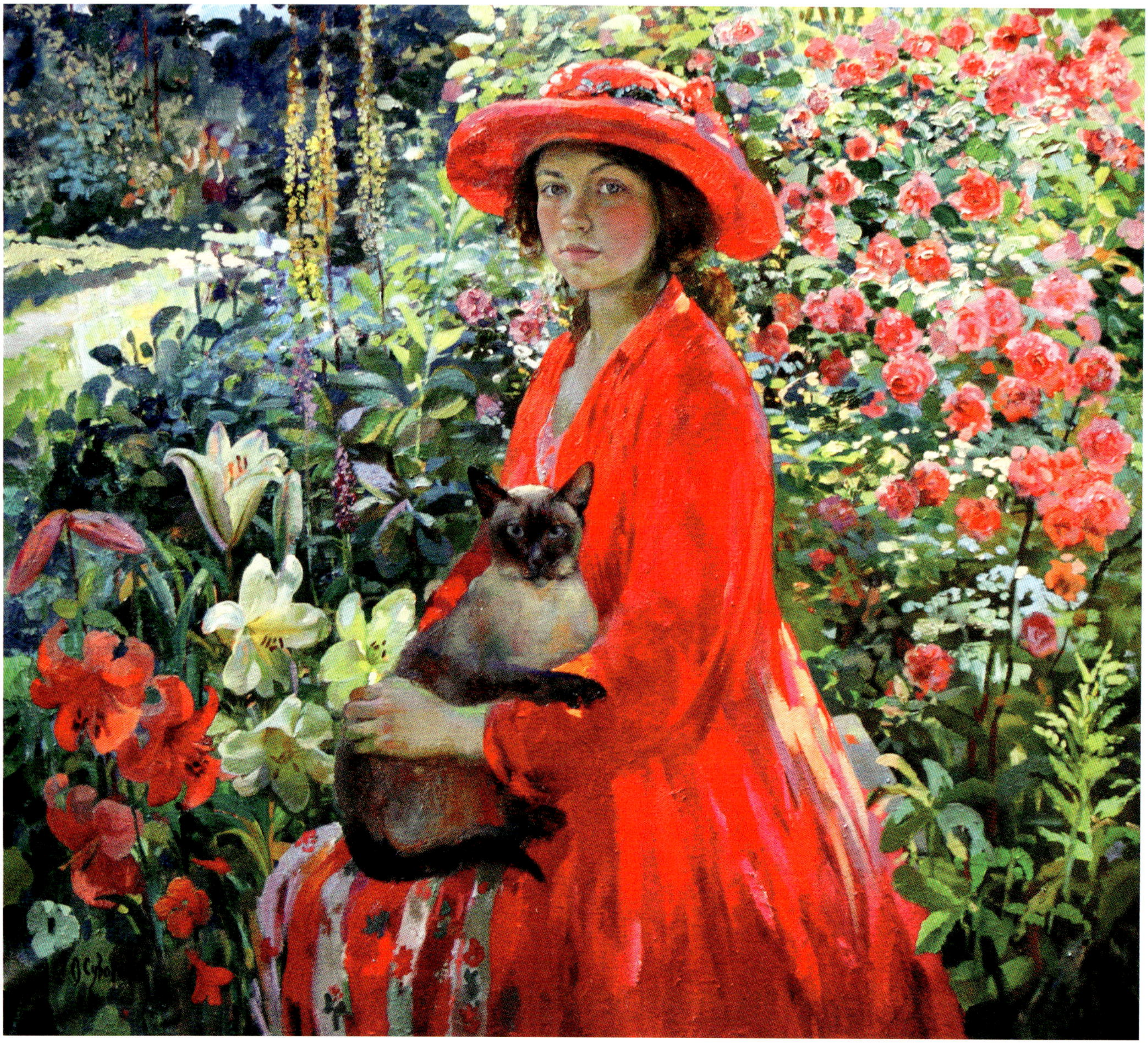

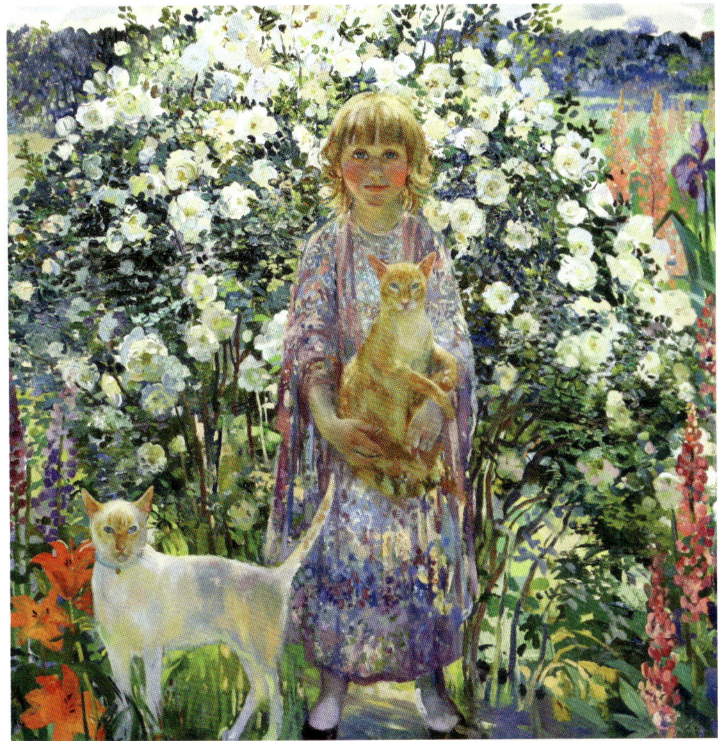

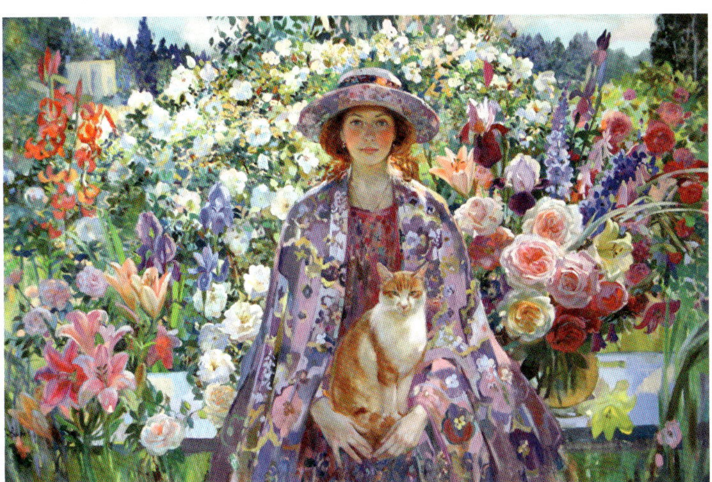

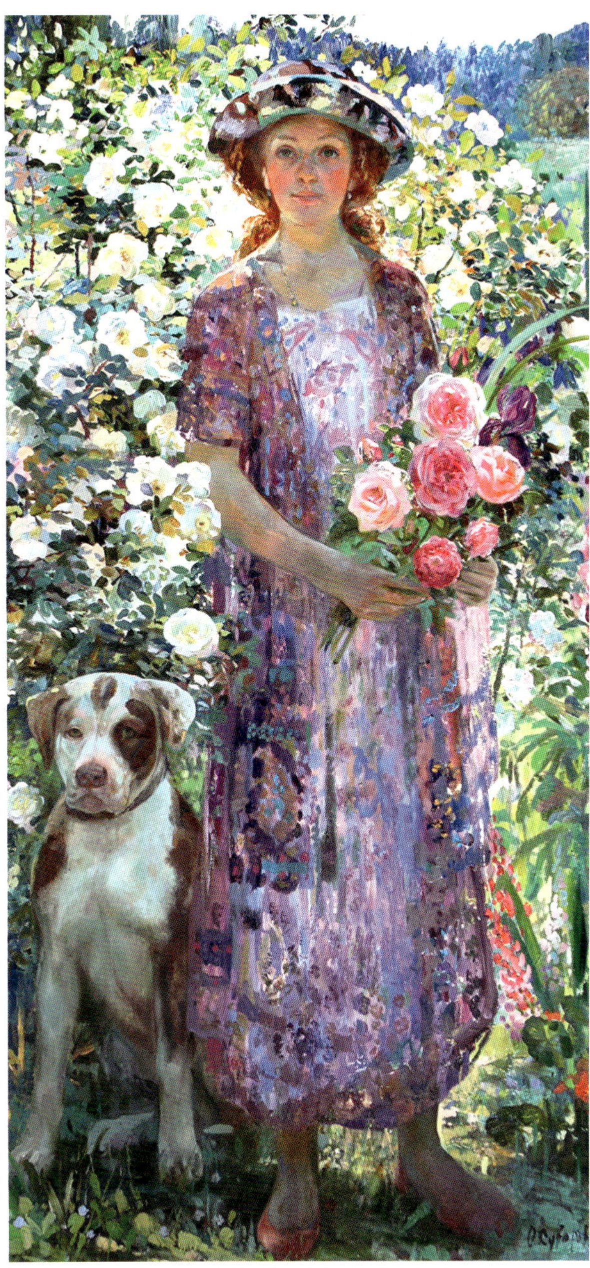

July II, by Olga Suvorova, oil on canvas, 99 × 108 cm (2001)
Portrait with Roses, by Olga Suvorova, oil on canvas, 90 × 125 cm (2015)
White Dog Rose, by Olga Suvorova, oil on canvas, 140 × 76 cm (2011)

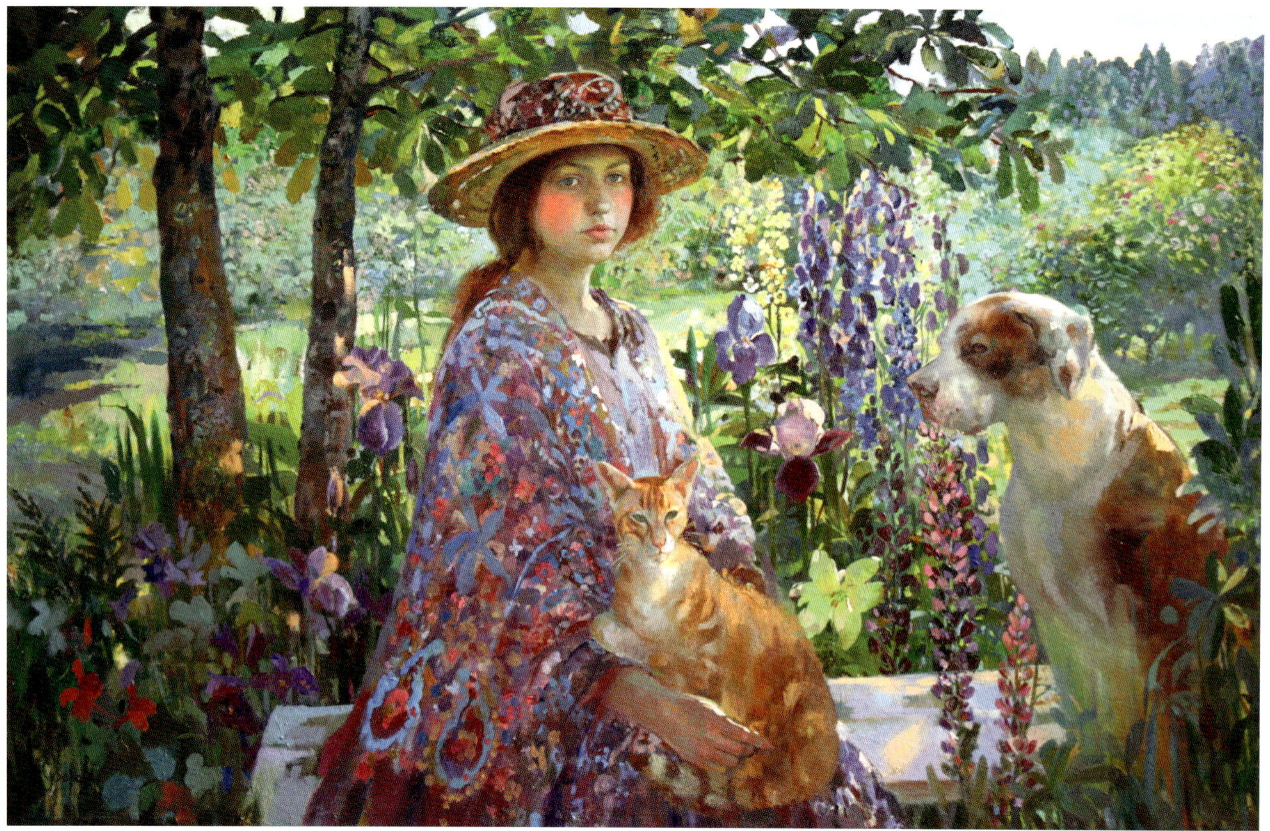

Friends I, by Olga Suvorova, oil on canvas, 80 × 135 cm (2015)

The hardest thing has always been drawing my animals. They are like small children, constantly in motion. Sometimes I have to catch a moment when my cats sit directly on the still life and fall asleep, purring. I've tried taking photos, but the camera is not able to convey a natural scene faithfully. When I work on the street, I try to paint *alla prima*, or immediately. Each painting takes no more than three days. This is a different type of painting than my usual decorative works. Here I draw everything quickly, focusing on the weather.

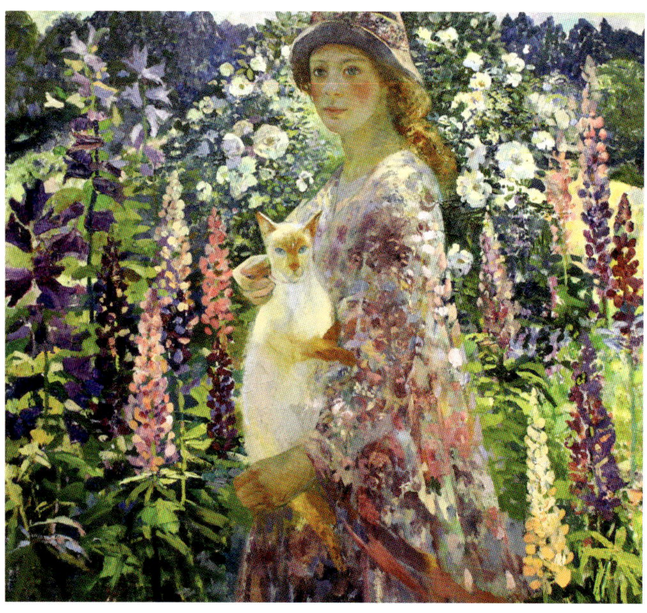

Garden, by Olga Suvorova, oil on canvas, 97 × 107 cm (2006)

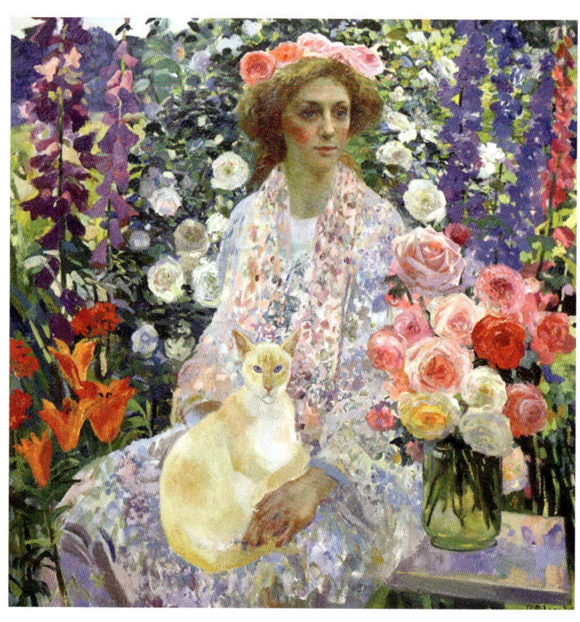

White Cat, by Olga Suvorova, oil on canvas, 95 × 96 cm (2010)

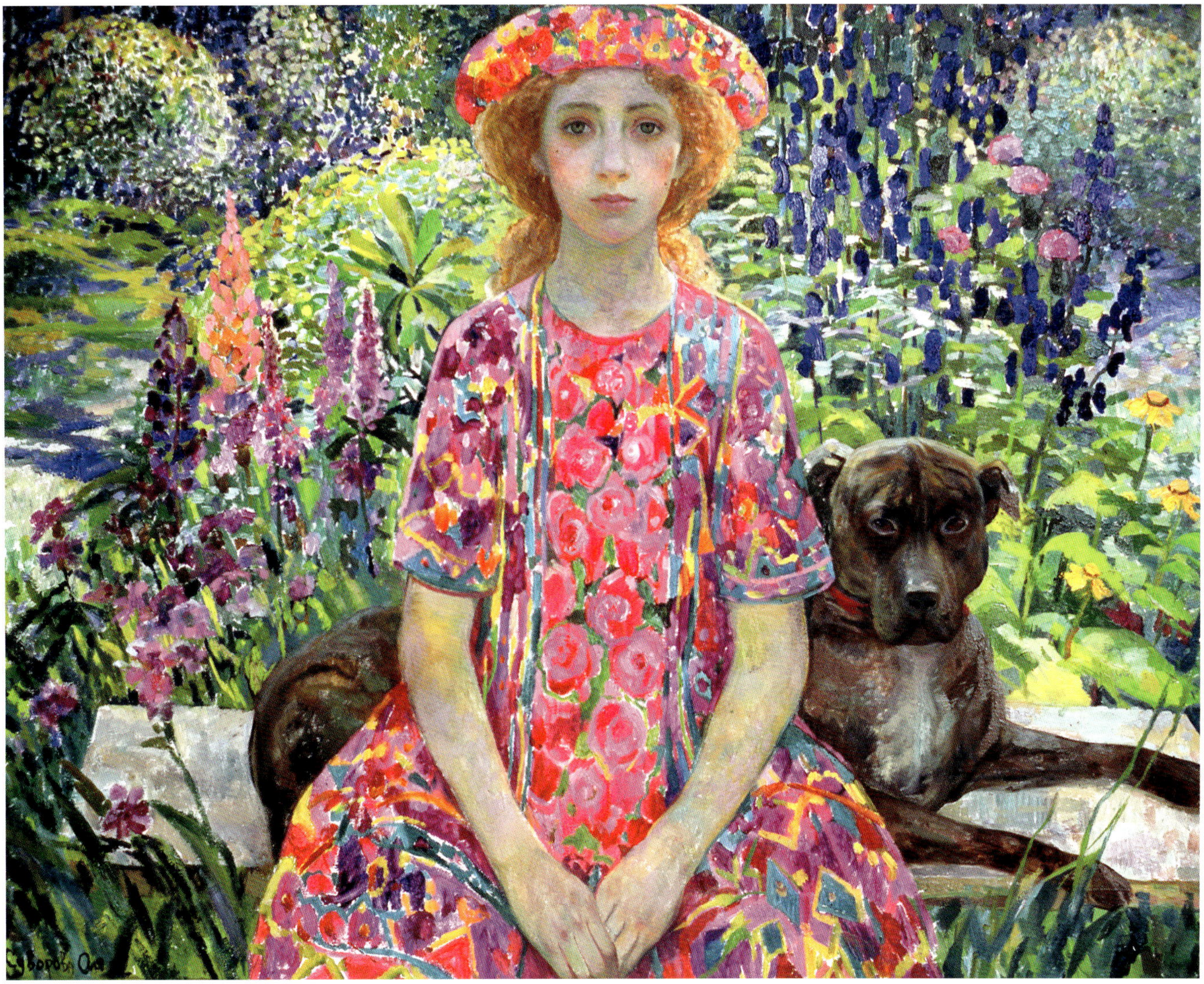

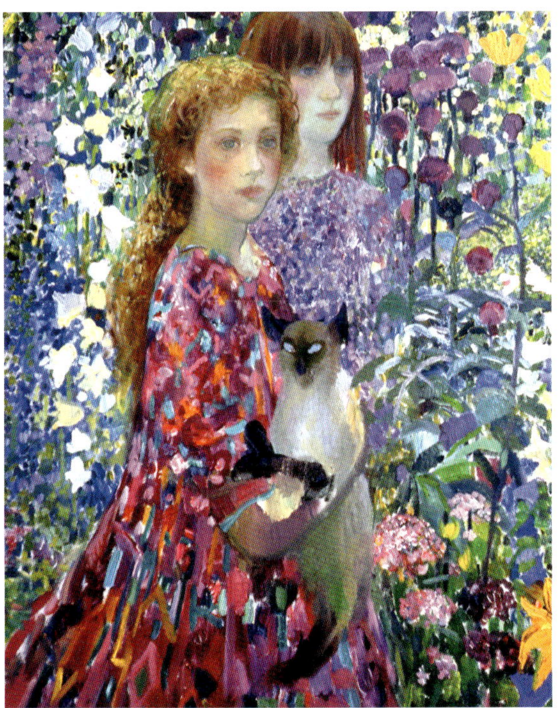

Paintings created in the garden and the studio are equally important. Portraits done on the street are more traditional and do not express my decorative style as vividly as my other work does. But drawing in the garden—with my family, my ginger cats, the flowers, or my favorite dog as subjects—is my favorite activity. It's like a breath of fresh air. You do not need to invent anything; nature tells you what to portray.

Friends II, by Olga Suvorova, oil on canvas, 95 × 110 cm (1998)
Sisters I, by Olga Suvorova, oil on canvas, 120 × 125 cm (1998)

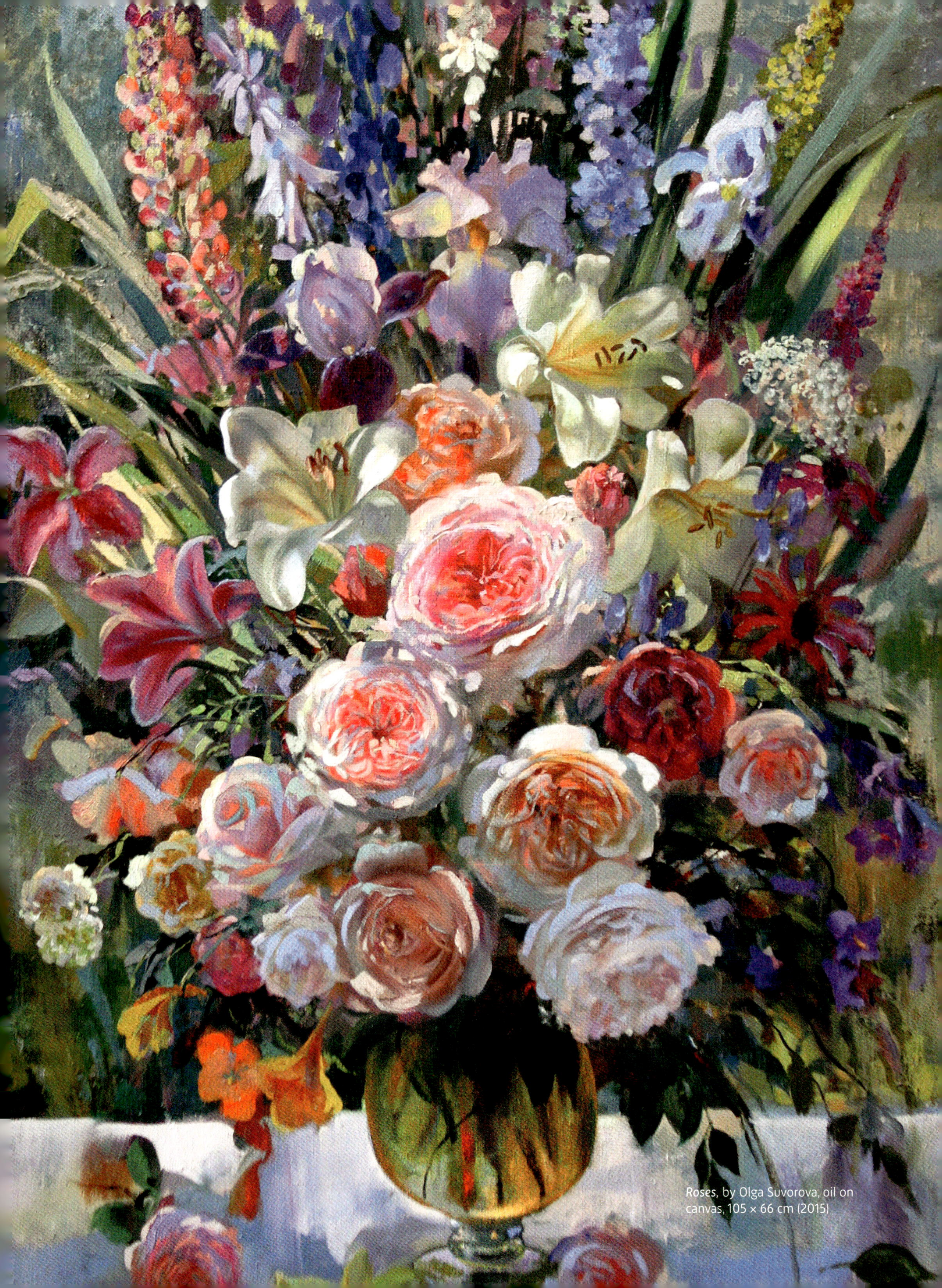

Roses, by Olga Suvorova, oil on canvas, 105 × 66 cm (2015)

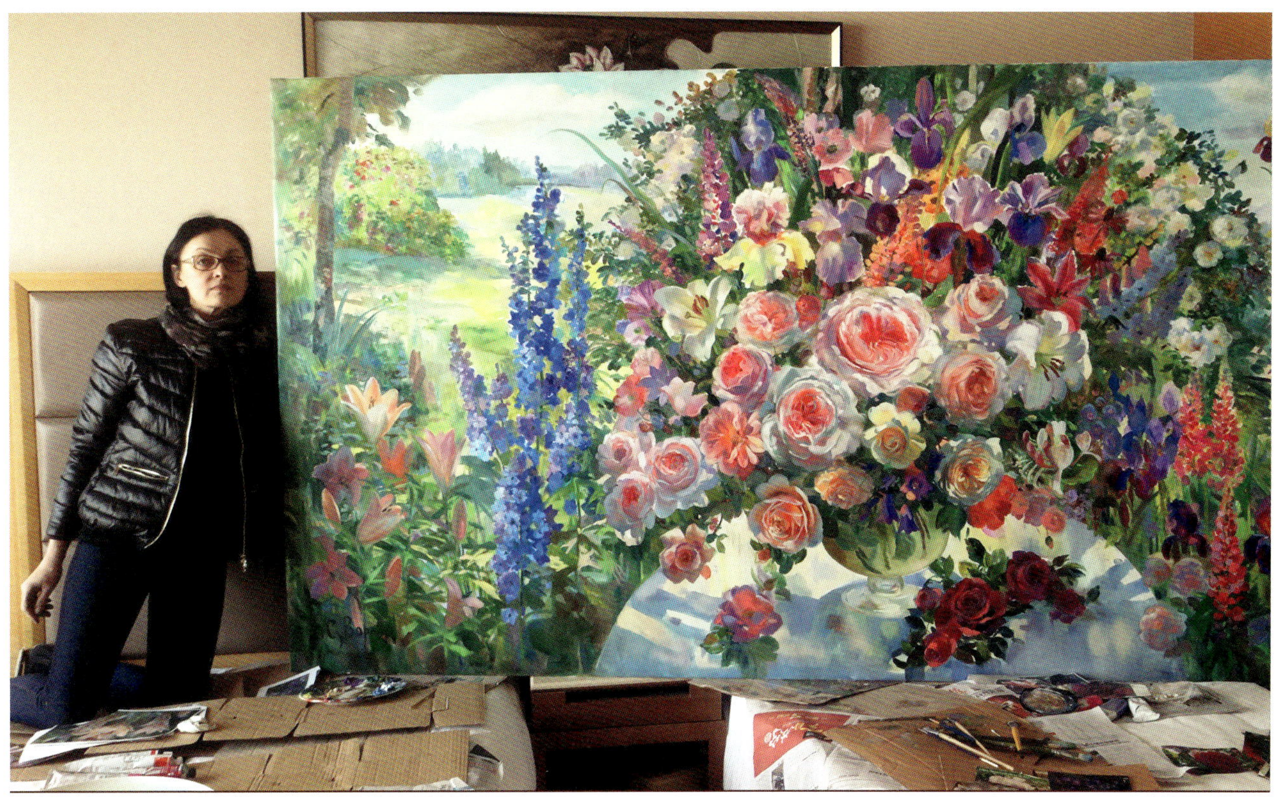

Suvorova in her studio, photo courtesy of Olga Suvorova (2016)

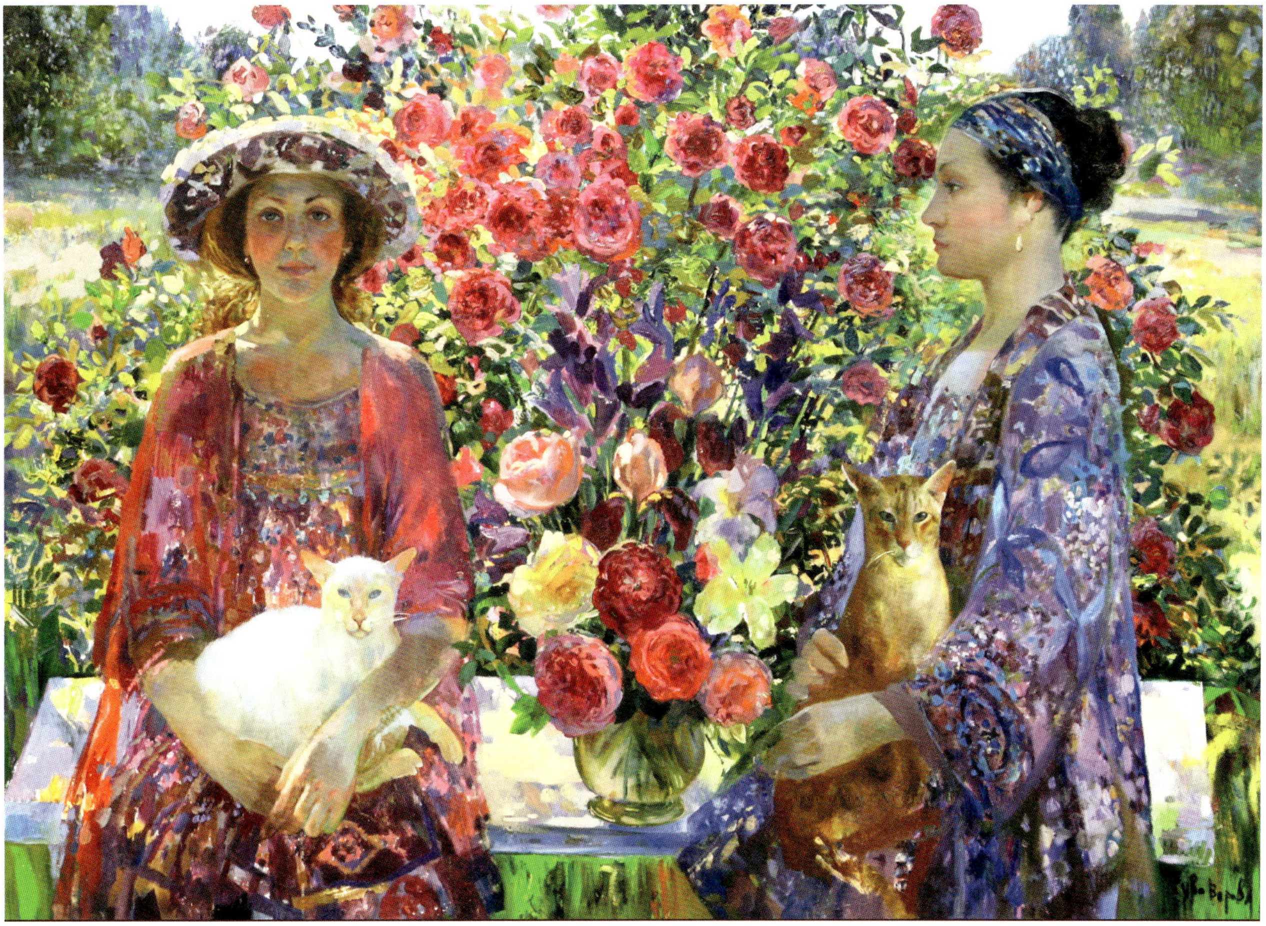

Sisters, by Olga Suvorova, oil on canvas, 98 × 139 cm (2014)

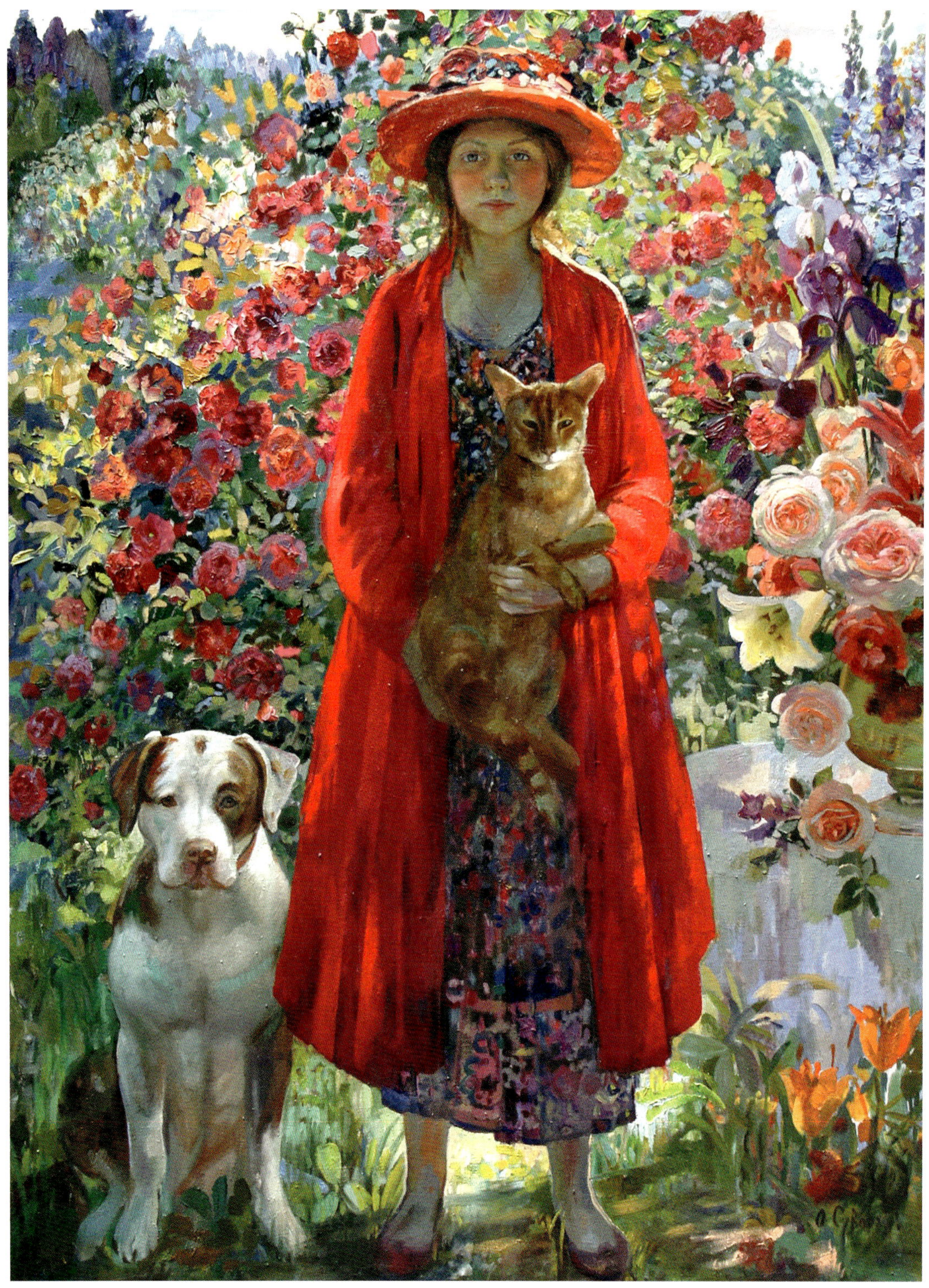

Friends III, by Olga Suvorova, oil on canvas, 115 × 90 cm (2015)

Every flower that I plant will surely be depicted in some picture. I especially like white rose hips; even though they bloom only once in a summer, it is an unforgettable scene. There are so many white flowers that you cannot even see the green foliage. For a short time, the rose hips become the center of the garden—bees, bumblebees, and colorful butterflies rush to enjoy this miracle of nature. I too hurry to capture this nature festival before it rains. After the rain, the land turns white from the abundance of fallen petals and I feel deeply sad that the flowering was so short. Closer to autumn, when everything is fading away, I return to my workshop.

Creative Maturity

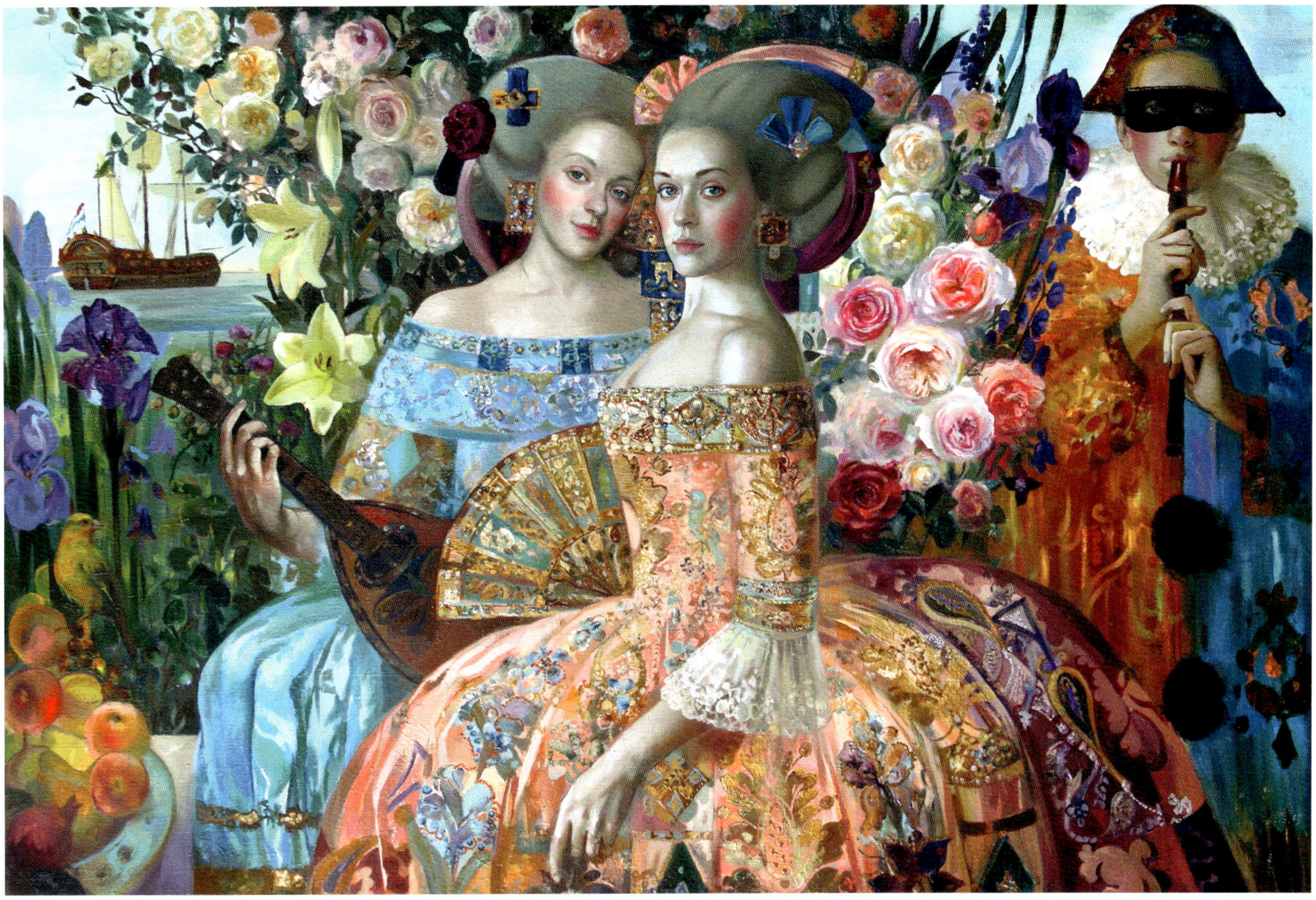

Sisters V, by Olga Suvorova, oil on canvas, 98 × 139 cm (2014)

Suvorova in her studio, photo courtesy of Olga Suvorova (2015)

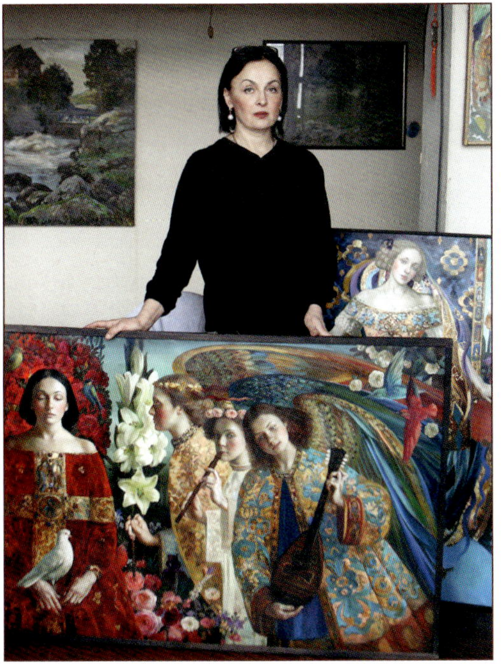

As I grew older and gained creative experience, I began moving away from simple decorative works such as a colored rug, where the image of a person was conditional. I wanted more personal details, elaboration of the characters' hands and faces. Hands are the hardest to draw. I also began to think about lighting—how the light will fall, what details will push forward, what will remain in the shadows and be left unsaid. I considered the individuality of different characters, looking for suitable models to express the idea of the picture. For example, the main idea of *Duel* is the eternal struggle between good and bad. There is a party-draw on the chessboard, because everything is in a certain balance in our world, and we know the tacit truths that without light there is no darkness, and vice versa.

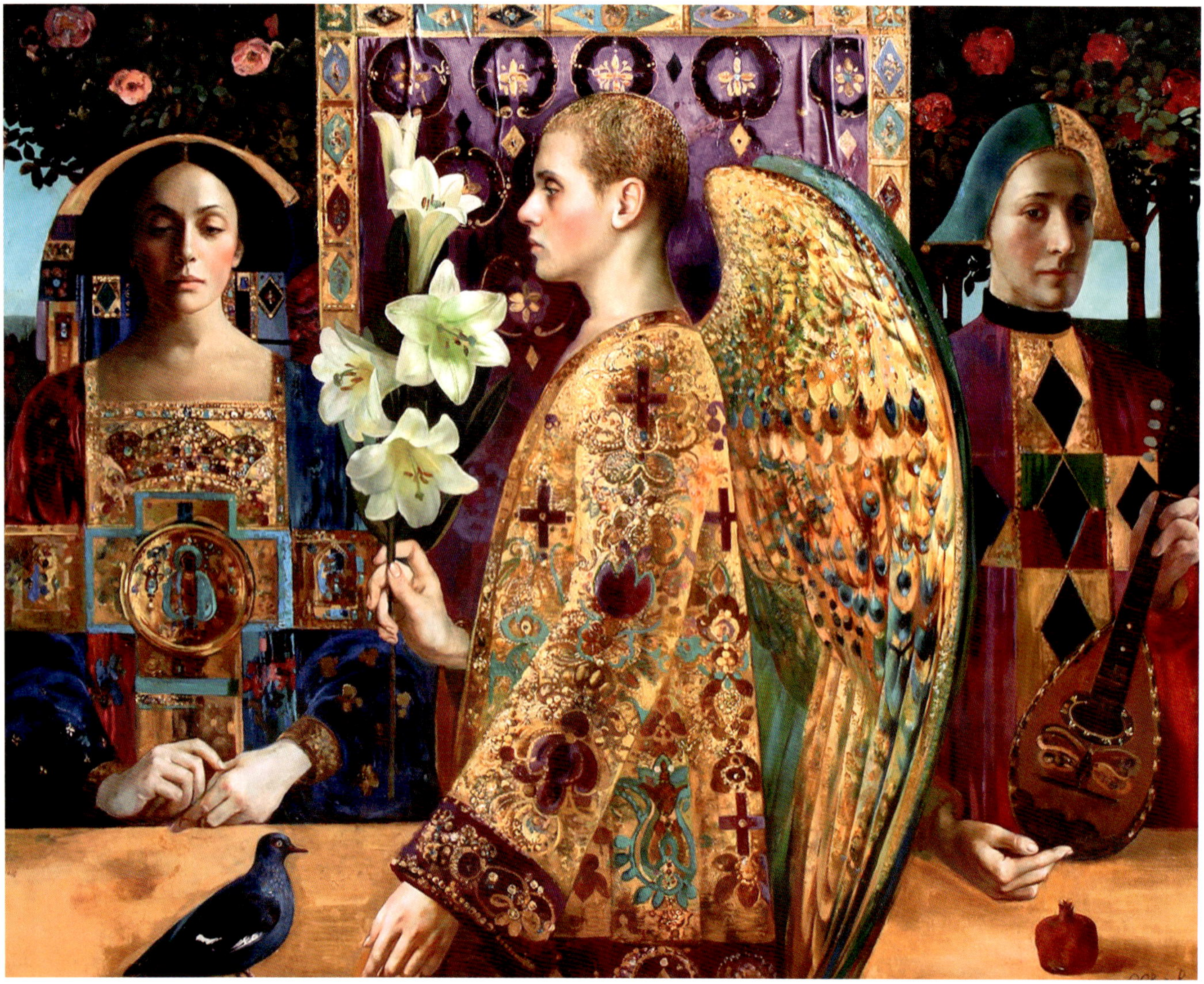

Golden Annunciation, by Olga Suvorova, oil on canvas, 132 × 109 cm (2011)

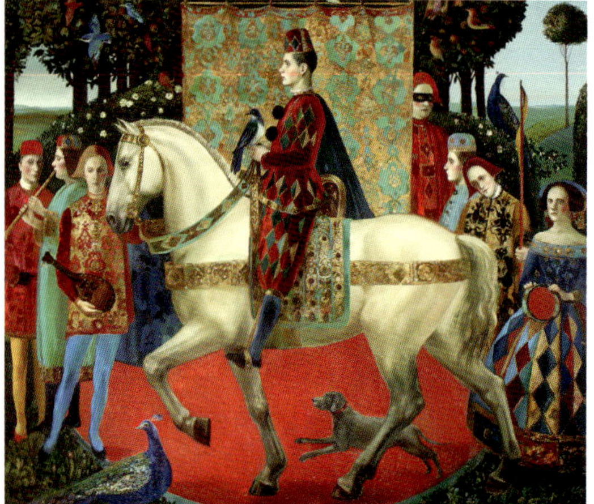

Theatre I, by Olga Suvorova, oil on canvas, 100 × 120 cm (2011)

Many of my pictures are devoted to theatrical topics. One of the earliest is *Theater*. I wanted to express the idea of an ordinary clown entertaining the crowd while sitting on a white horse, which characterizes him as a winner. He is in charge, and the theater revolves around him. Everyone expects jokes from him, which sometimes tell us the bitter truth. I also created a series of paintings on the love triangle, where a woman disguised as Columbine chooses between two men. Usually they are Pierrot and Harlequin, opposite characters—indecisive Pierrot and boorish Harlequin, who is used to getting everything he wants immediately. In life, it is often difficult for us to make a choice; we want our chosen ones to combine all the best human qualities. I see Harlequin and Pierrot as two halves of a whole. *Pierrot's Dream* continues this theme. It depicts a hand in the sky, and people often ask me what it means. The plot is simple: Pierrot, who is asleep, dreams about himself and his beloved Columbine. But in life everything is predetermined, and only in the sky are all the answers to our questions.

The hand symbolizes help for Pierrot in love, since all marriages are made in heaven.

I am impressed with the Symbolist movement. It was characterized by experimentation, a desire for innovation, the use of symbolism, understatement, hints, and mystery. The Symbolists were looking for deep meaning in fantasies, dreams, consciousness, and emotions. Whereas realists and naturalists sought to reproduce objective reality, their ideas were focused on expressing the ideal image.

In my paintings, I try to explain to the viewer the absolute truths, using metaphorical images and allegories. I want to convey with a brush not a literal image, but the combination of feelings and emotions. In this vein, I adore Russian artist Mikhail Vrubel. His Demon series is fascinating. His work stands alone among others of this trend. Sometimes I want to understand the hidden meanings, to go in-between the visible and invisible worlds.

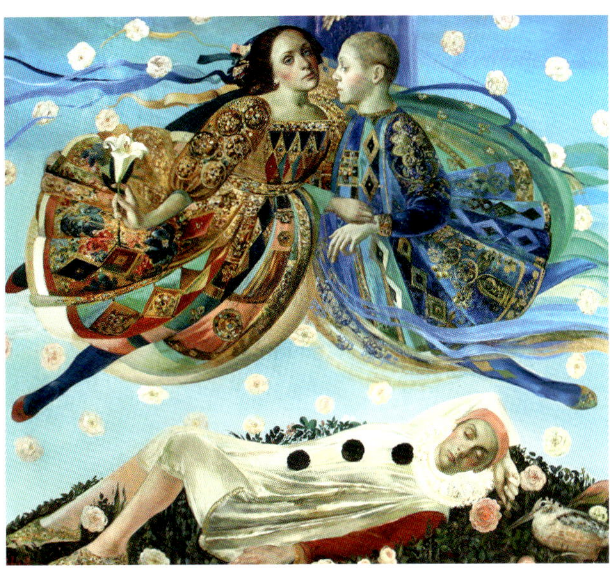

Pierrot's Dream, by Olga Suvorova, oil on canvas, 97 × 115 cm (2010).

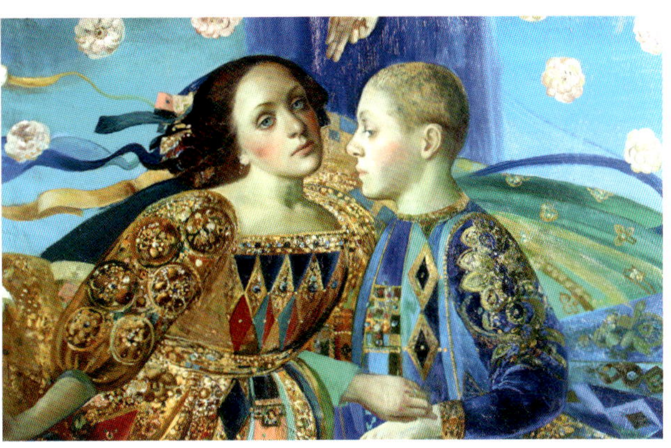

Pierrot's Dream (detail)

My recent work is devoted to the theme of carnivals and masquerades. When I immerse myself in the world of beautiful maids of honor and their secrets, I forget about the monotony of everyday life. I invent dresses, fans, and hairstyles for them. Sometimes it seems that our modern world is too minimalistic in its clothes, and even the feelings between people. The life of a modern person is full of conflicts, tension, overload, unfulfilled hopes, and disappointments. Art succors, leads to the world of dreams, and brings harmony to one's inner state, restoring mental balance. I want to believe that creating harmony in this crazy world compensates for loss and brightens everyday lives.

The French sociologist Edgar Morin, for example, believes that looking at a work of art helps to diffuse internal tension.

I surely cannot ignore my religious works. My favorite artist, Sandro Botticelli, pushed me toward this profound topic; his works are so majestic and sometimes full of true drama. Interesting fact: his painting *Spring* depicts 170 species of plants, at least that is what good botanists have assured us. With surprising delicacy, his work combined ancient humanism and Christianity. This gave birth to the phenomenon of the Italian Renaissance. In the middle of the nineteenth century, Botticelli's work was reinterpreted and highly appreciated by the British Pre-Raphaelites, who honored the fragile linearity (the technique of creating linear images of clothes, contours of figures, and a certain brush style and limitation of color spots) and spring freshness of his mature paintings as the highest point in the development of world art. His work is filled with features of delicacy and aristocratic elegance. The paintings are extremely emotional and ingrained with personal experiences that reflect the complex inconsistencies of the era and absorb the best tradition of fifteenth-century Italian art.

I wanted to paint a big picture of the universe that would reflect the great meaning of our existence. With the help

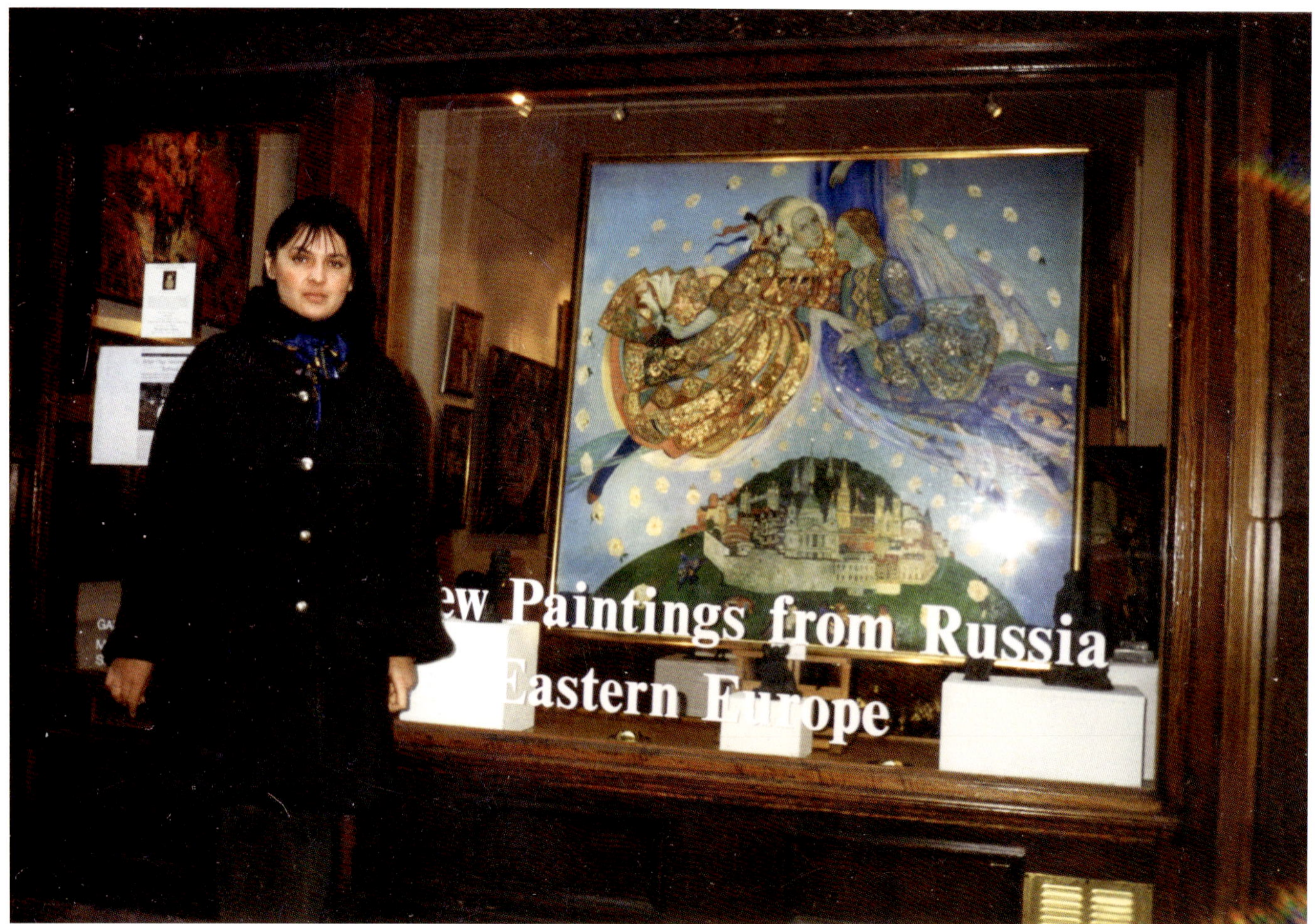

Suvorova at the Alberti Gallery in London, photo courtesy of Olga Suvorova (1998)

of a brush, I wanted to send a message to the viewer that our universe is the Supreme mind—design and thought-form. Clear, bright, positive thoughts bring prosperity to our world. Evil and ignorance lead to the destruction of civilization. The Mother of God is depicted in blue clothes, where blue is symbolic of the sky, eternal peace, clarity, and purity. Her head is graced with a crown and she is leading the Son of God by the hand, Christ, with a goldfinch sitting on his hand. In art, this little bird represents the Passion of Christ, as the goldfinch's red mask, in the eyes of the first Christians, symbolized the blood on the face of Christ from the crown of thorns. In Renaissance art, the infant Christ is often portrayed with a goldfinch in his hands, reflecting his future suffering and death. Legend tells that during Christ's journey to Calvary, a little goldfinch sat on his shoulder and pulled a thorn out of the Savior's forehead, and the blood of God's son remained as an eternal red stain around his beak.

Demon, by Mikhail Vrubel, size, medium, and date unknown.

OPPOSITE

The Riddle, by Olga Suvorova, oil on canvas, 94 × 131 cm (2017)

Music II, by Olga Suvorova, oil on canvas, 90 × 140 cm (2014)

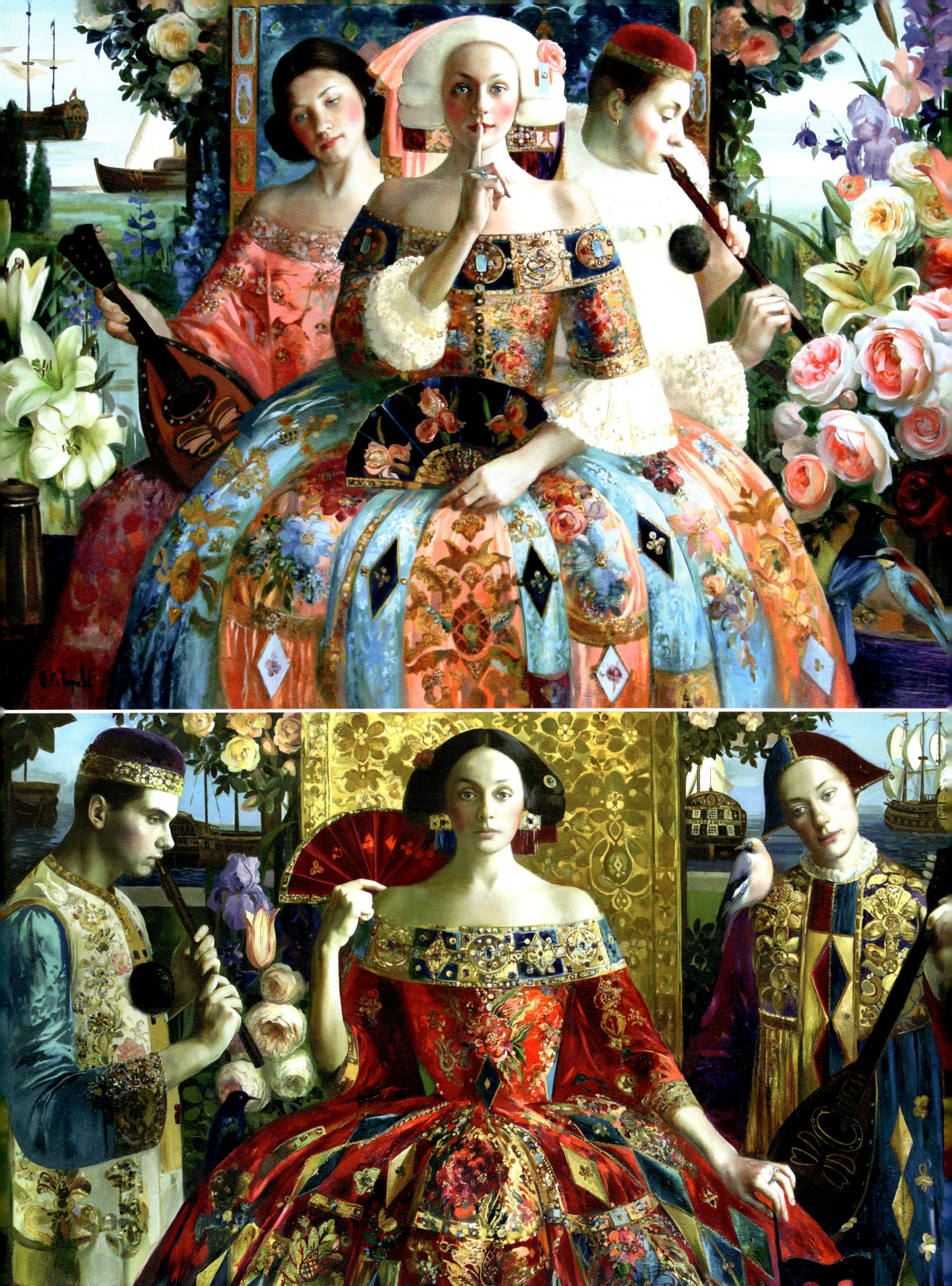

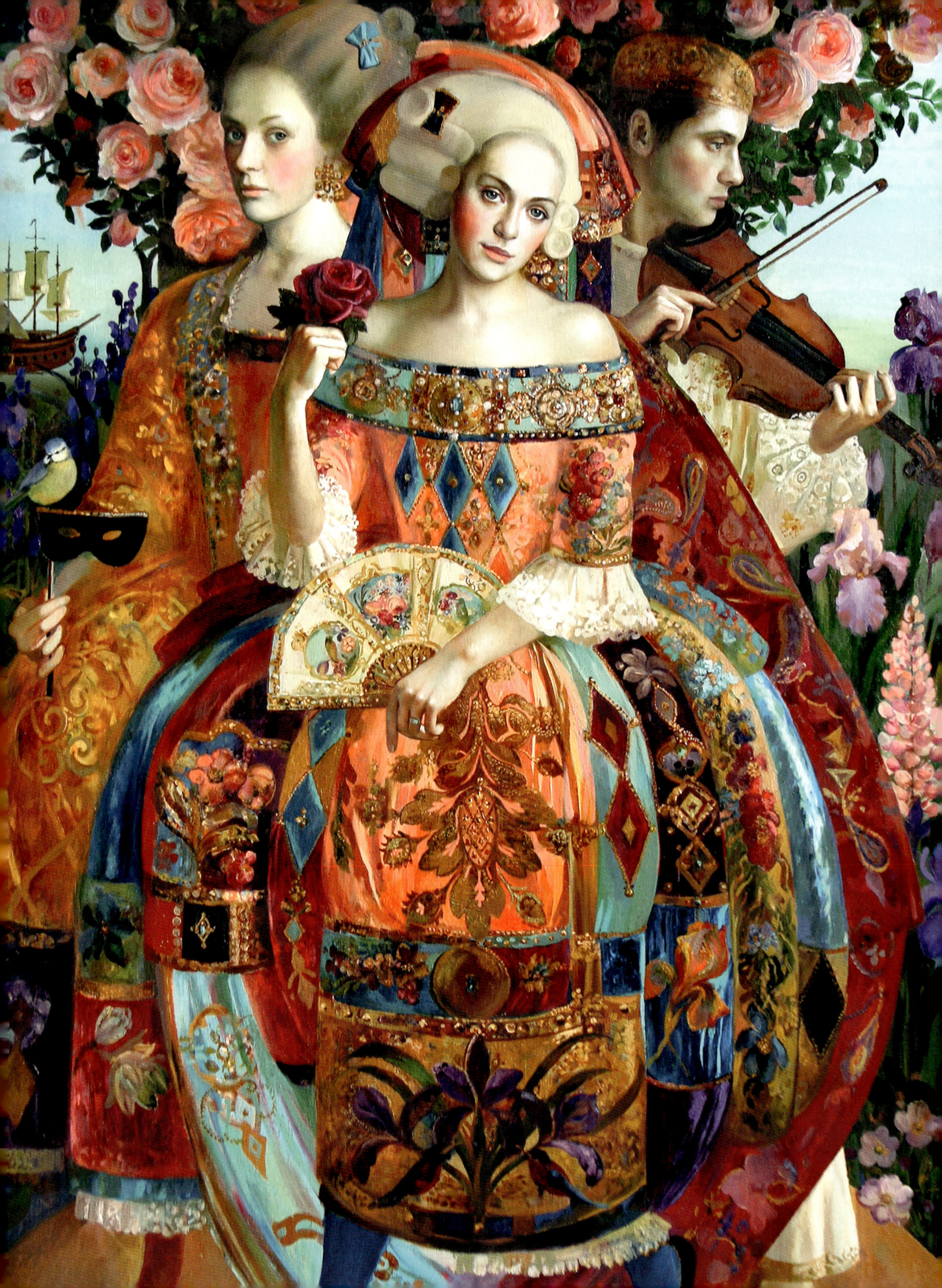

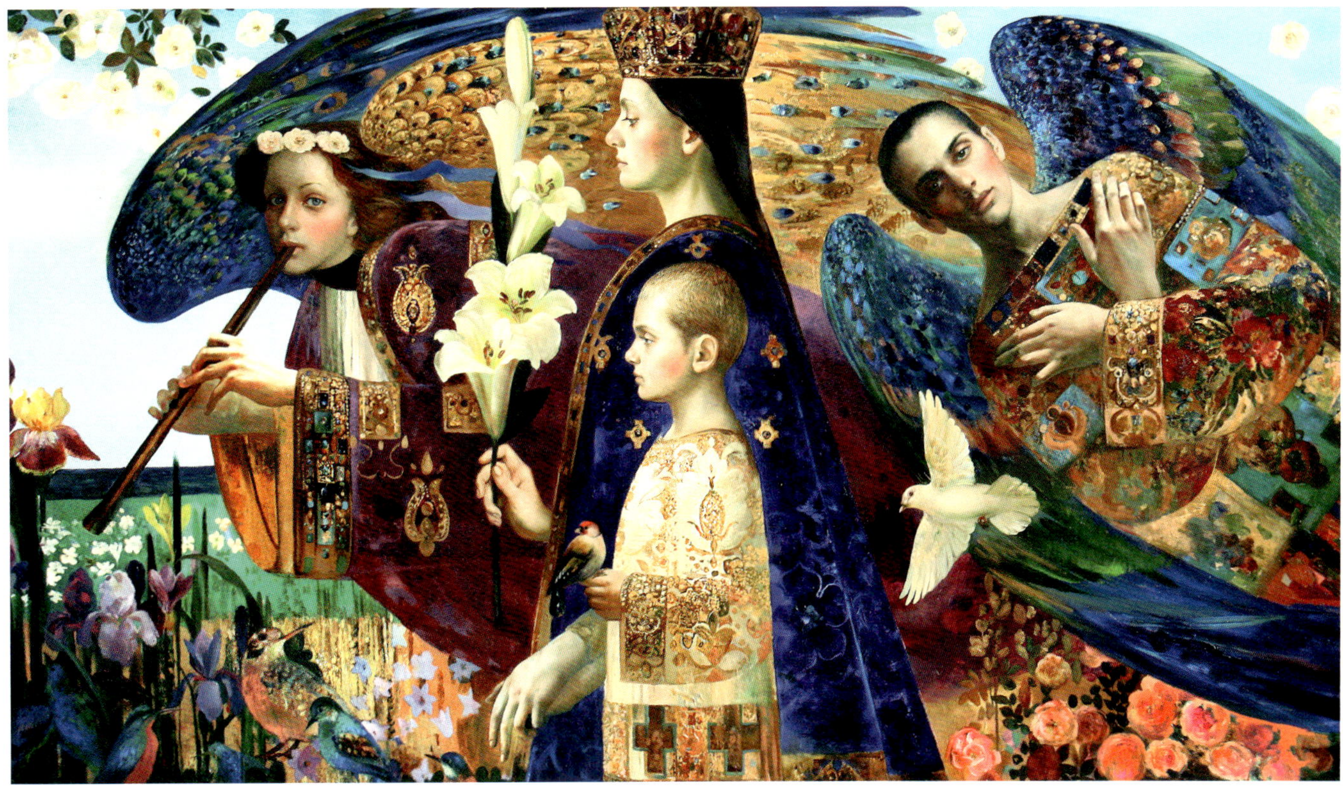

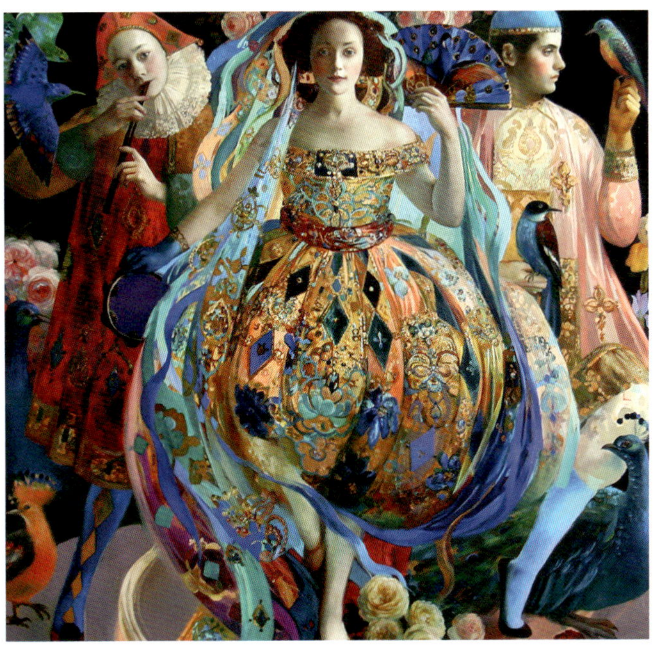

The Universe, by Olga Suvorova, oil on canvas, 101 × 163 cm (2013)

Moon Light, by Olga Suvorova, oil on canvas, 115 × 120 cm (2019)

OPPOSITE

Venice, by Olga Suvorova, oil on canvas, 145 × 95 cm (2018)

The white dove, flying with the Madonna, represents the Supreme mind that always accompanies the Mother of God. The angel, flying ahead in this picture, is depicted in purple clothes—this color is also not accidental, as it symbolizes intimate knowledge, silence, and spirituality. In early Christianity, the color purple symbolized sadness and affliction. The angels are depicted with sad faces because they know of the Savior's future sufferings. Birds and flowers tell us that all life on Earth is created by the Supreme mind.

Most of humanity is deeply convinced that a person has a soul, but a robot cannot have one. However, none of the believers can clearly define what is hidden within this belief. One thing is known for sure: the soul is a nonmaterial substance. The dilemma of the primacy of spirit or matter has been fruitlessly discussed for centuries. There are two official concepts of consciousness: On the one hand, the spirit is defined by living matter and is secondary. On the other hand, in the cosmic concept of consciousness, the spirit is the Supreme mind that creates matter. The energetic-informational system, having an unimaginable magnitude, embraces the whole of infinite space. Based on this, I want to answer the question of whether the

To quote Van Gogh:

"Our canvases must speak for us. We created them, and they exist, and this is the most important thing."

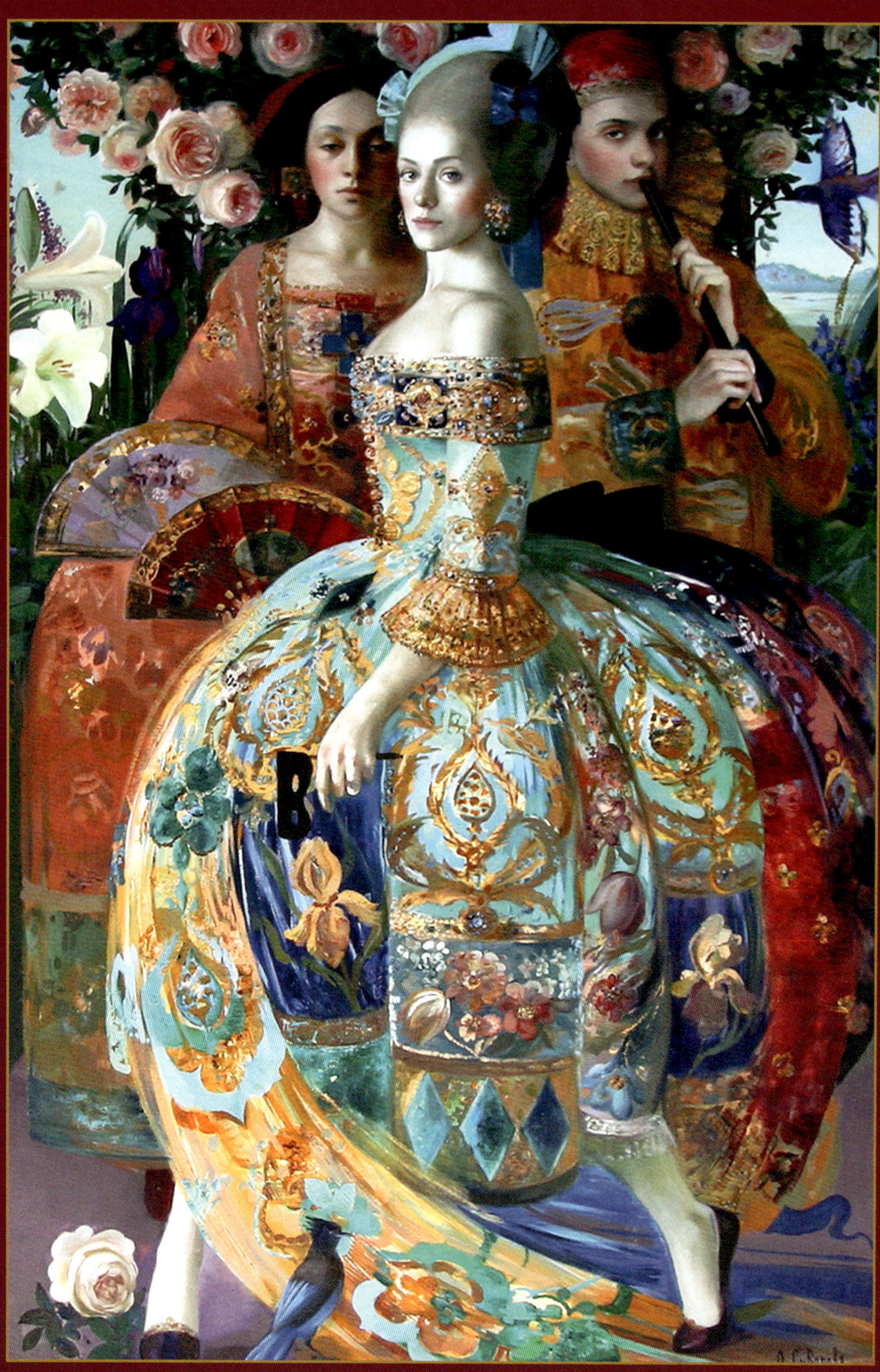

Music IV, by Olga Suvorova, oil on canvas, 145 × 95 cm (2016)

human spirit is in the brain or in the higher mind. If we consider spirit to be the product of the human brain, everything is simple; but if it is the activity of the higher mind, the situation is more complicated.

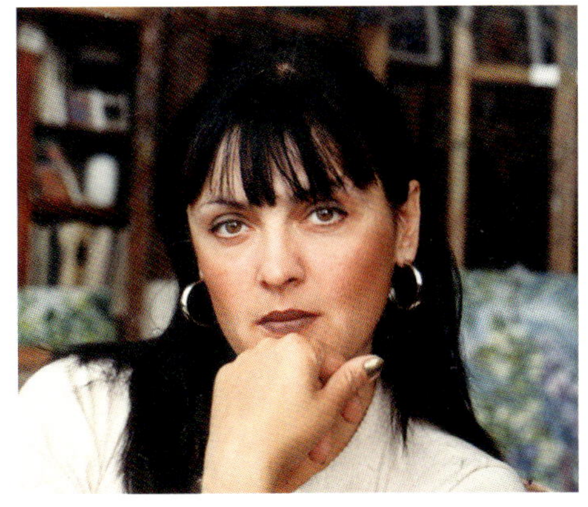

Suvorova in her studio, photo courtesy of Olga Suvorova, (2004)

If we state that the unconscious is the sum of past evolution, then the Supreme mind is its future. The latter statement represents our standard, never-sleeping consciousness. The mystery is to find the eternal in the temporal, the boundless in the limited, and the all-embracing completeness even in the darkest part of existence. Every person is a reflection of the Universe. This is some kind of a microworld that keeps to the same laws and stores the same energy. We ordinary people are not meant to solve the origin of mankind, we only have our faith. Perhaps, in the future, humanity will come to the solution of the origin of mankind and all things. To believe or not to believe in God is a personal matter, but for me the theme of religion is very important. In my paintings, I try to remind people of that bright and important feeling, which must be preserved in every one of us.

The main thing for me is that people at exhibitions or in social networks react with interest to my paintings. Everything I do, I do for you, beloved viewer, and people's indifference to art seems to be the most terrible thing for me. Try to find time to go to a museum or exhibition, because there you can learn the true diversity of our world.

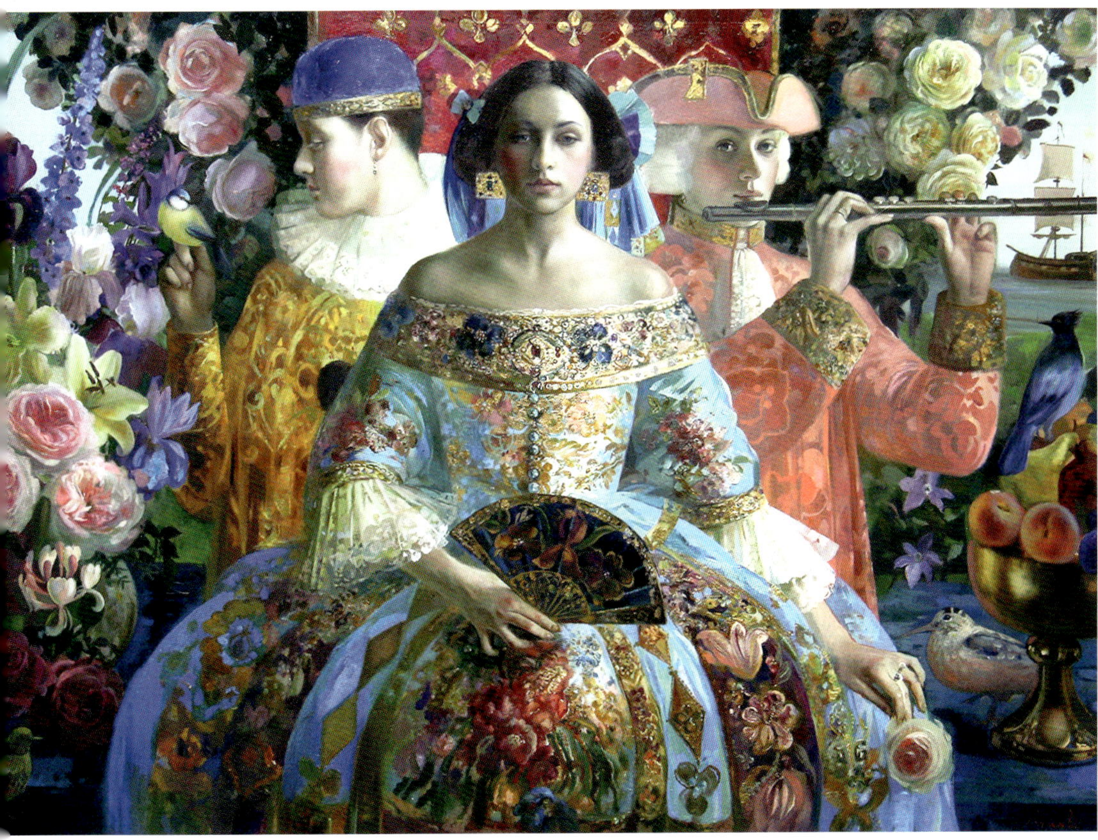

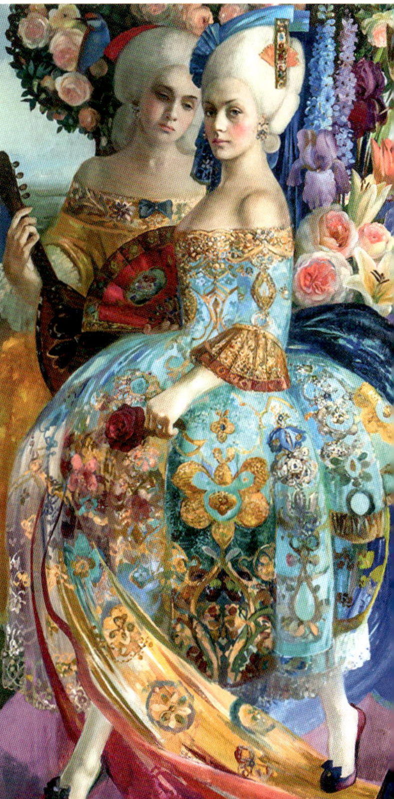

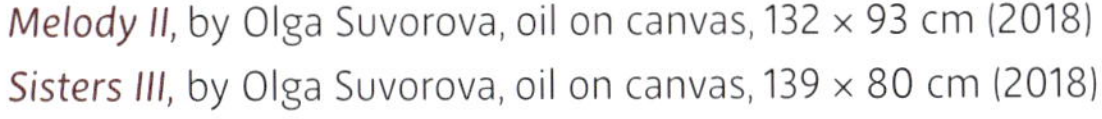

Melody II, by Olga Suvorova, oil on canvas, 132 × 93 cm (2018)
Sisters III, by Olga Suvorova, oil on canvas, 139 × 80 cm (2018)

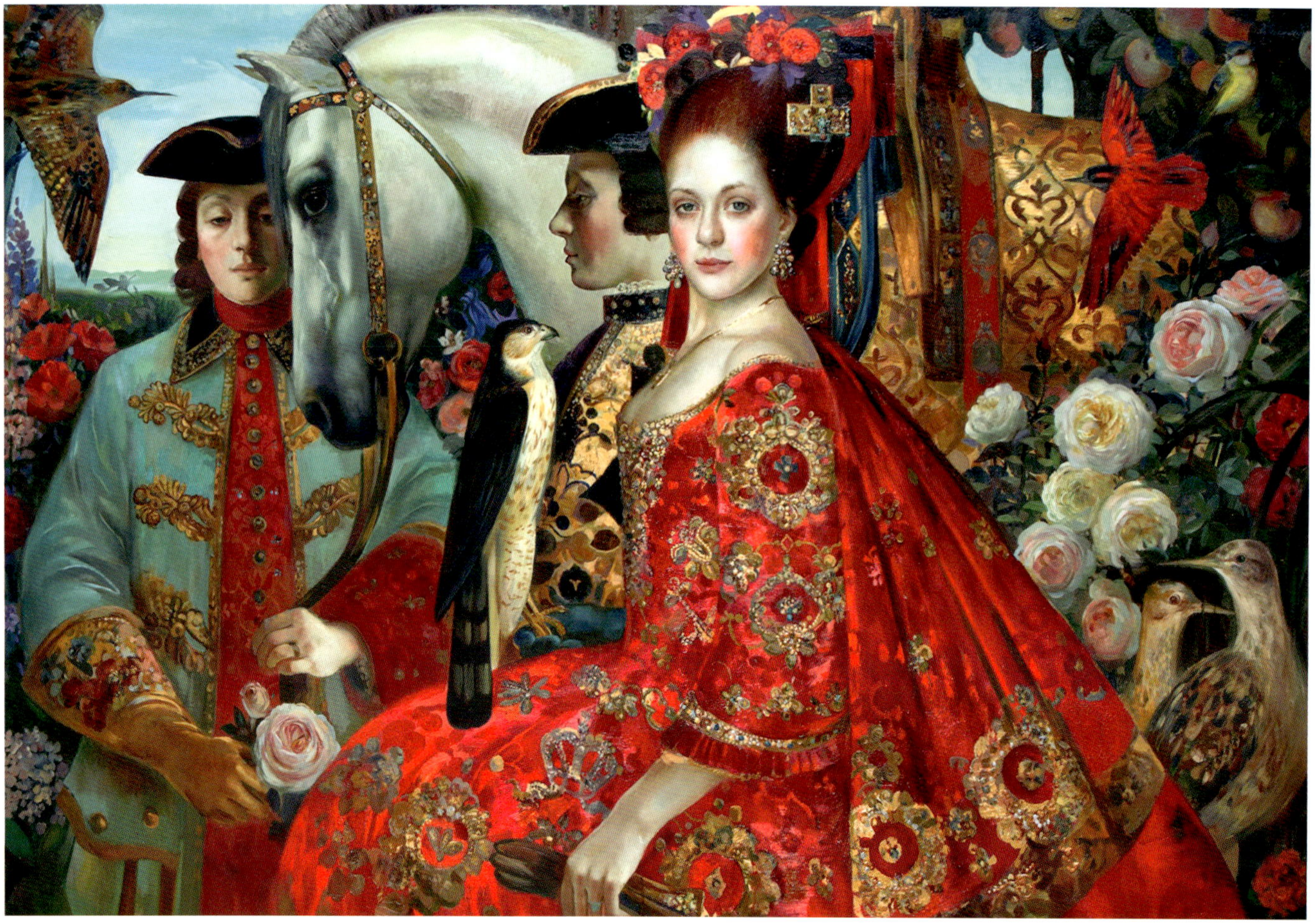

Tsar's Hunting, by Olga Suvorova, oil on canvas, 135 × 90 cm (2018)

On the Hunt, by Olga Suvorova, oil on canvas, 93 × 130 cm (2017)

OPPOSITE

Friends IV, by Olga Suvorova, oil on canvas, 135 × 90 cm (2018)

Expectation, by Olga Suvorova, oil on canvas, 93 × 135 cm (2018)

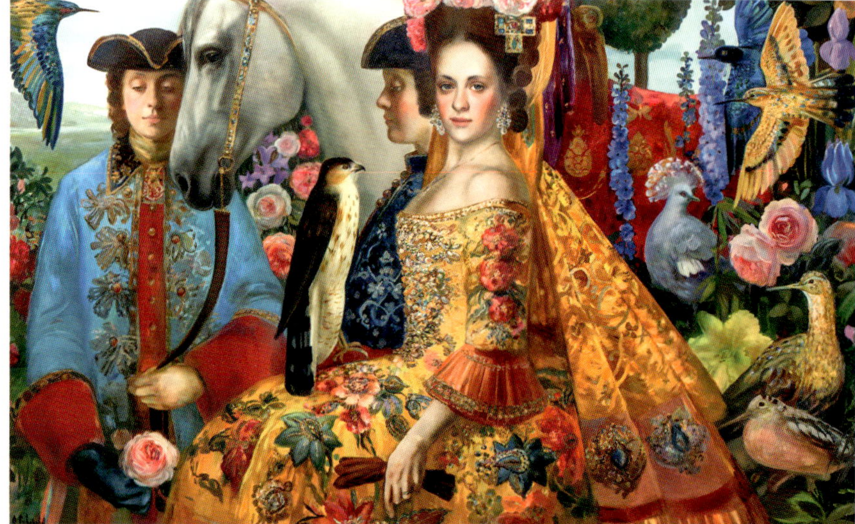

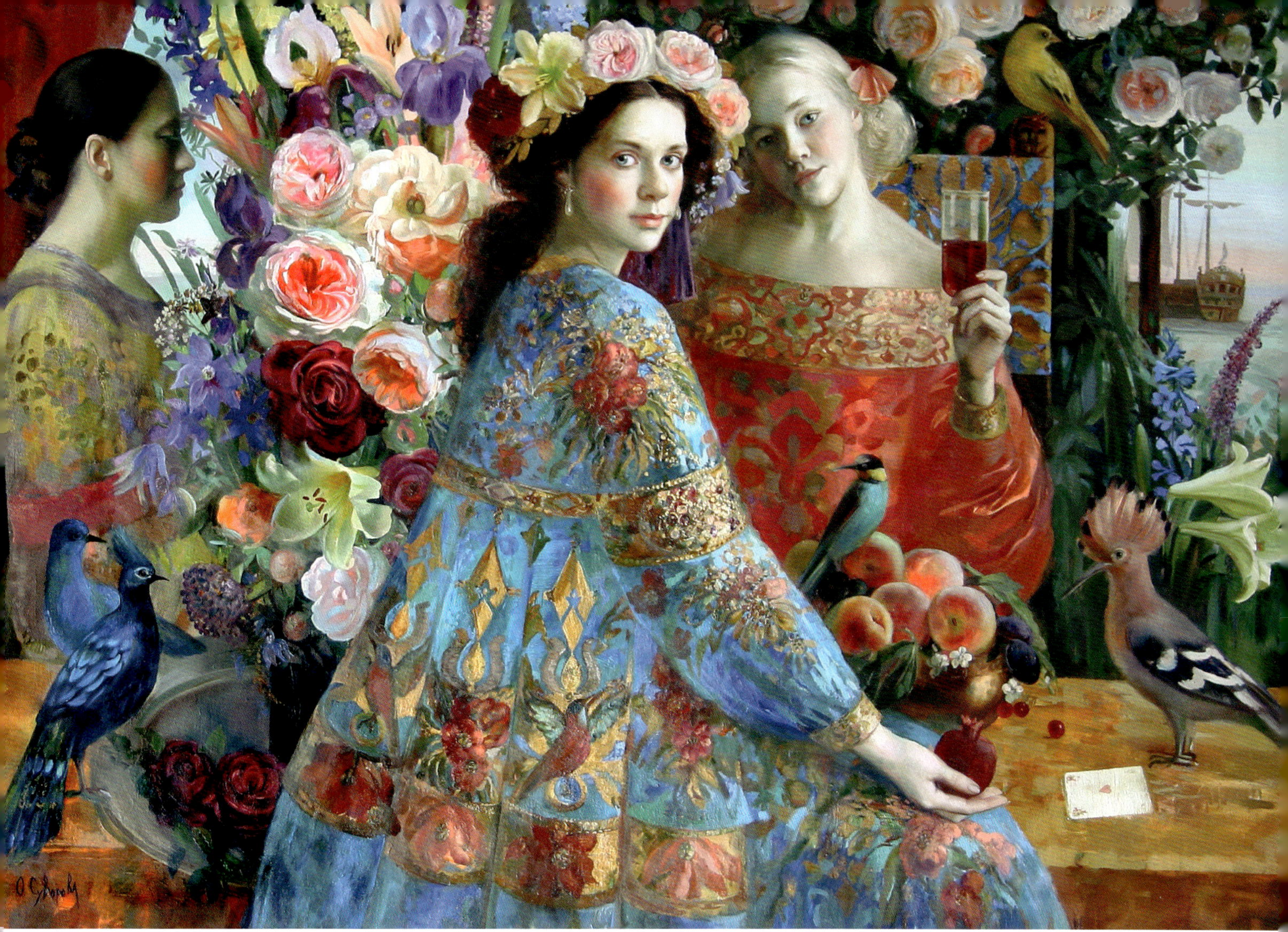

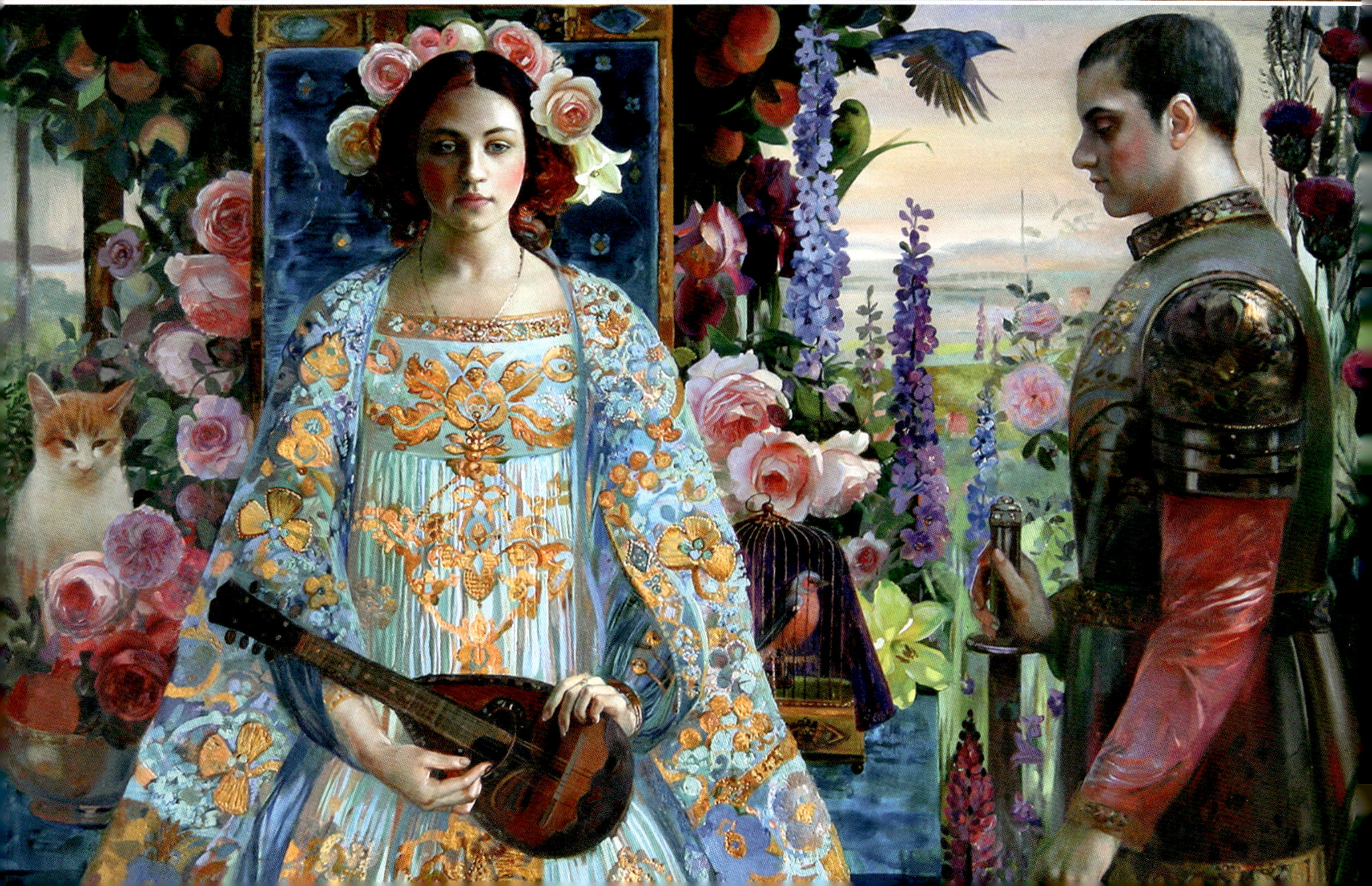

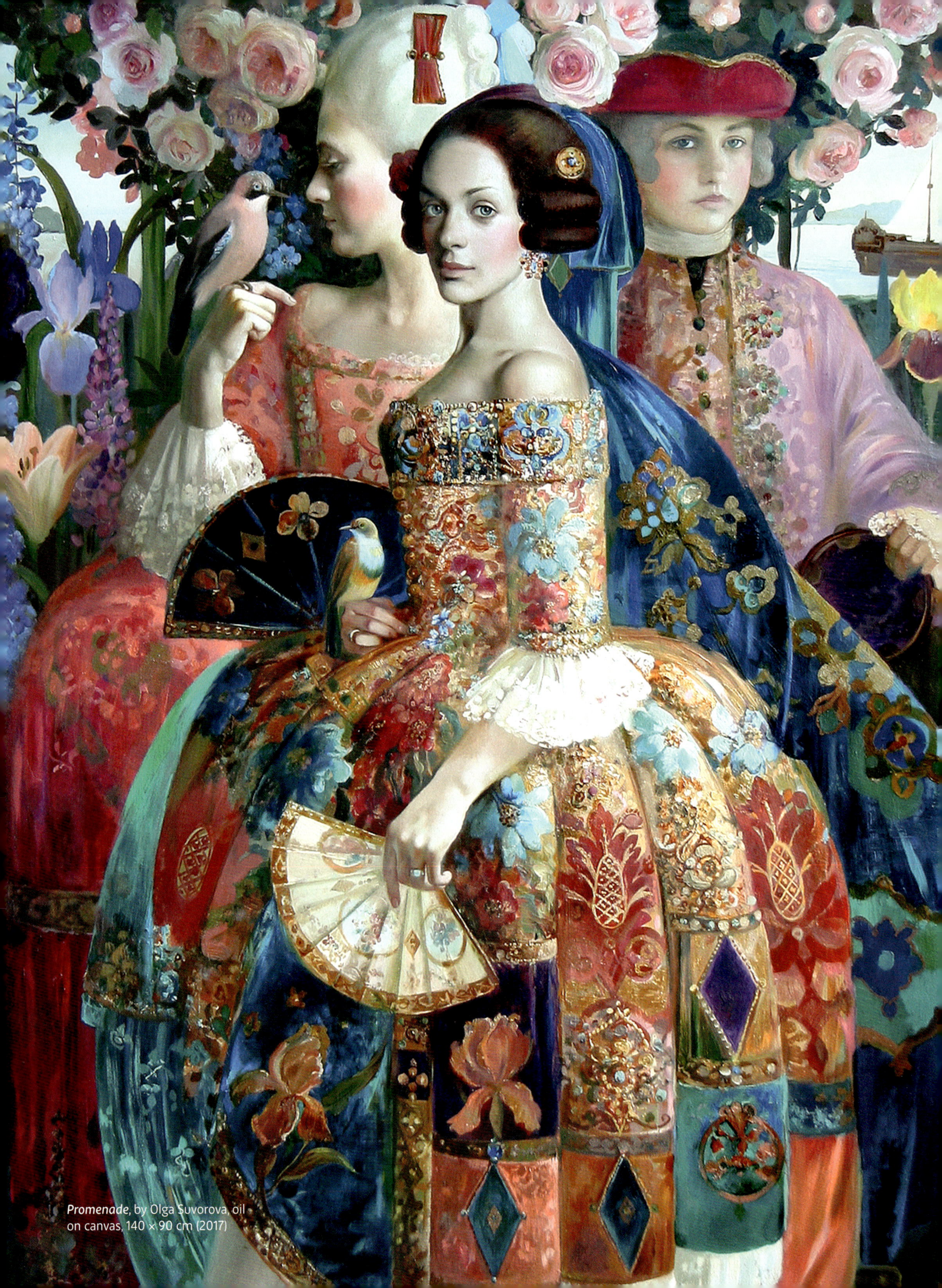

Promenade, by Olga Suvorova, oil on canvas, 140 × 90 cm (2017)

Annunciation

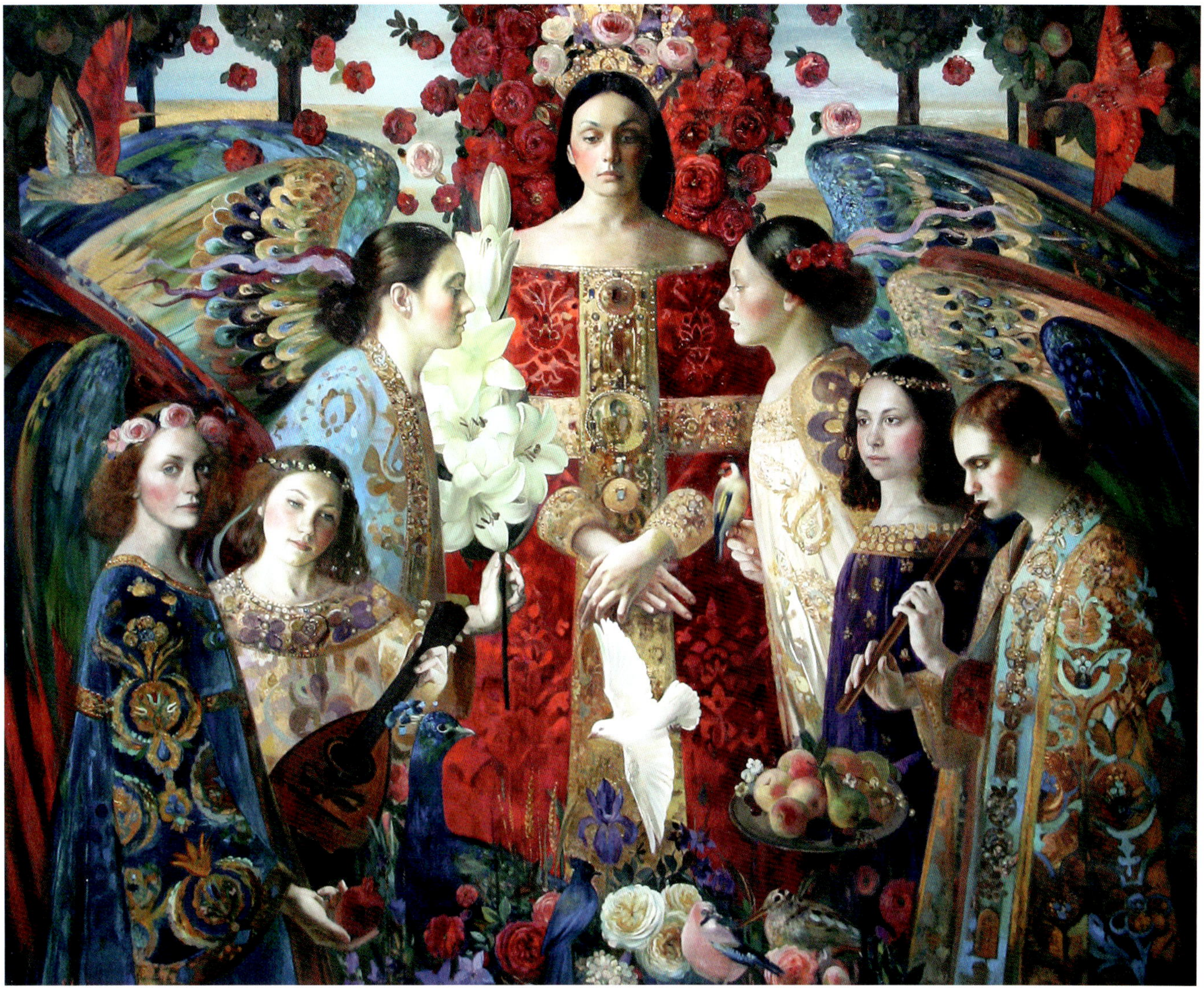

The Annunciation V, by Olga Suvorova, oil on canvas, 120 × 150 cm (2017)

My next painting was *The Annunciation*. No detail in this work was drawn without reason. Almost all the colors and characters are symbolic. I wanted to show joy and drama at the same time. The purple vestments of the Mother of God merge with the flow of red roses. In Christianity, red symbolizes the blood of Christ, shed for the salvation of people, and therefore his love of humanity. This is the color of the fire of faith, martyrdom, and passion of the Lord, as well as the royal triumph of justice and the victory of good over evil. A large group of red roses over the Virgin Mary's head points to the wounds of Christ, and in this context is a tribute to his rebirth. The hands of the Mother of God are powerlessly lowered, a golden crucifix on her clothes connects heaven and earth. The white dove, representing the Holy Spirit, serves as an accent of the whole asymmetric composition. The branch of

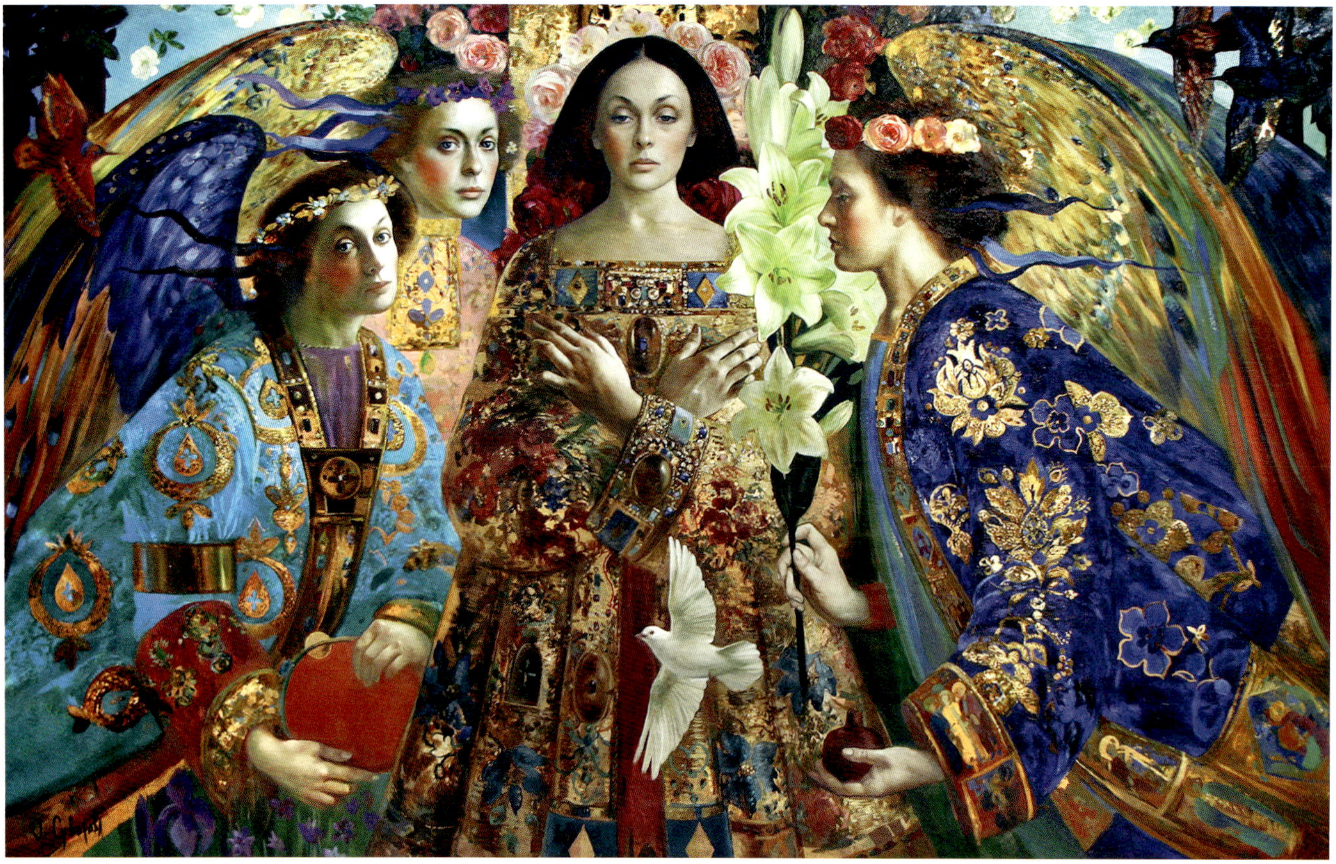

The Annunciation II, by Olga Suvorova, oil on canvas, 105 × 170 cm (2015)

the white lily, in the hands of the Archangel Gabriel, is a symbol of the purity and innocence of the Virgin Mary. His golden clothes are also not accidental, as the color gold has special meaning in Christian symbolism. The magi brought gold to the newborn Savior. The Ark of the Covenant of ancient Israel was also decorated with gold. The most precious material on earth, gold is the expression of the world's most valuable spirit. We meet gold in the halo of saints, the aura around the figure of Christ, the raiment of the Savior, virgin, and angel—all this is an expression of holiness and belonging to the world of eternal values. Gold has always been an expensive material, so it was often replaced by other close colors—yellow and ochre. Why gold? Because in Christianity it is a rich symbol of everlasting illumination.

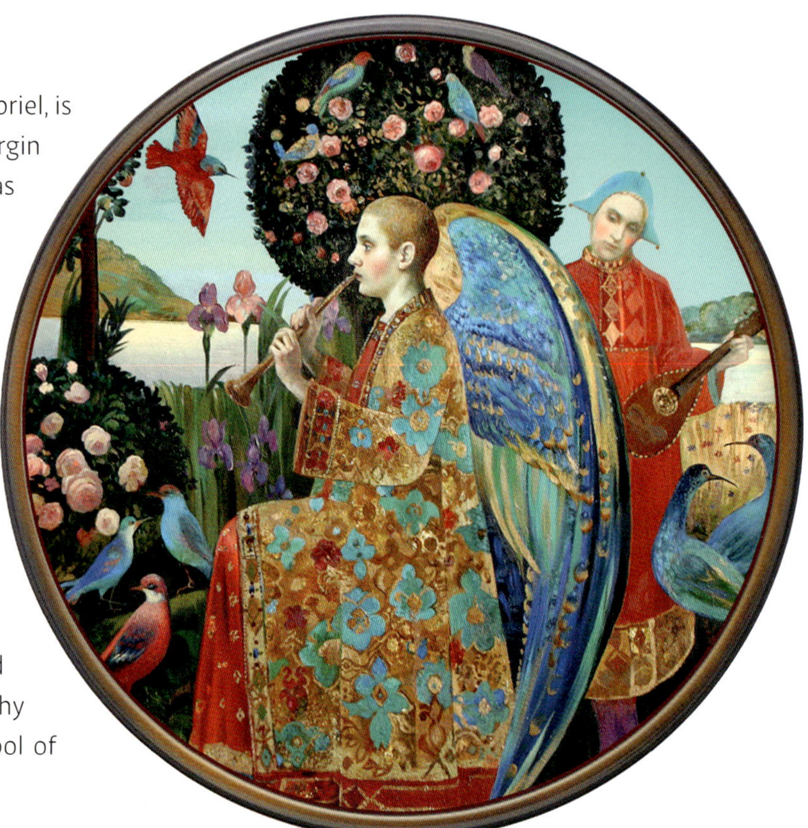

Angel, by Olga Suvorova, oil on metal, diameter 60 cm (2009)

The other angel, playing the flute, symbolizes the resurrection of the Savior. There are three angels depicted,

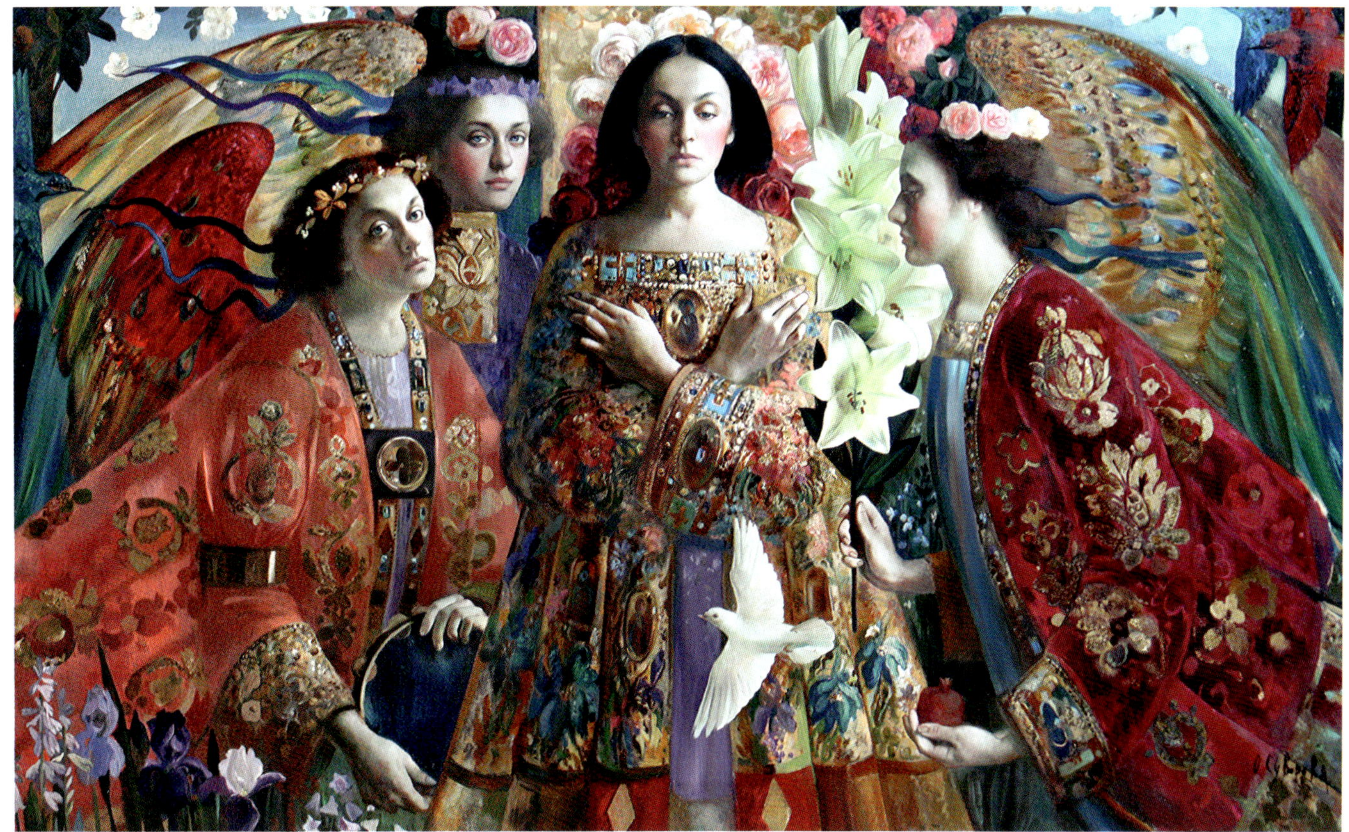

The Annunciation IV, by Olga Suvorova, oil on canvas, 97 × 168 cm (2016)

representing the theological: faith, hope, and love. As messengers of God, angels are intermediaries between heaven and earth. They are beyond the earthly laws of time and space. They are like the spirits of the middle ages—sylphs, undines, salamanders, and dwarves—who rule over the forces of nature but have no soul. According to Christian teaching, angels stand closer to man than to God. In John's "Revelation," the angel appears to the evangelist and reveals the holy city of Jerusalem. John falls to his knees before the angel, but the angel says: "Do it not; for I am of thy fellow servants, and of thy brethren." The flowers at the bottom of the painting symbolize new life: God came to Earth and flowers bloomed. In future I would like to create more pictures on this serious topic. In the history of world art, artists have always turned to this important theme for mankind.

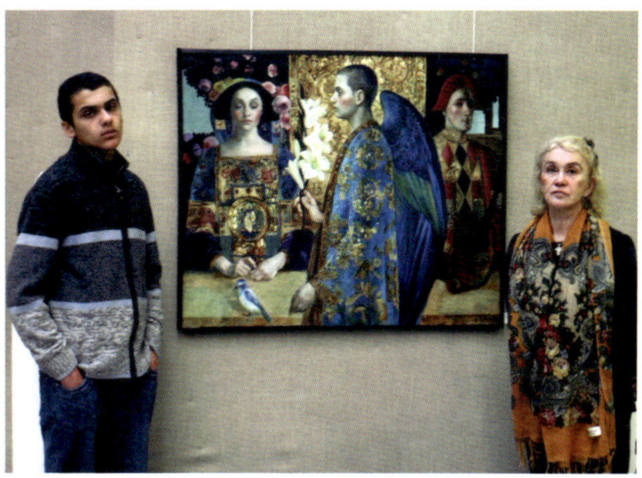

Son Andrey with Suvorova's mother, Natalia, St. Petersburg, Russia, exhibition of Olga Suvorova paintings, photo courtesy of Olga Suvorova (2006)

Alongside the religious theme, I worked on a completely different idea—creating a picture dedicated to Rembrandt van Rijn. A commission from a young family pushed me to do it. They had got married recently and decided to order a joint portrait, in which I used Rembrandt's painting *Flora* as reference. I have often visited the State Hermitage Museum in St. Petersburg, and every time I walked through the hall with Rembrandt's works, I was fascinated by this Dutch

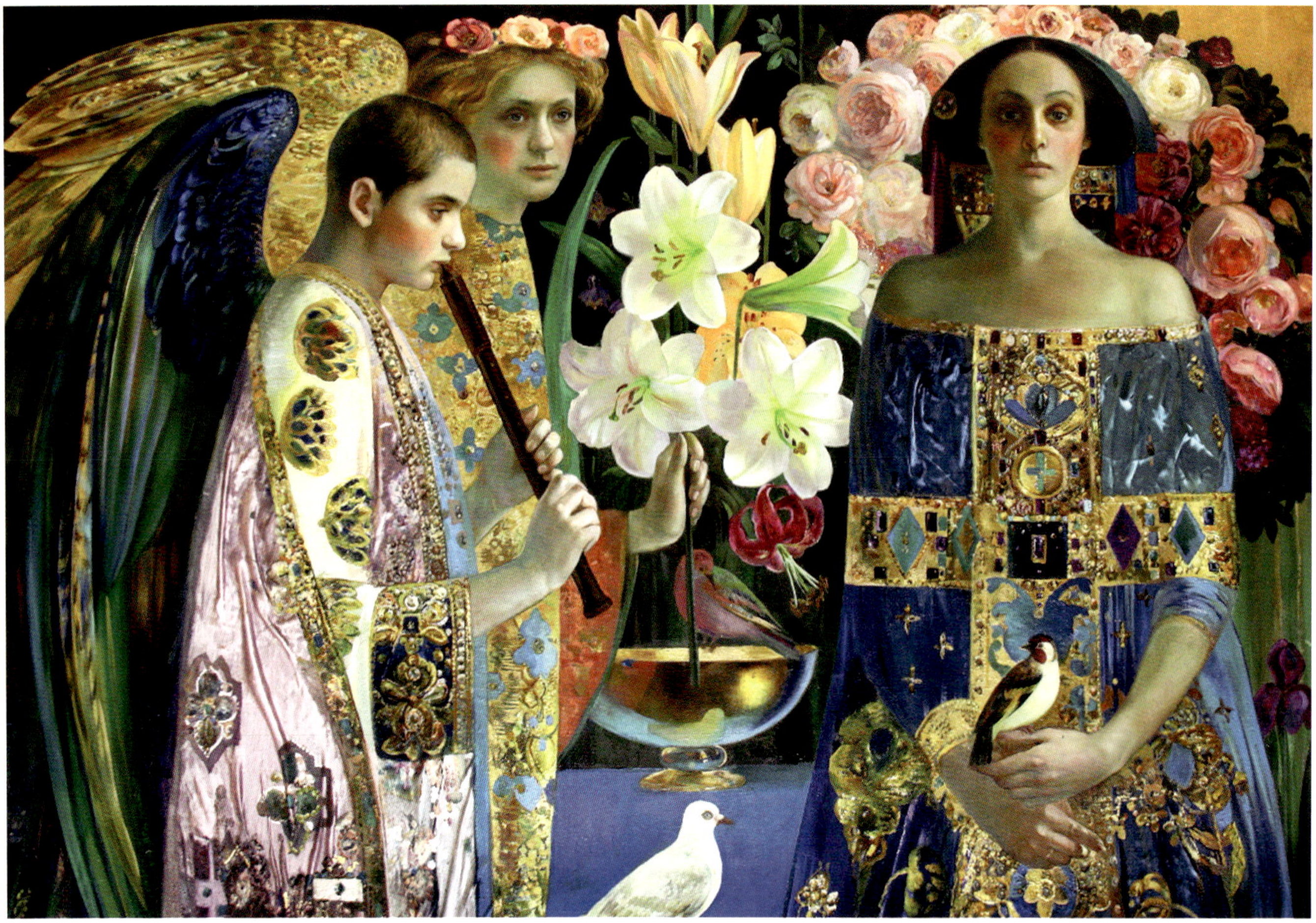

The Annunciation I, by Olga Suvorova, oil on canvas, 95 × 140 cm (2011)

masterpiece. The artist portrayed his wife many times, but for me this particular picture surpasses all his other works taken together. This is a real world of beauty and poetry. I wanted to create an image of a young bride, so it would be thoughtful and at the same time slightly sad. After all, she is on the threshold of a new life, when careless teenage habits are left in the past. Now she needs to rely on her beloved, and no one knows how long this union will last. The headdress entwined with flowers certainly points to Flora, the ancient Roman goddess of spring, as does the rich clothing of that time, covered with ornate gold patterns. All this creates a festive atmosphere. According to ancient legends, the pomegranate fruits, lying on the table, foretell a young couple's endless love and many children. A luxurious bouquet behind the bride tells us of an unforgettable moment. On the right side of the picture, the groom's mother is shown in the role of a friend. She seems to instruct the young bride; a blue magpie—a bird endowed with cunning and wisdom—sits on her hand.

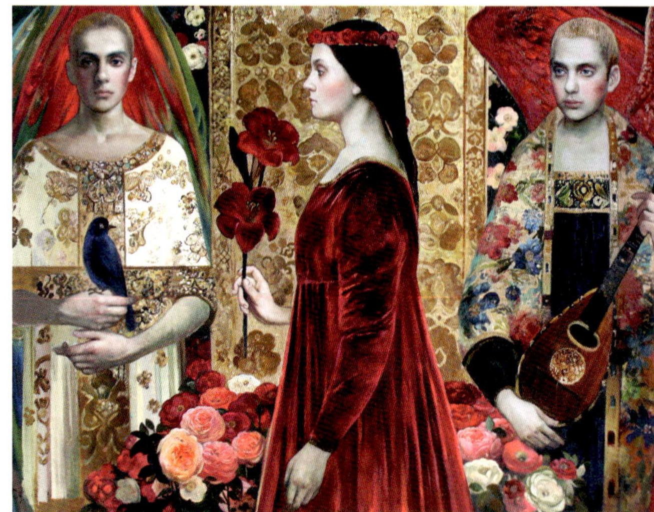

Red Annunciation, by Olga Suvorova, oil on canvas, 95 × 133 cm (2009)

In general, the picture turned out to be festive, replete with many details. But I was not satisfied, and over and over again I returned to the topic, trying different color combinations. Perhaps my best picture has not yet been created, and this is good. It means I still have something to strive for.

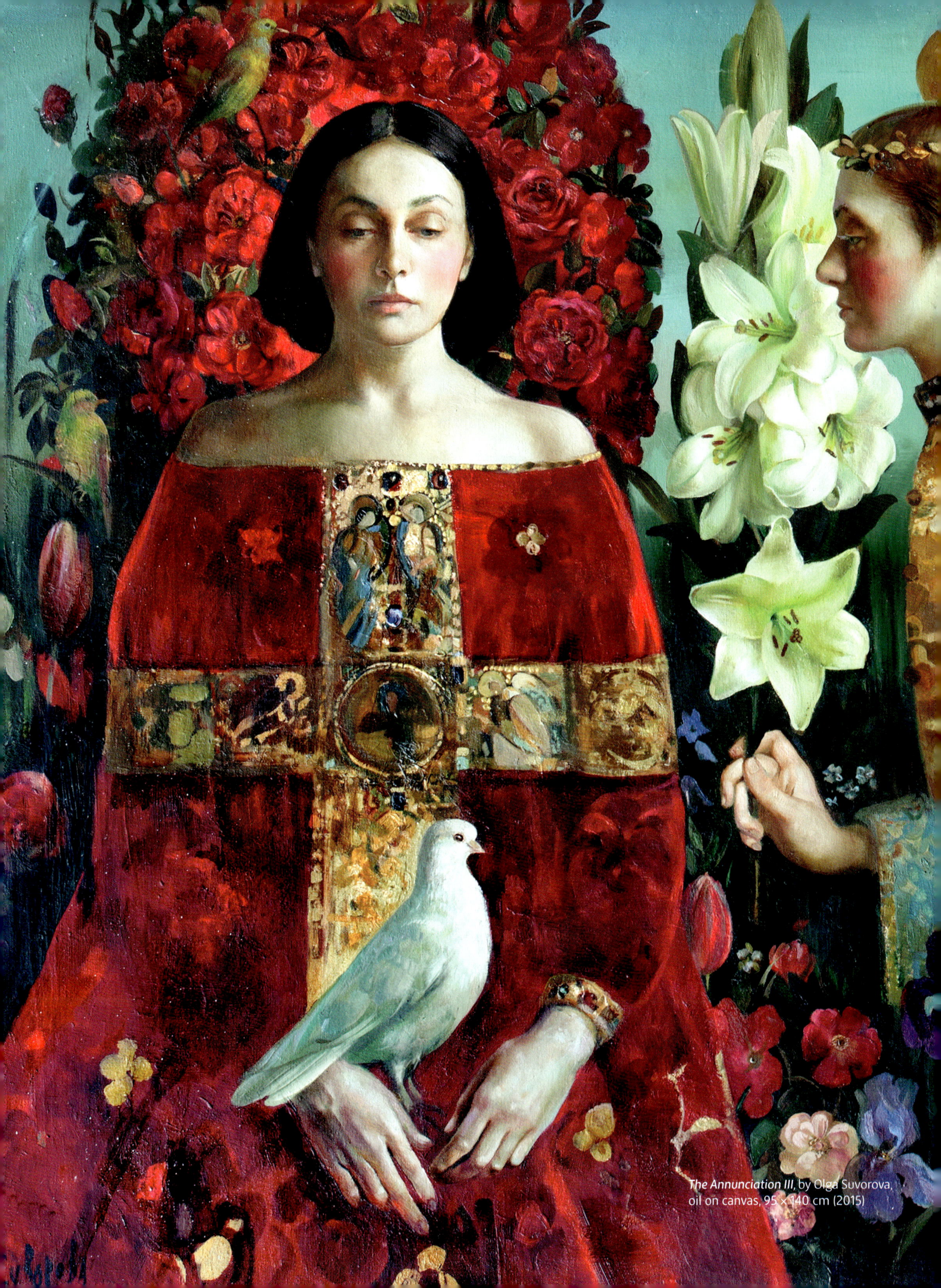

The Annunciation III, by Olga Suvorova, oil on canvas, 95 × 140 cm (2015)

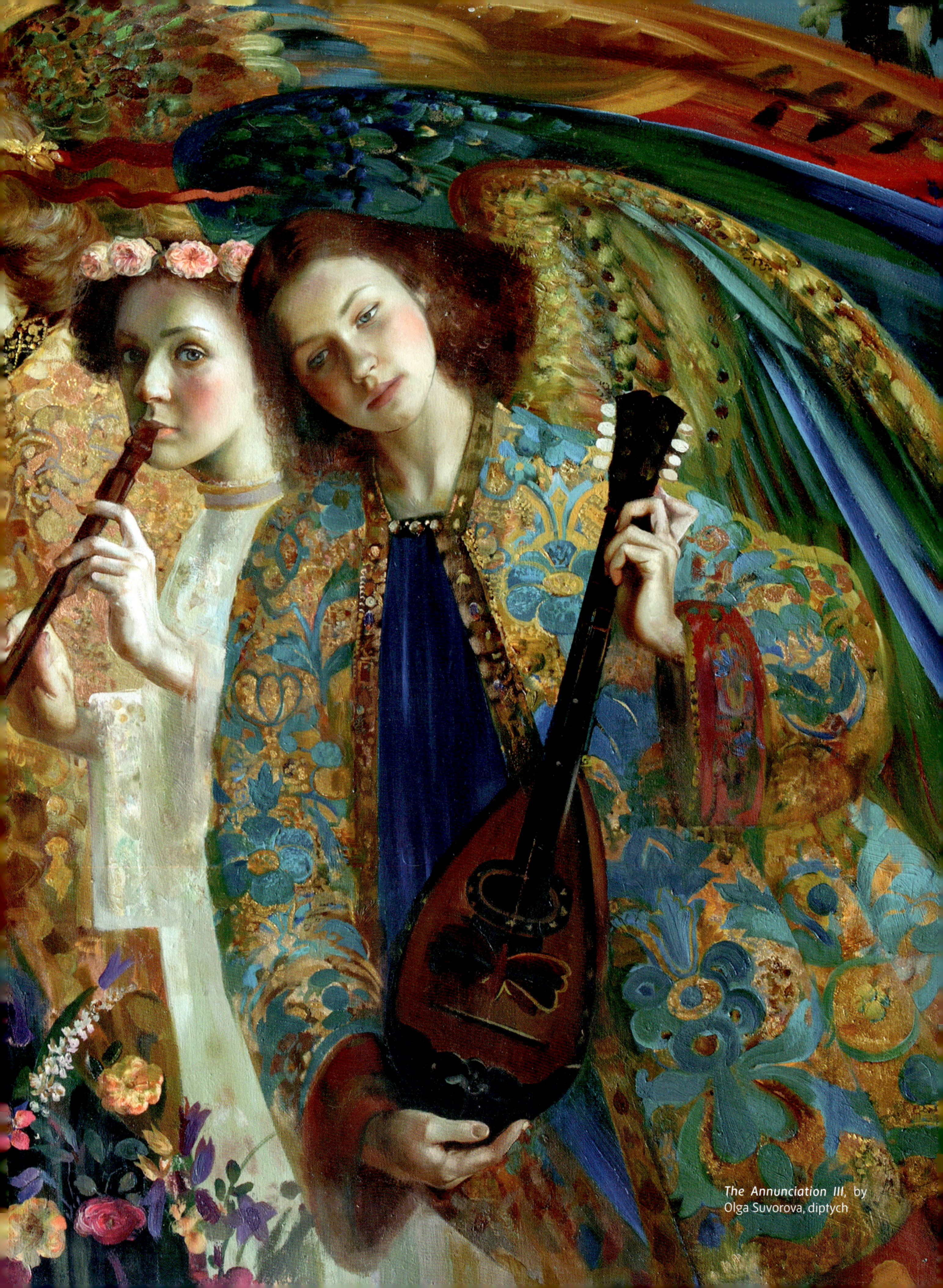

The Annunciation III, by Olga Suvorova, diptych

Fortune & Game

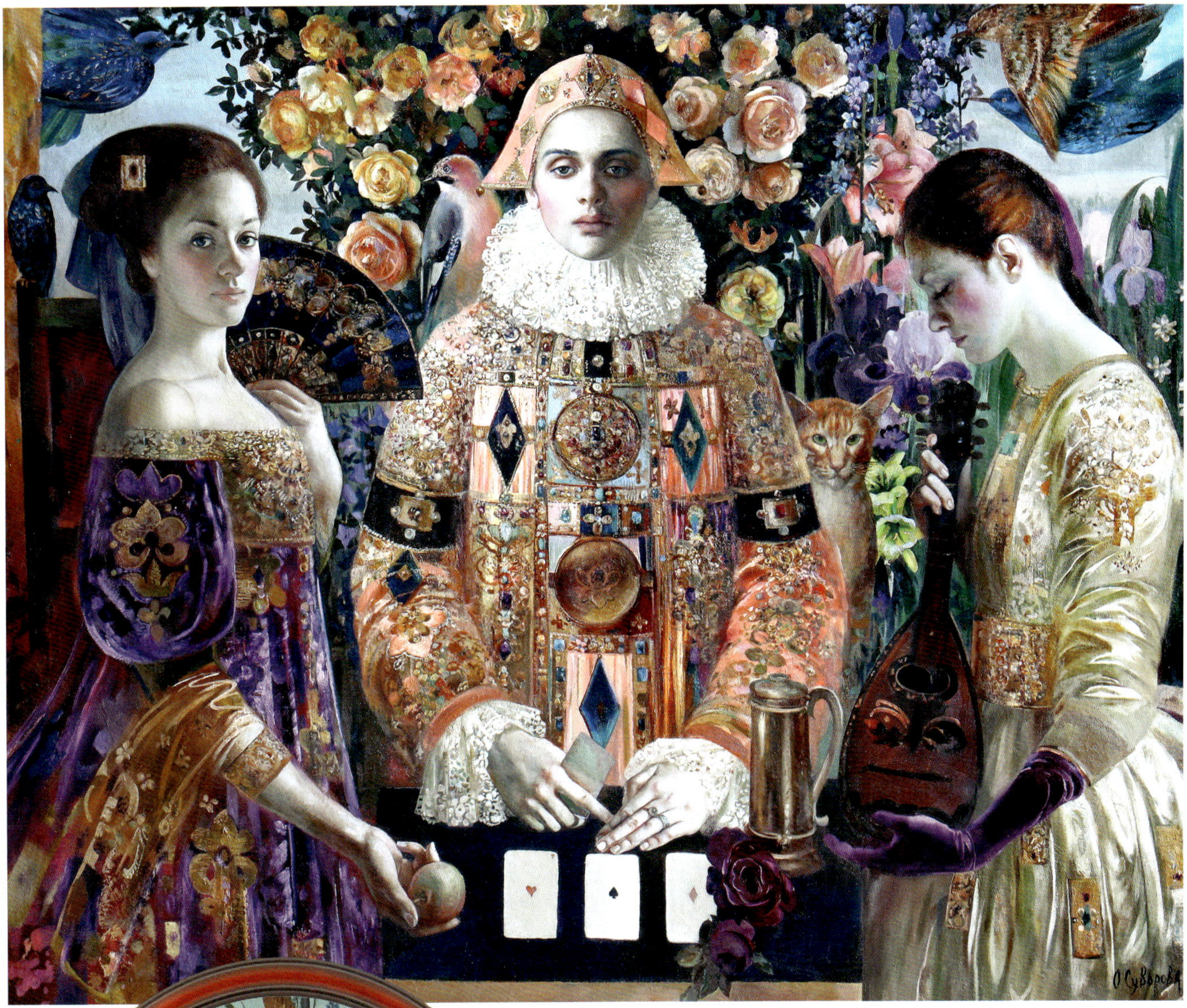

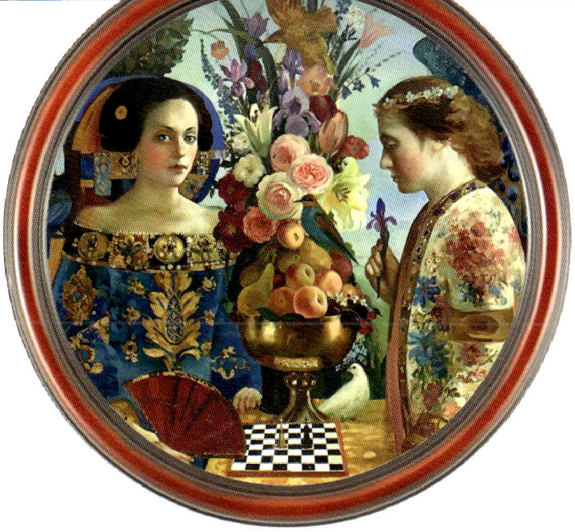

This is a series of works devoted to the theater and the psychology of human relationships. In *The Game*, the main role is played by the Harlequin-Joker holding a playing card in his hand. On either side of him are two beautiful ladies, each hoping to claim the heart of the elusive Harlequin, but the women are unlikely to capture his sympathy.

Game, by Olga Suvorova, oil on canvas, 109 × 132 cm (2013)
Decorative tray, by Olga Suvorova, diameter 60 cm (2013)

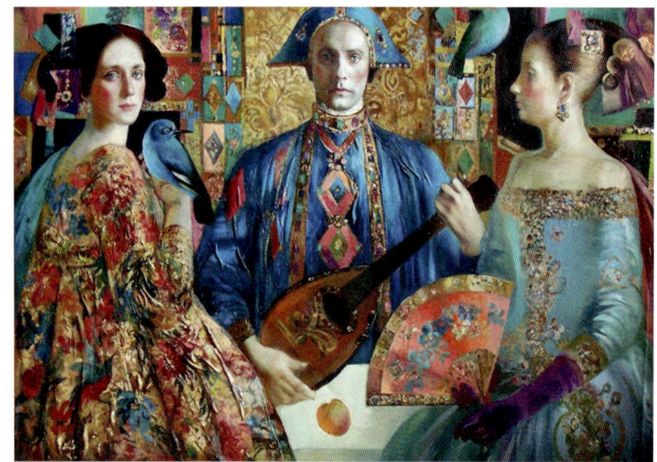

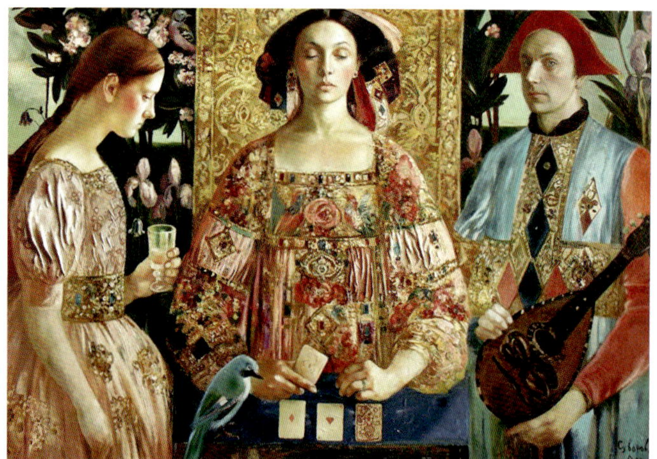

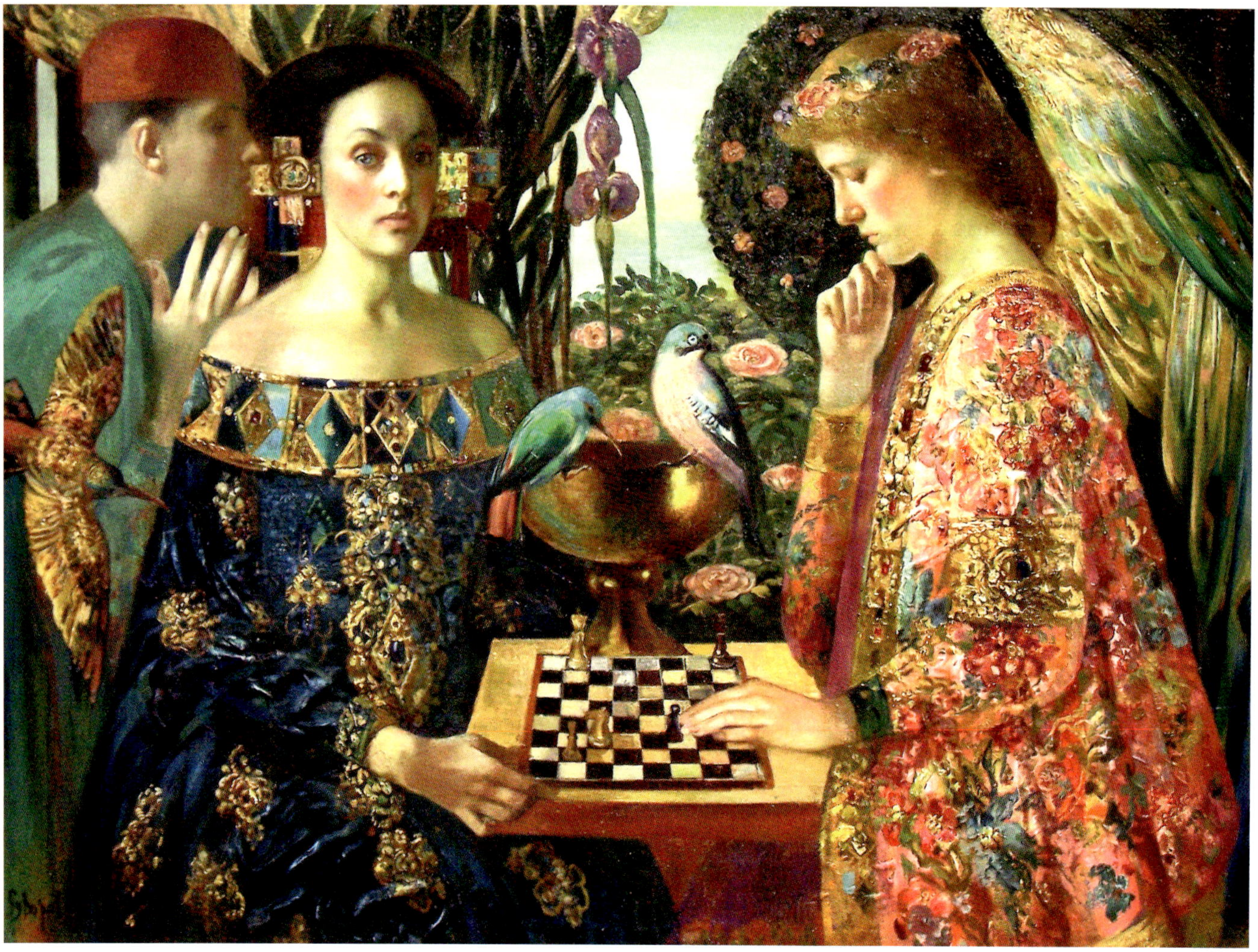

CLOCKWISE

Harlequin, by Olga Suvorova, oil on canvas, 95 × 140 cm (2005)
Fortune Teller I, by Olga Suvorova, oil on canvas, 95 × 120 cm (2005)
Duel I, by Olga Suvorova, oil on canvas, 95 × 120 cm (2006)

OPPOSITE

Game II, by Olga Suvorova, oil on canvas, 83 × 147 cm (2016)
Duel (Draw), by Olga Suvorova, oil on canvas, 101 × 148 cm (2013)

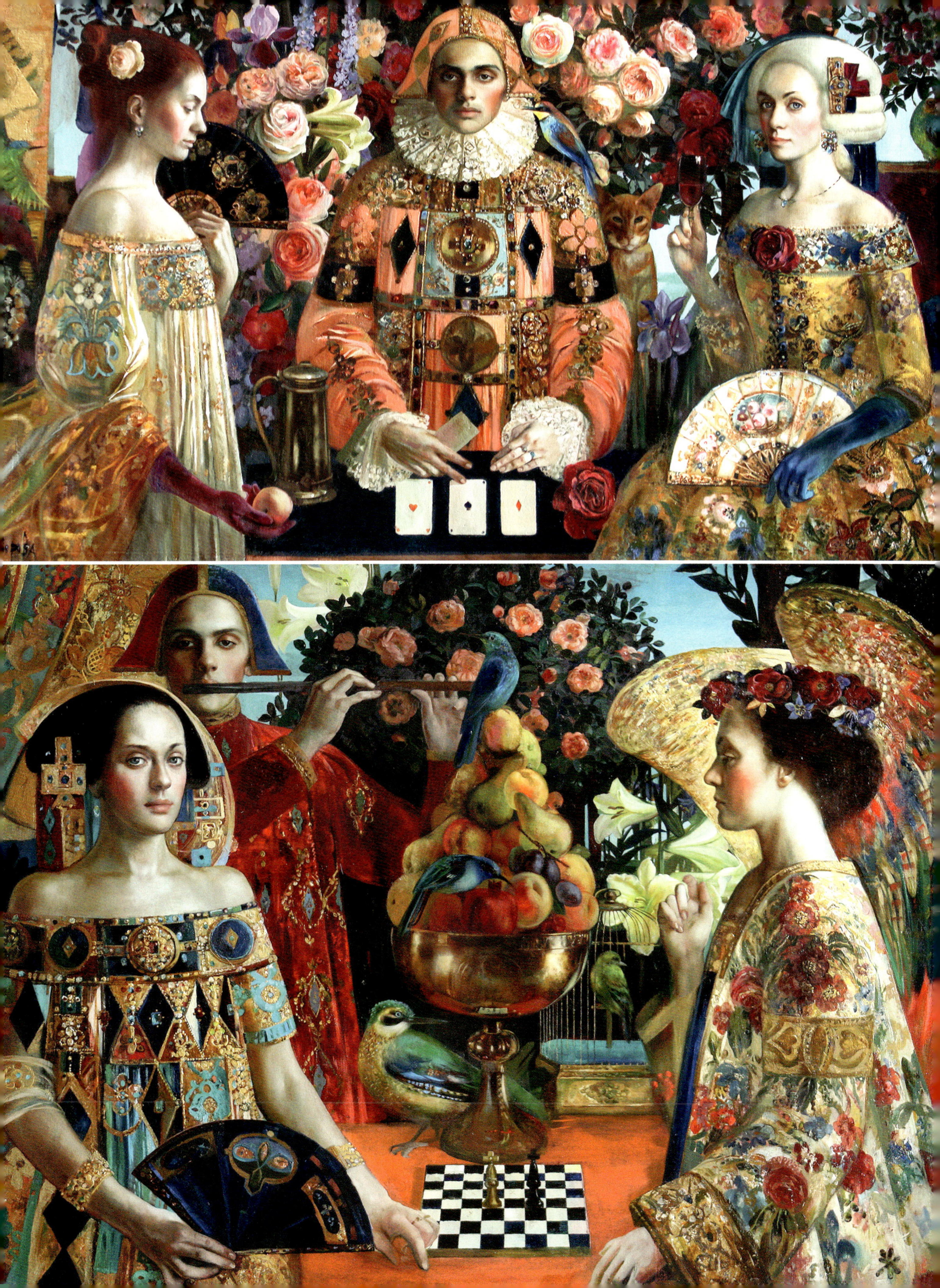

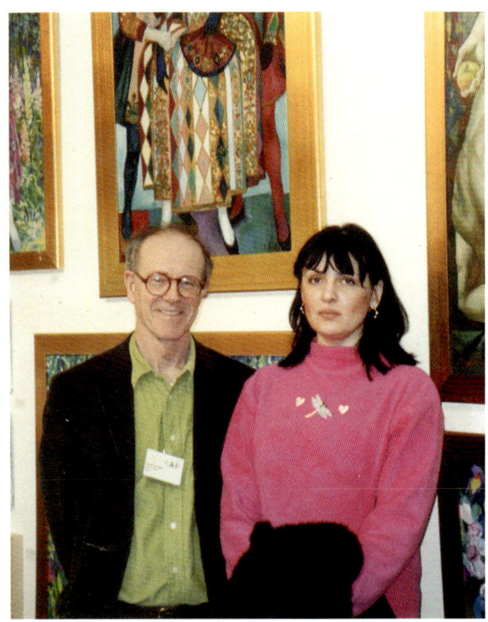

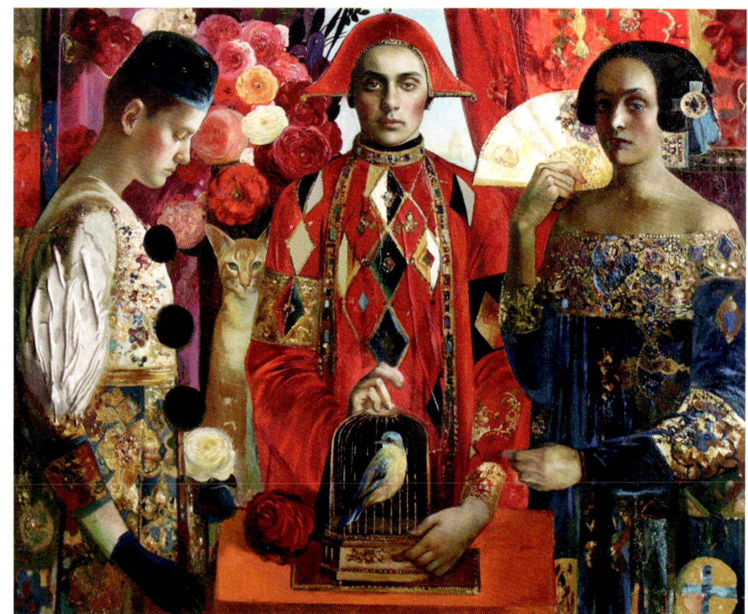

A red, cunning, autocephalous (acknowledging no higher authority) cat sits behind him. Pictures of cats are often found in medieval heraldry. Cats have an understanding of freedom, since they do not want to be caught or imprisoned. As English author Terry Pratchett wrote in *The Unadulterated Cat* (1989), "Cats have a way of always having been there even if they've only just arrived. They move in their own personal time. They act as if the human world is one they just happened to have stopped off in, on their way to somewhere that is possibly a whole lot more interesting."

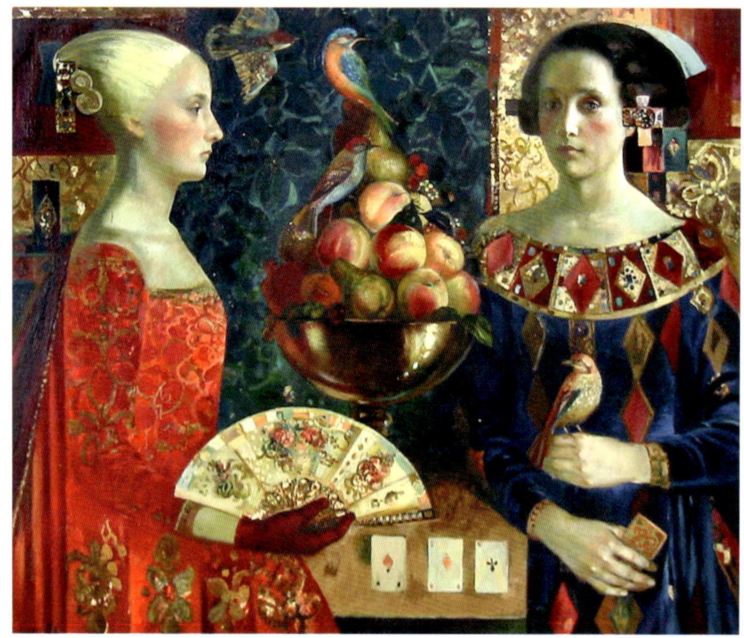

An apple is in one of the ladies' hands—a juicy and everyday fruit, but in the visual arts, the apple is a paradoxical object. It is a mysterious and ambiguous symbol that reveals a lot of meanings and unites a lot of opposite meanings. In my painting, the apple stands for love and temptation. The head of one lady is lowered; she is looking at the cards. Her black fan symbolizes sadness, and at the opposite end of the table sits her competitor. Her burgundy rose also speaks of infinite love. The open fans of both ladies tell us that they feel sympathetic to this particular man. Of course there will be a winner in this card game, and most likely it is Harlequin. The ladies will be left with nothing, sighing and indulging in romantic thoughts.

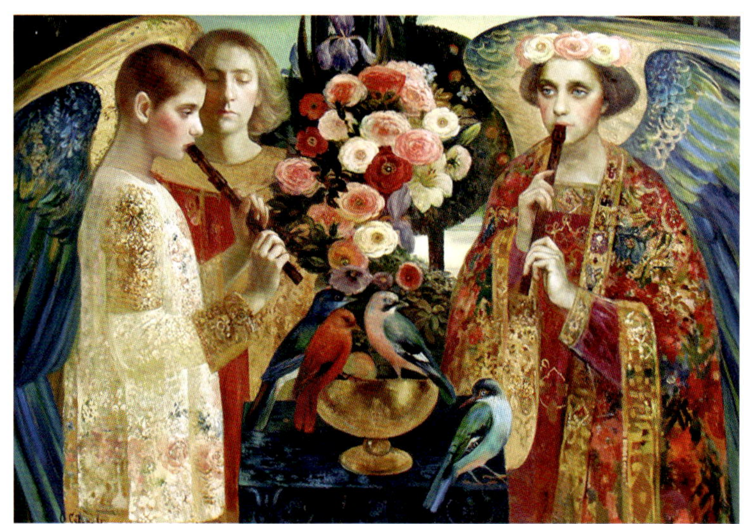

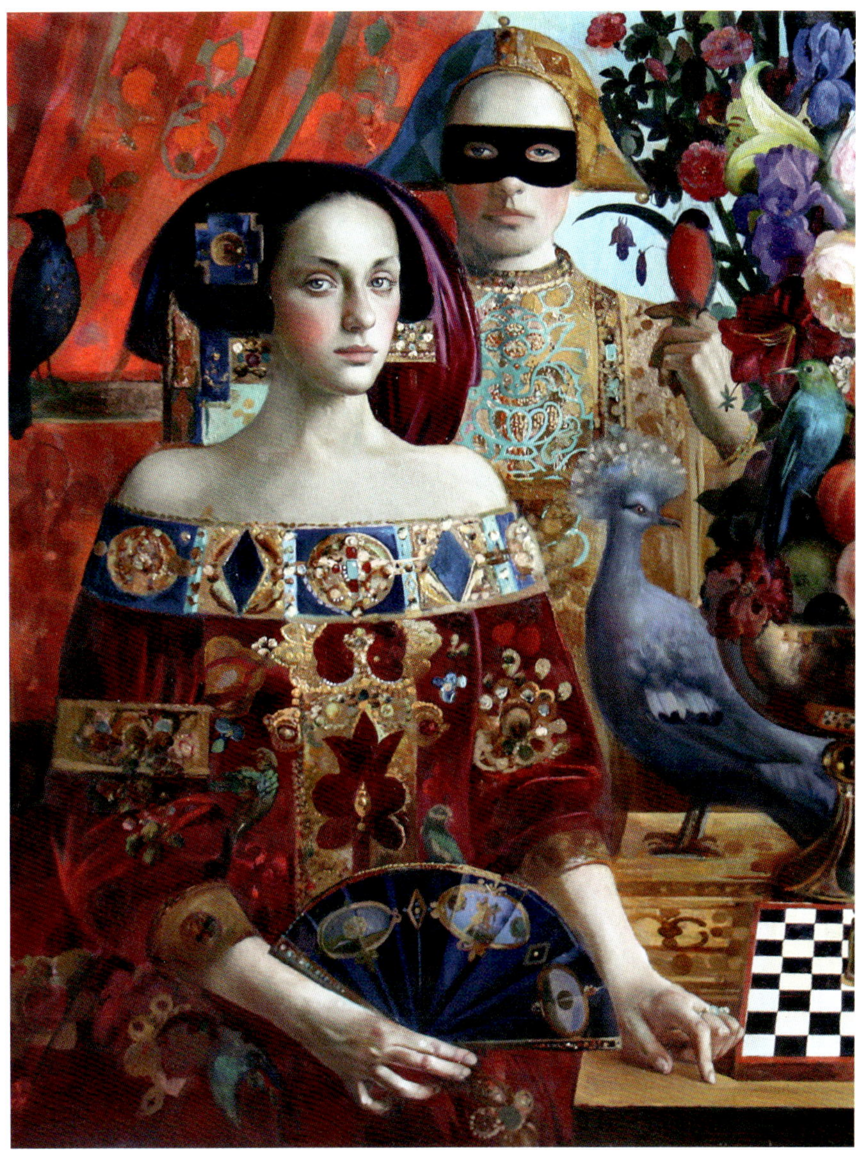

Duel II, by Olga Suvorova, oil on canvas, 95 × 140 cm (2015)

The main character is the Harlequin-Joker or Jester—he can be called different names but has one meaning as a combination of opposites—black and white, truth and falsity, love and hatred. His goal is to extract joy and pleasure from life, and to playfully accumulate experience. The other side of Joker's symbolism lies in his connection with the principle of initial and constant movement. He is enterprising, inquisitive and open, and trusts his instincts. Experiencing everything himself is one of the basic drives of his existence. That is why Joker chooses the direction of going anywhere and doing anything he wants, as all his actions are subordinated to this hidden agenda. He goes on the road, not having a chance to turn around—fate itself leads him on. And he needs to continue his path, relying on intuition, luck, and the protection of the Supreme forces. The divine genius directing him is able to create or destroy the Universe through the Joker's hands, and the absolute freedom of this formation contains all existing opportunities.

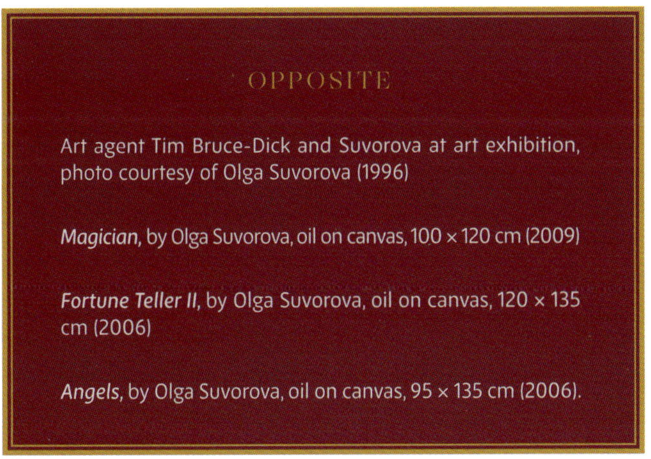

OPPOSITE

Art agent Tim Bruce-Dick and Suvorova at art exhibition, photo courtesy of Olga Suvorova (1996)

Magician, by Olga Suvorova, oil on canvas, 100 × 120 cm (2009)

Fortune Teller II, by Olga Suvorova, oil on canvas, 120 × 135 cm (2006)

Angels, by Olga Suvorova, oil on canvas, 95 × 135 cm (2006).

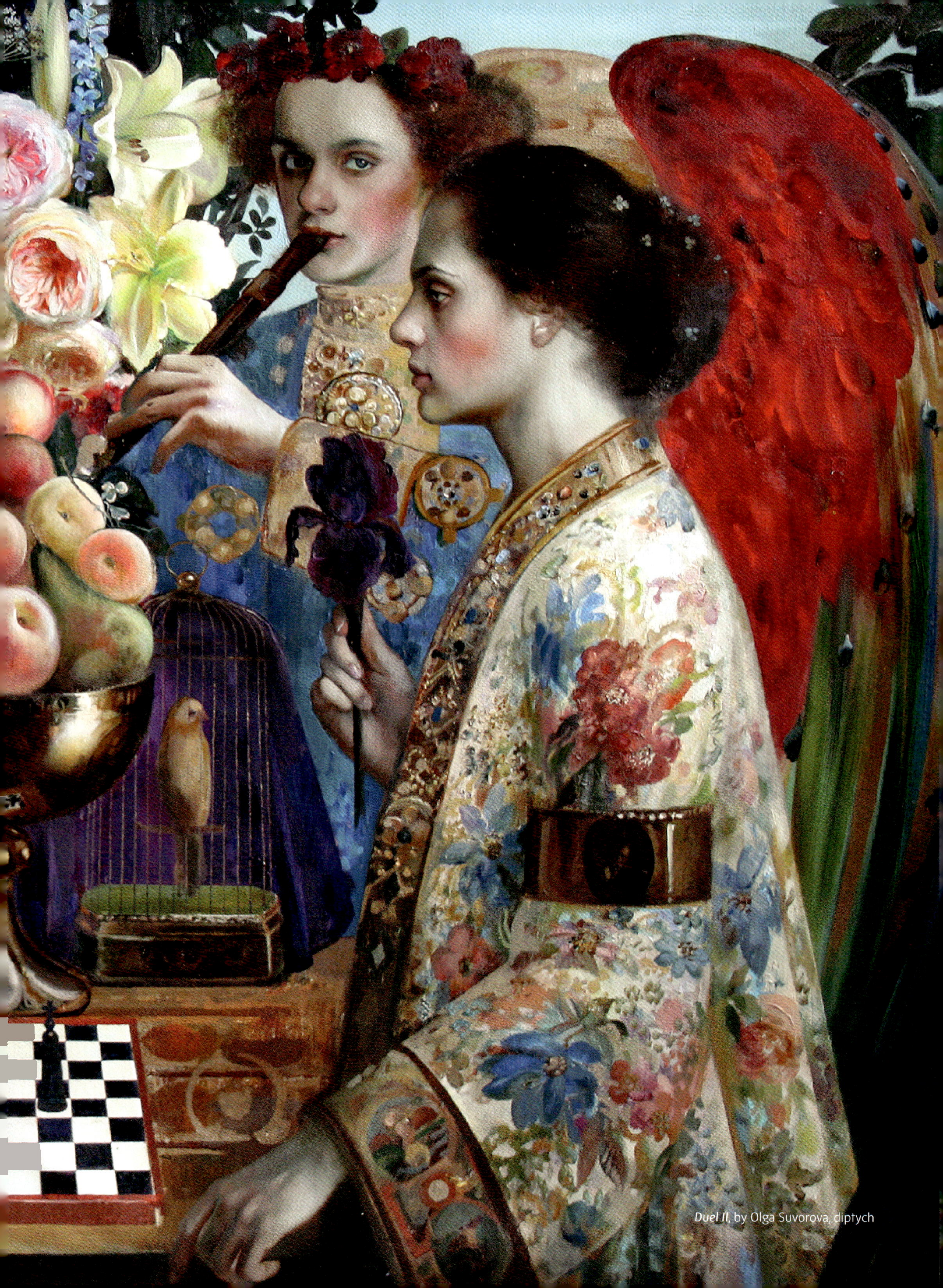

Duel II, by Olga Suvorova, diptych

Love & Masquerade

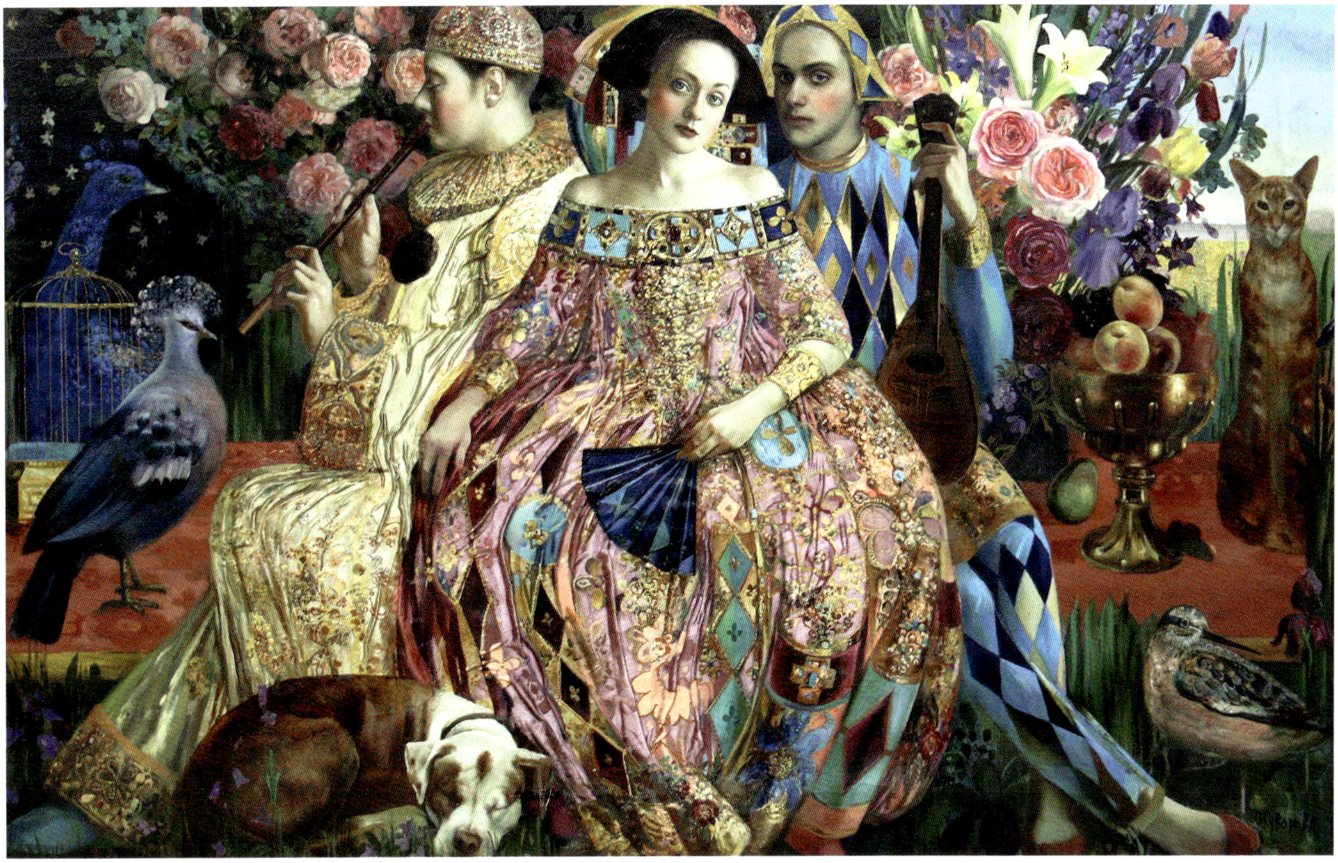

Fidelity, by Olga Suvorova, oil on canvas, 95 × 149 cm (2013)

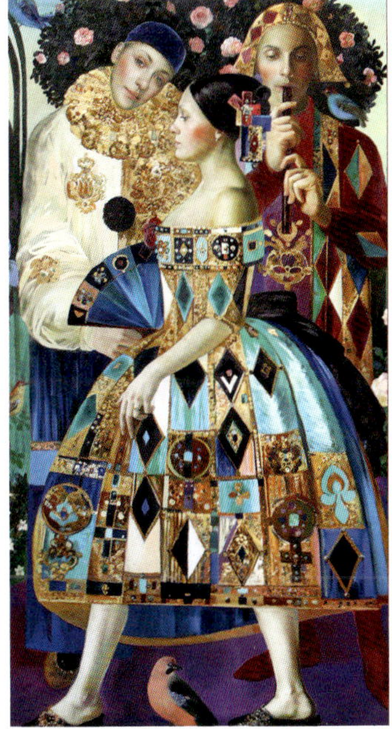

Love Triangle I, by Olga Suvorova, oil on canvas, 140 × 75 cm (2013)

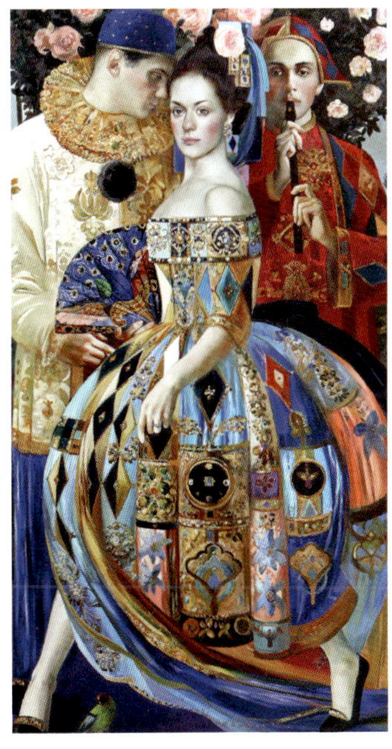

Choice, by Olga Suvorova, oil on canvas, 140 × 95 cm (2014)

A series of paintings dedicated to masquerades and carnivals is not only visually spectacular but reflects my desire to show the essence of this action. Traditional heroes of the celebrations were Pierrot, Columbine, and Harlequin—the collective images from the Commedia Dell'arte—the carnival's most popular characters. Only during the carnival did everyone become equal to each other: Jester became equal to his master and had the right to sit at the same table. Many people wore masks and therefore could do anything, regardless of their rank in society. The rich and the poor just wanted to have fun at the festival, where almost anything was allowed. It was a time of endless dancing, excitement, and flirting. For a short time you had a chance to break away from your everyday worries and immerse yourself in the atmosphere of fun, without thinking about the consequences. The grandiose and enchanting spectacle turns into some kind of theatrical performance; everyone plays their role.

My paintings on this topic are perceived to be very modern, as you can watch the same carnival in virtual reality on the internet. Now, in our time, people can afford to do anything via the internet, remaining anonymous. After all, human essence does not change. We all sometimes put on masks and want to seem to be people we are not. On the internet, people can do anything—it corrupts the human essence, as they will not get punished for their actions.

By choosing a decorative style in painting, I wanted to reflect this fairy tale, to show the cooperation of the spiritual and material worlds, their constant influence on each other. My desire for a clear structural composition on the canvas, the harmony and brightness of paintings, is the desire to find a language, an opportunity to reflect the beauty of our world. I want to achieve some kind of harmony, which is reflected in symmetrical compositions, in the softness of coloristically consonant tones, in golden texture. All this shows my attachment to certain origins, the art of the Russian baroque and early Italian Renaissance.

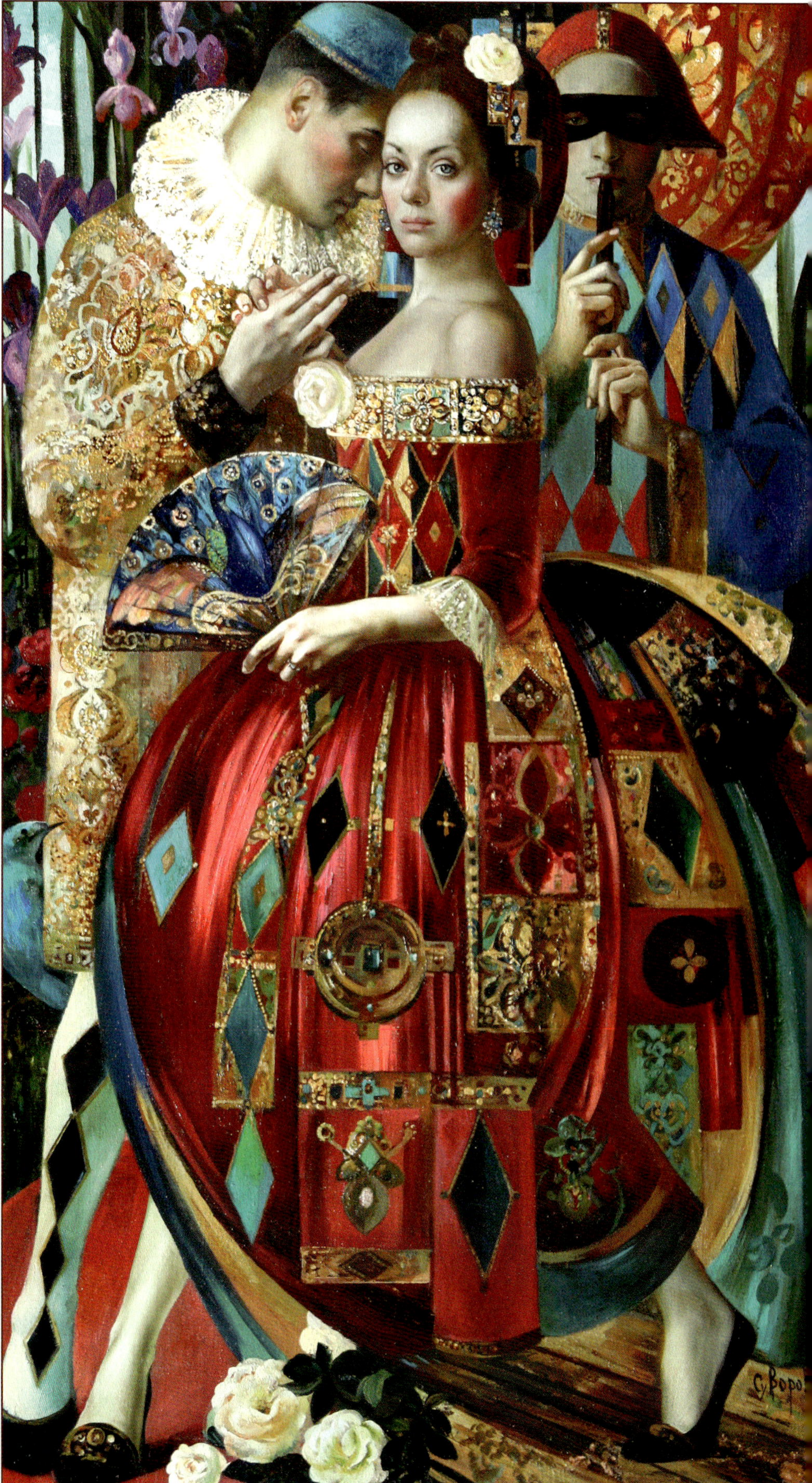

Love Triangle II, by Olga Suvorova, oil on canvas, 117 × 71 cm (2013)

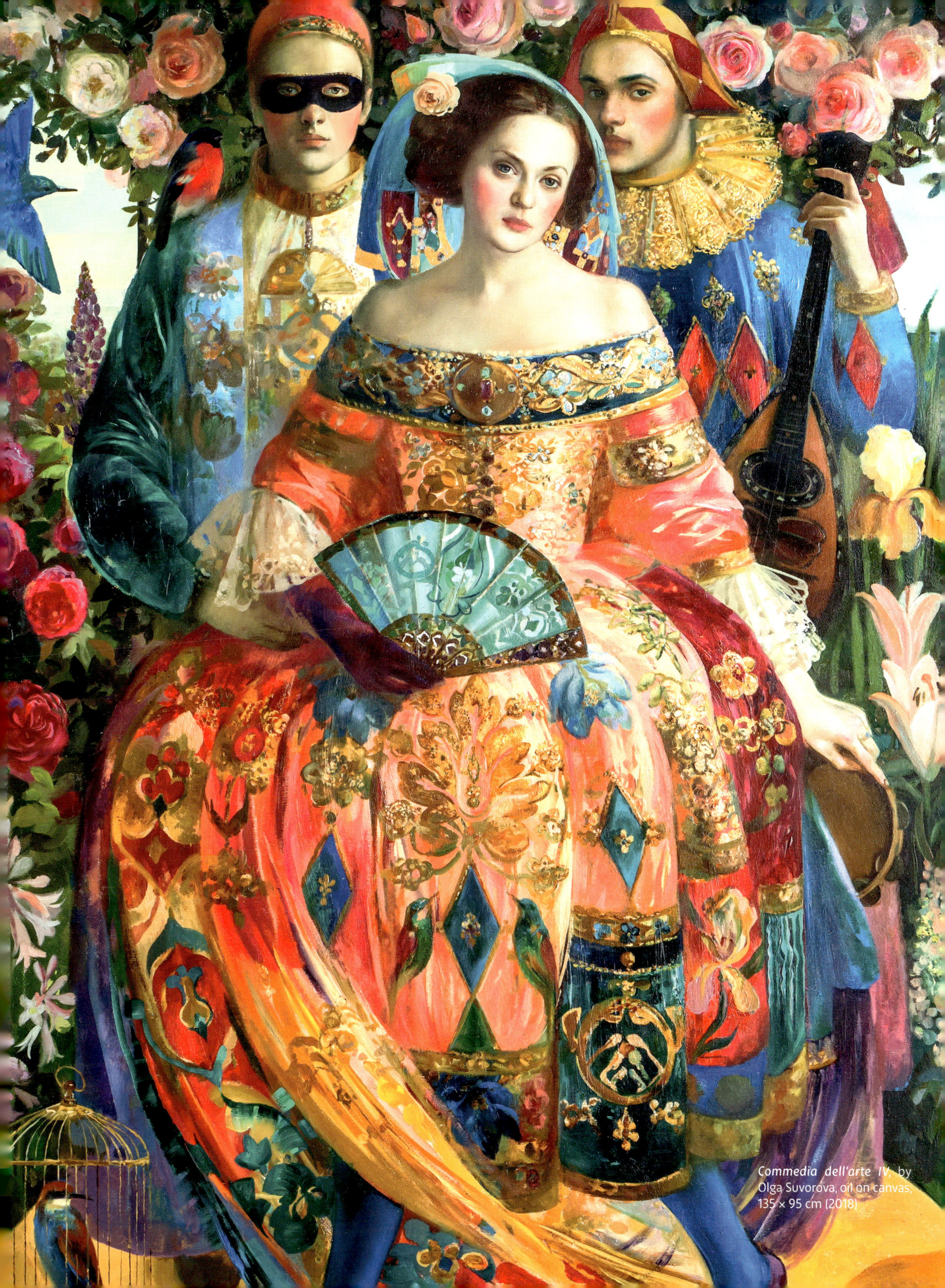

Commedia dell'arte IV, by Olga Suvorova, oil on canvas, 135 × 95 cm (2018)

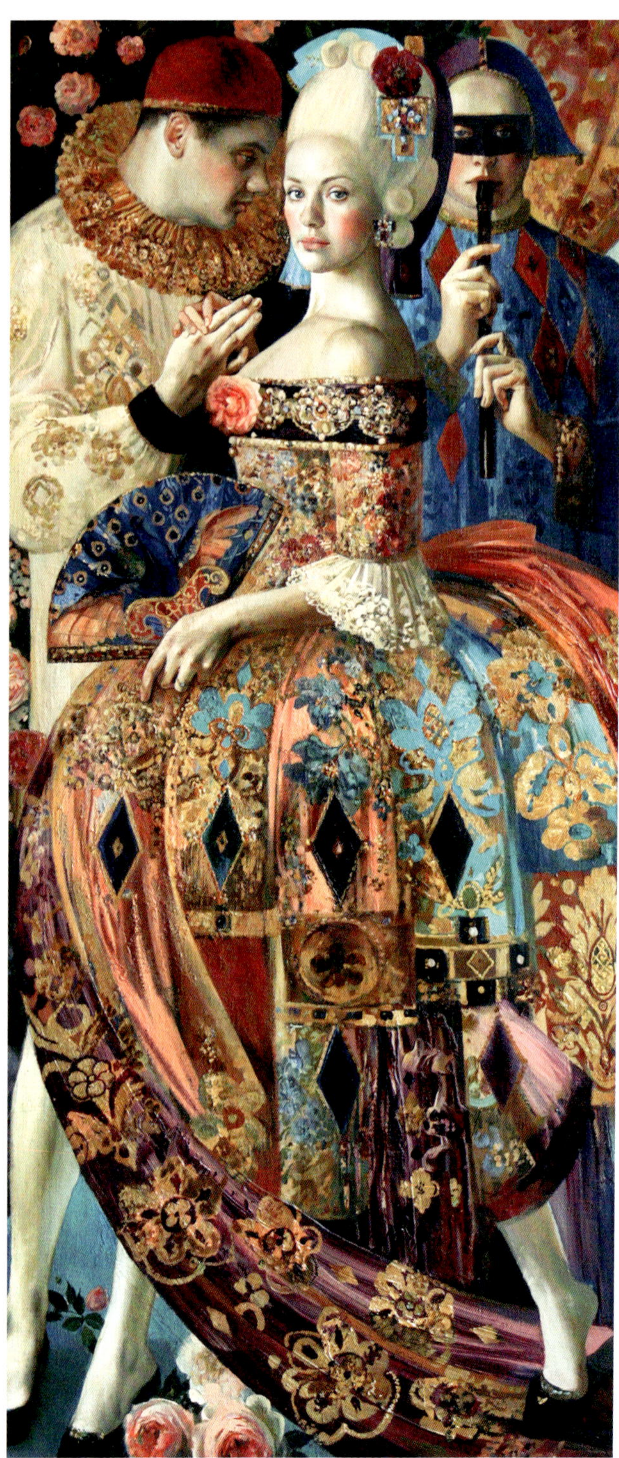

Dancer I, by Olga Suvorova, oil on canvas, 80 × 145 cm (2015)

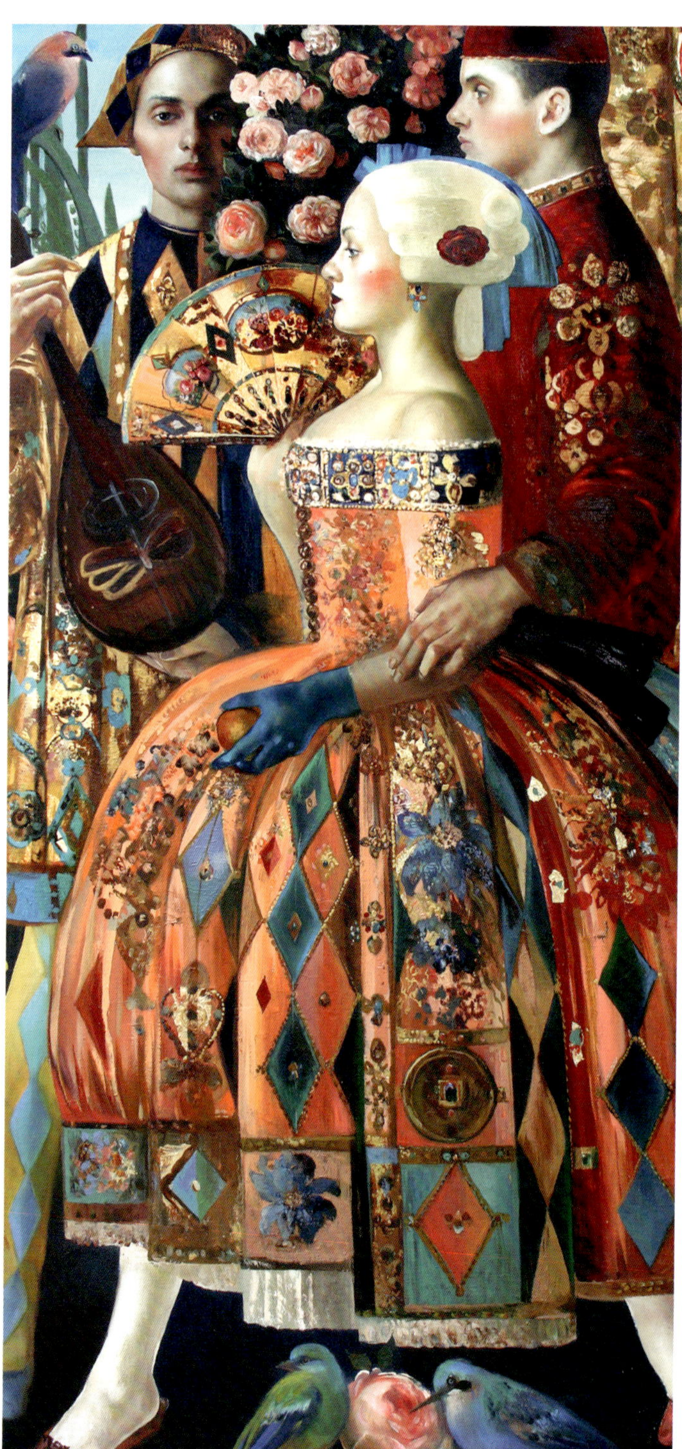

Love Triangle III, by Olga Suvorova, oil on canvas, 129 × 79 cm (2013)

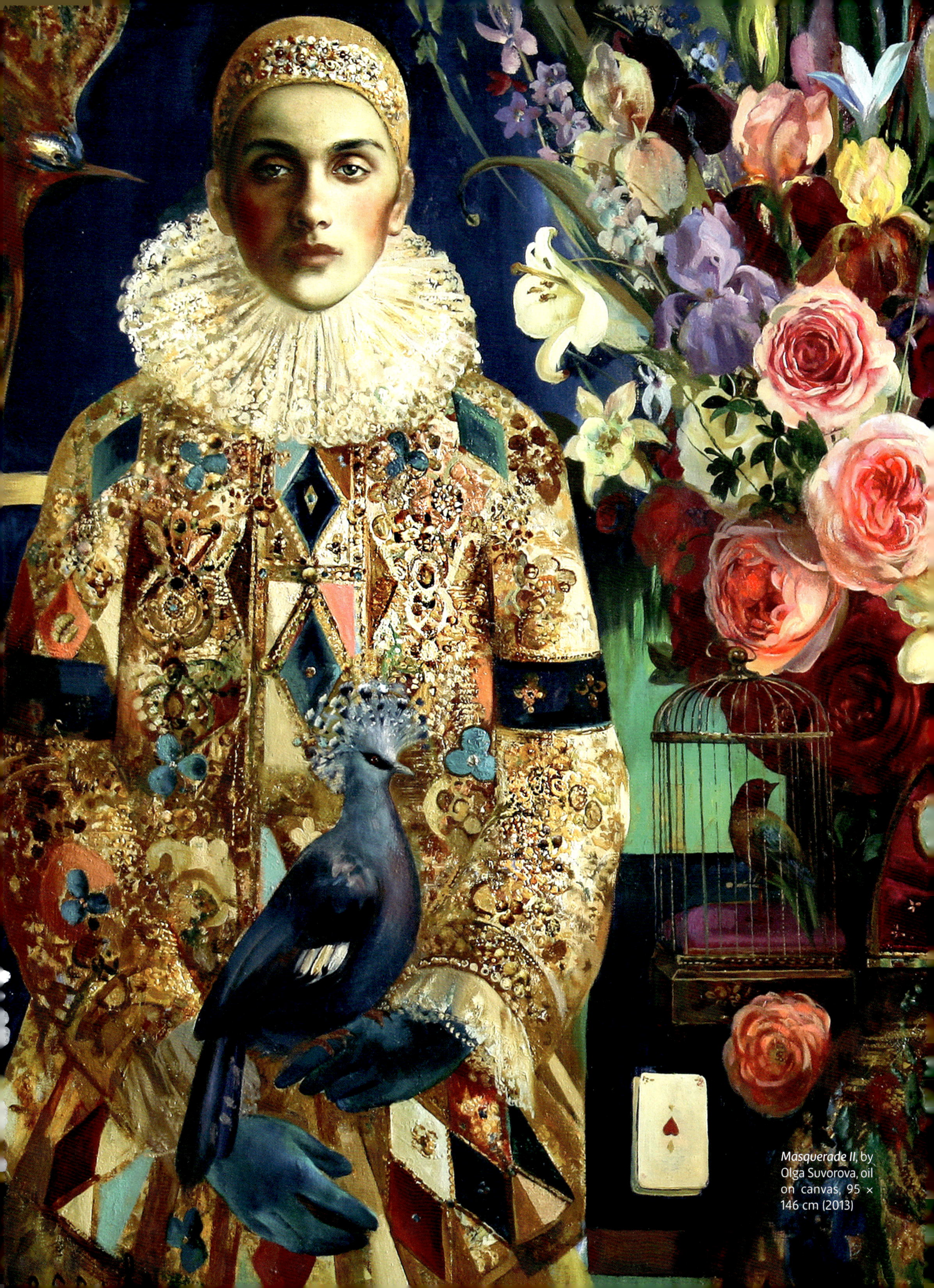

Masquerade II, by Olga Suvorova, oil on canvas, 95 × 146 cm (2013)

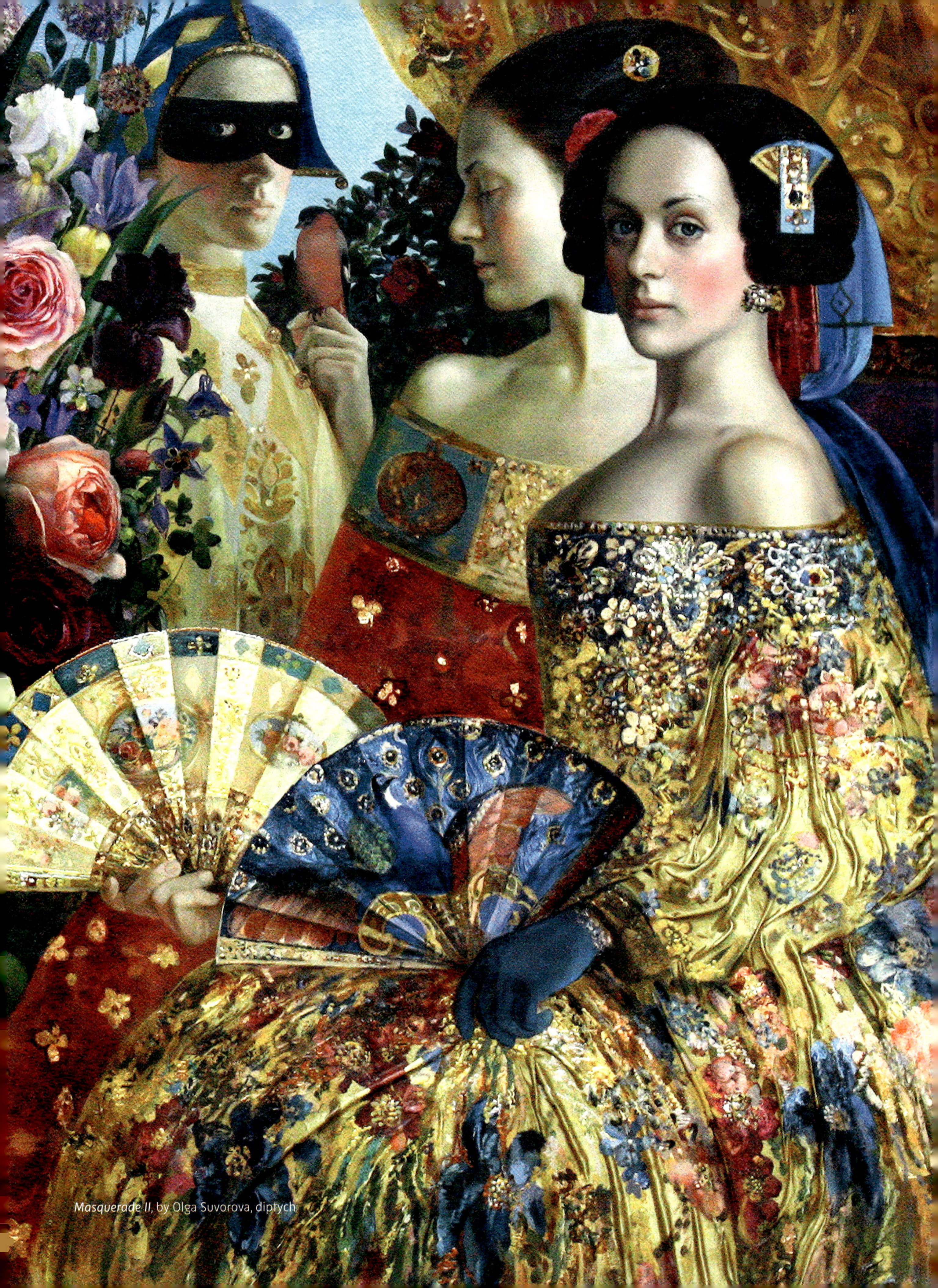

Masquerade II, by Olga Suvorova, diptych

Music & Dance

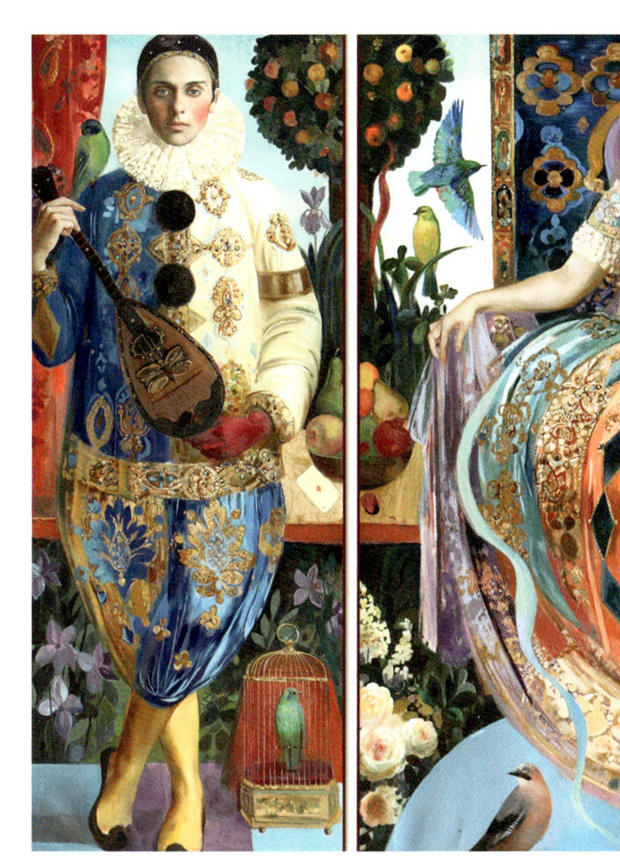
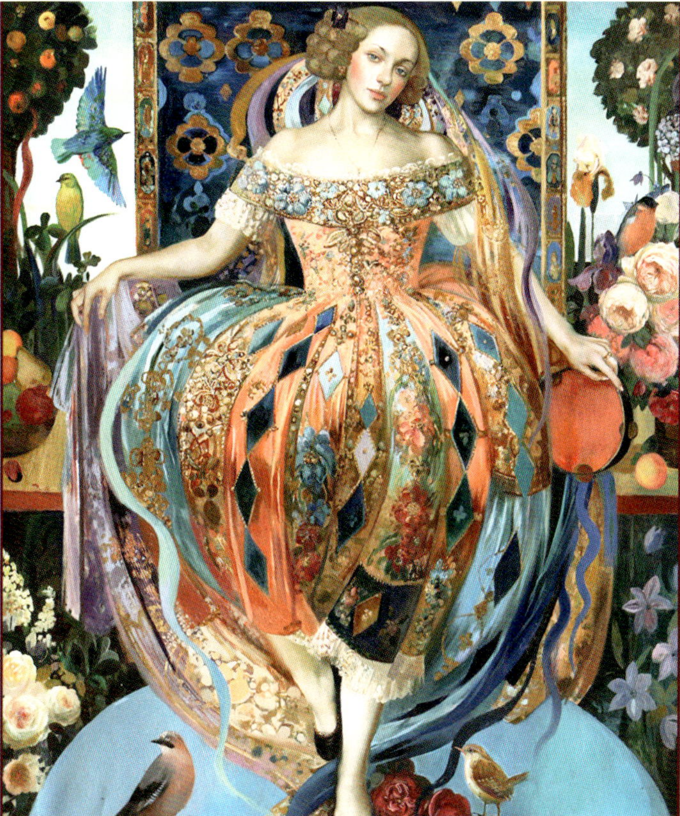
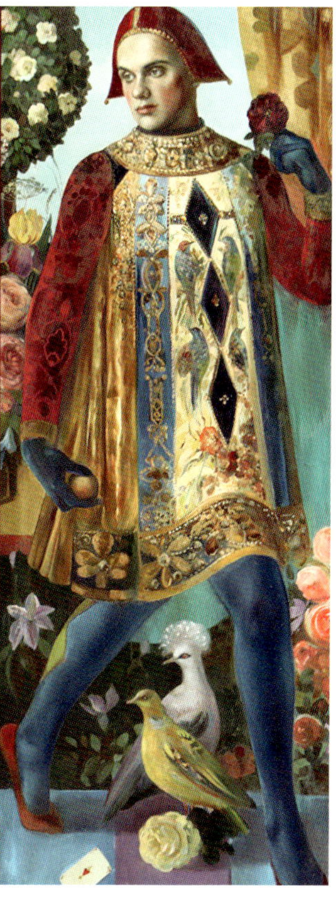

Dancer I, by Olga Suvorova, triptych, oil on canvas, 98 × 160 cm (2015)

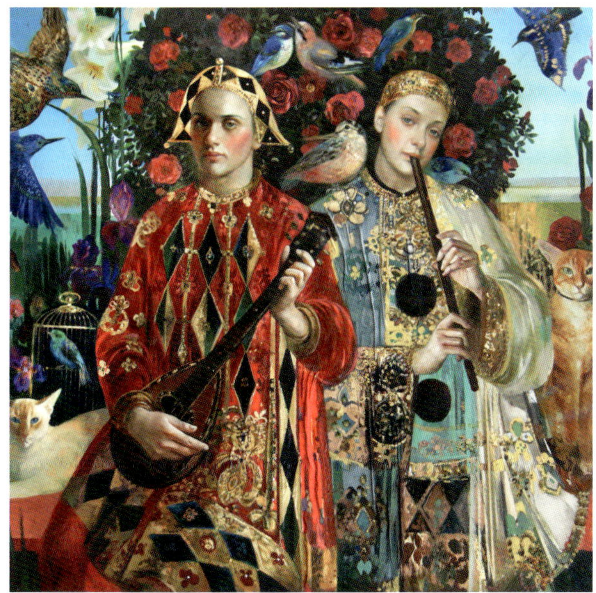

Spring I, by Olga Suvorova, oil on canvas, 110 × 115 cm (2012)

In a series of paintings devoted to music and dancing, I combined my love for the Pre-Raphaelite artists and the eighteenth-century rococo era. The Pre-Raphaelites taught me not just to create beautiful pictures, but how to animate the characters. I wanted each subject to have its inner life and fate, so that each figure could express a certain emotion. The Pre-Raphaelites strove for the ultimate naturalism. They painted only from nature, and the suffering of the artists' models (their roles were often played by friends and relatives) were commonplace. Everyone knows the sad story of how the English artist John Everett Millais painted his drowned *Ophelia*. After the painting was finished, the artist's model fell ill from posing, laying in a cold bath for hours. The artist had to pay for expensive treatment for the poor girl.

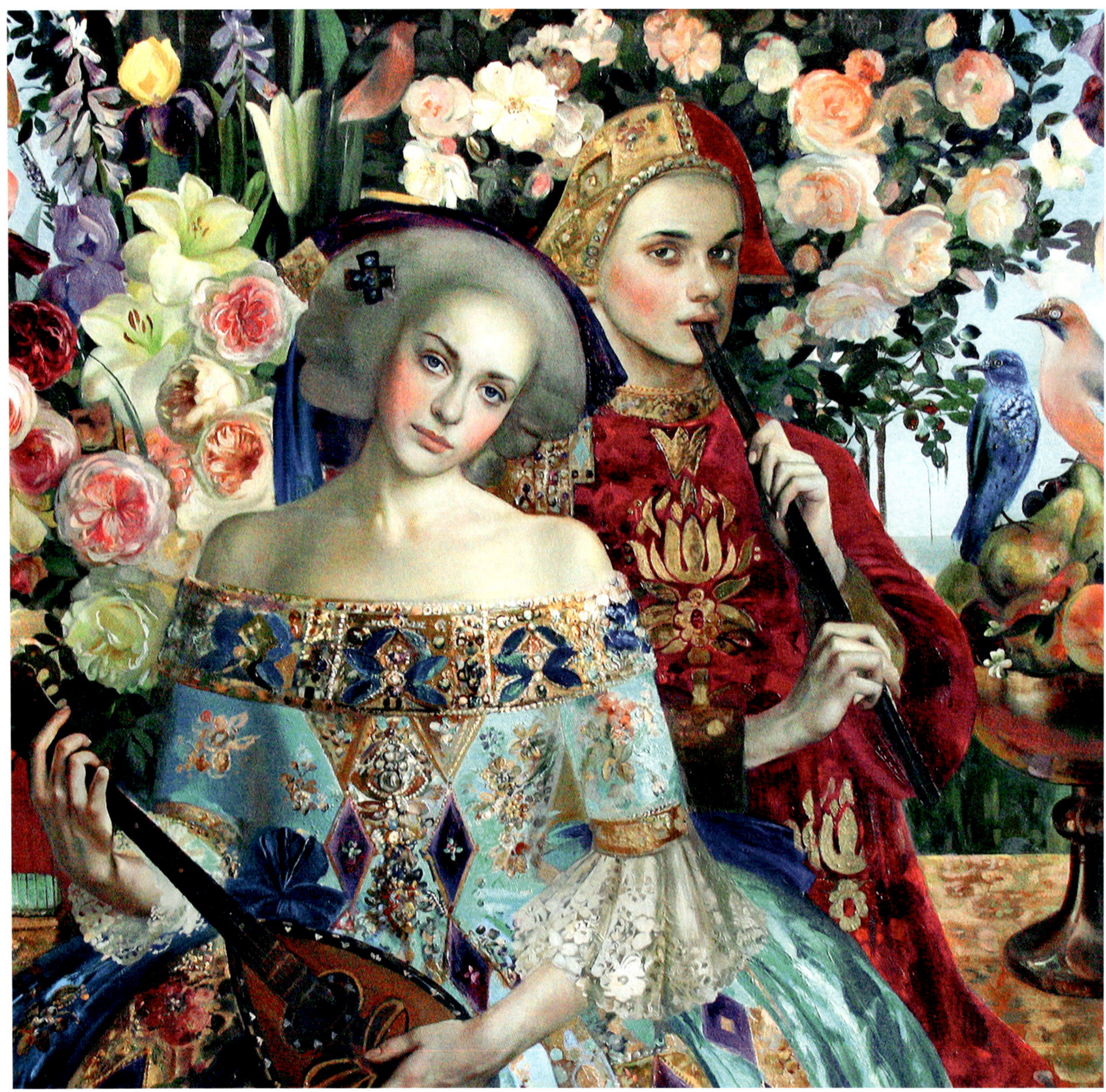

Spring II, by Olga Suvorova, oil on canvas, 125 × 130 cm (2015)

The English artists preferred story topics with a hidden drama, especially unrequited love. Today, these topics are of little interest. Our community looks differently at feelings between people. I do not seek to fully copy the Pre-Raphaelites, and it is impossible anyway. The level of their professional skills was very high, but they taught me to pay great attention to even the smallest details. Also, and with great pleasure, I execute sketches from nature for particular pictures. At the same time I am attracted to the rococo era. This style is considered feminine and aristocratic. The eighteenth century is regarded as the heyday of the rococo: hypertrophied and elaborate forms, deep necklines, metal corsets, skirts of incredible size, heels on which one could not stand without a special cane, white, blush, high hairstyles with jewelry and lace intertwined. Today, this fashion does not seem viable, but you can still meet elements of the rococo era in the modern wardrobe: lace trims, ribbons on the neck, and most importantly, floral print, which was popular on ball gowns of the eighteenth century. Fashion is cyclical not only in clothes but also

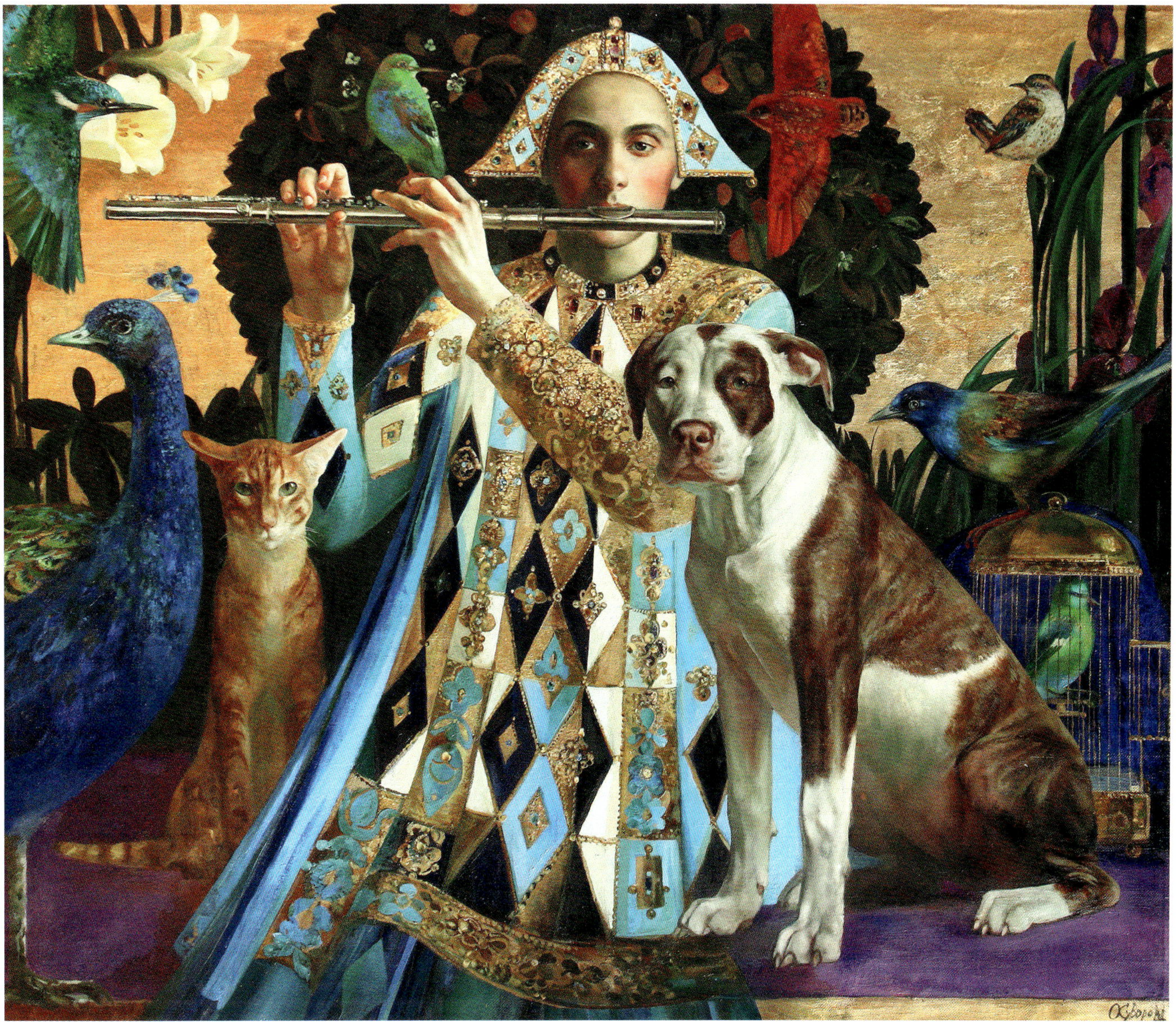

Clown, by Olga Suvorova, oil on canvas, 94 × 111 cm (2011)
Performance, by Olga Suvorova, oil on canvas, 140 × 95 cm (2017)

in many other spheres of our lives. I cannot stop admiring this era. Back then, any plain Jane in a lace ball dress looked attractive, because many figure shortcomings were hidden under the lush skirts.

At that time, it was traditional to arrange magnificent balls, take dance lessons, and have fun. Today, many filmmakers refer to this topic; for example, *Marie Antoinette*, the 2006 Sofia Coppola film about the life of

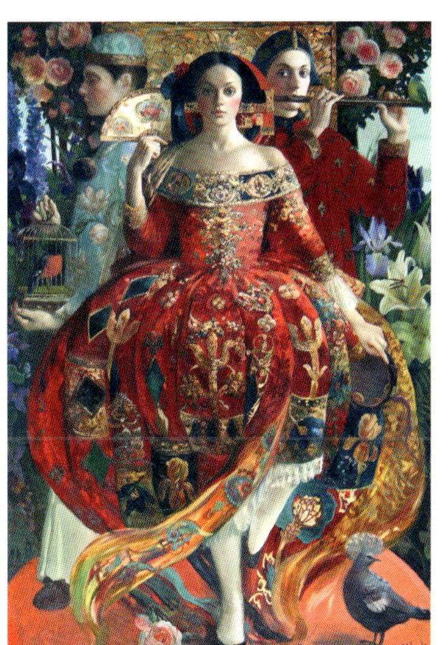

the infamous French queen. I'm no exception. I also want to bring this beauty and visual feast to my works.

I try not to miss any exhibition related to historical costumes. I recently visited an exhibition at the State Hermitage Museum that was dedicated to the famous artist-collector and couturier Mariano Fortuny. The famous Spaniard was known for his pleated dresses—Delphos—and printed fabrics, most often velvet, from which his pieces were made in medieval or ethnic styles. At first the velvet was painted in the necessary color, and then the picture was printed. Fortuny drew inspiration from Renaissance fabrics and paintings. Medieval ornaments are delightful. I often turn to ancient fabrics, wanting to transfer the beauty of silk or velvet to my pictures, and fill the entire space of the canvas with gold brocade and floral ornament. I want to display all the best that was created by the famous masters of past centuries in my paintings. The experience gained over many years of plein air practice helps a lot. I use garden motifs in my theatrical and decorative works. Watching the birds in my garden is of great interest to me. The most beautiful, in my opinion, are jays. They are also called the northern parrots, and I often portray this loud bird in my paintings. I like to depict Columbine dancing with her constant companions—Pierrot and Harlequin. These characters serve as a background for the main character in each picture. From painting to painting, my Columbine is reinvented. No longer a servant, she becomes more aristocratic; her clothes look more luxurious; her dress is overloaded with fragments and details, a mass of ribbons and laces. I put velvet gloves with gold embroidery on her hands. One thing remains unchanged—she has to choose between her two beloveds. Her movements are dynamic; the dress moves to the beat of her body. And perhaps, in this precise dance, she will finally make up her mind. Dance is thought to be one of the oldest arts. It reflects the human need to show one's feelings to others through one's body, which dates to the earliest times.

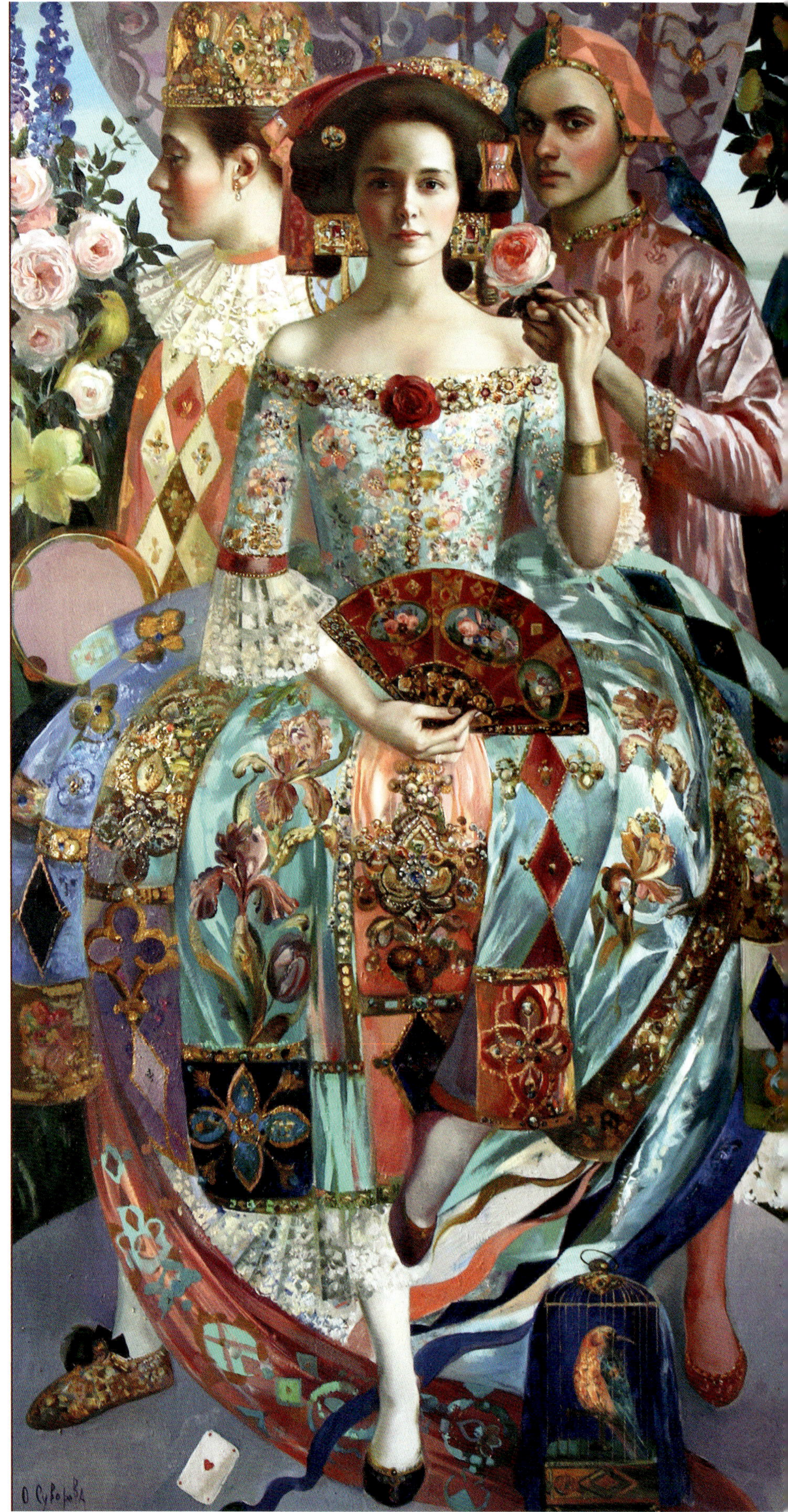

Columbine II, by Olga Suvorova, oil on canvas, 140 × 85 cm (2016)

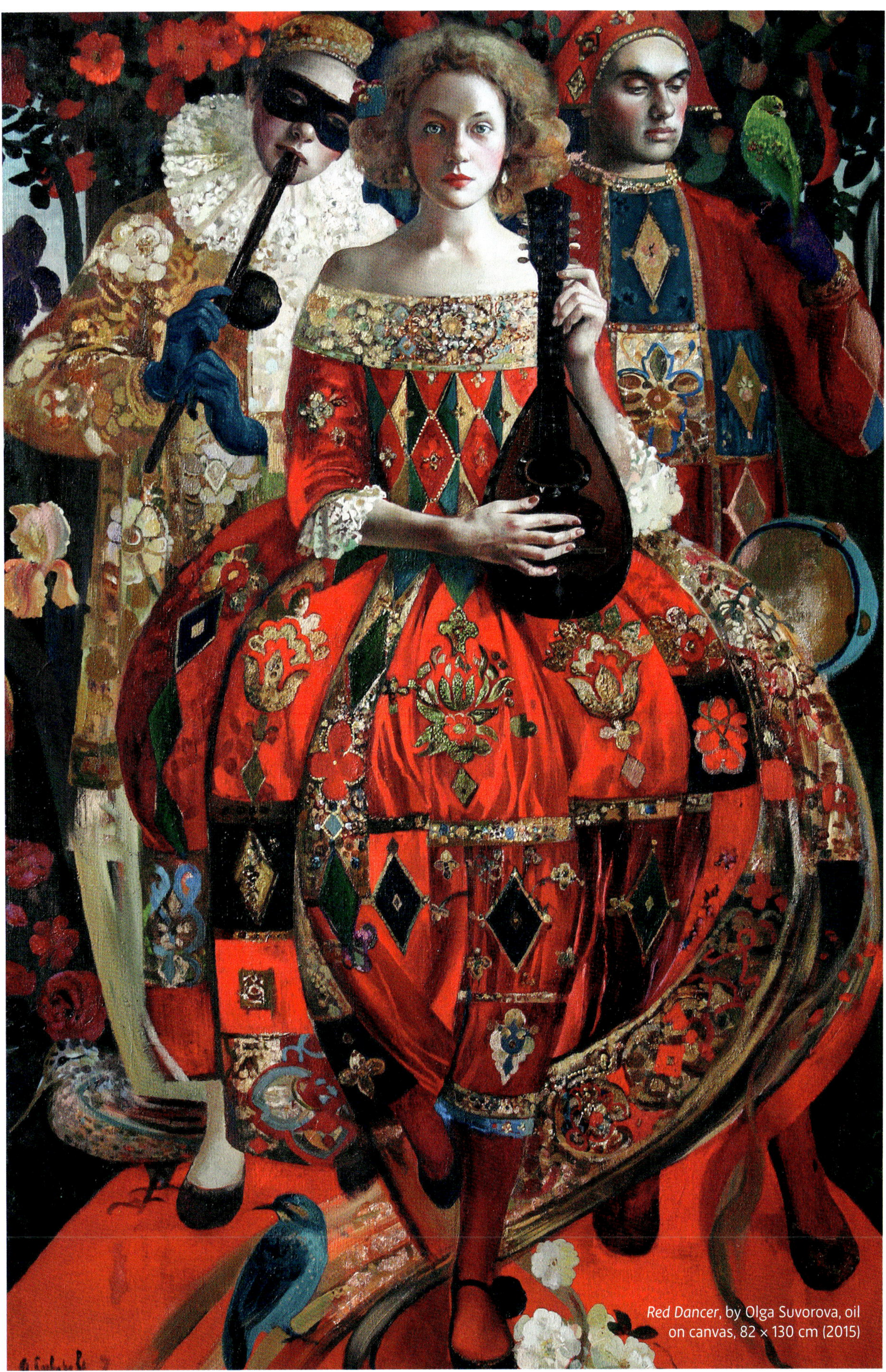

Red Dancer, by Olga Suvorova, oil on canvas, 82 × 130 cm (2015)

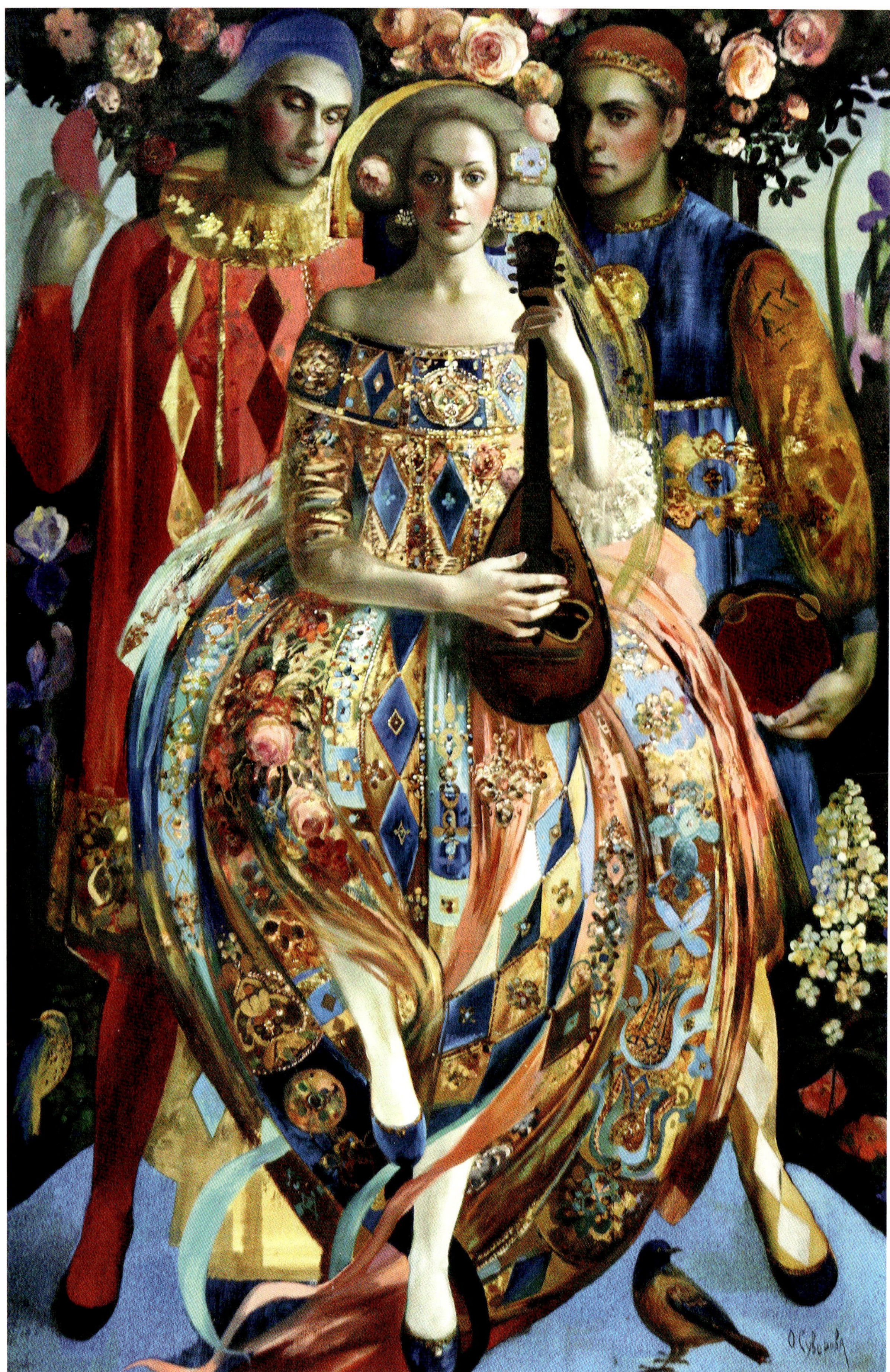

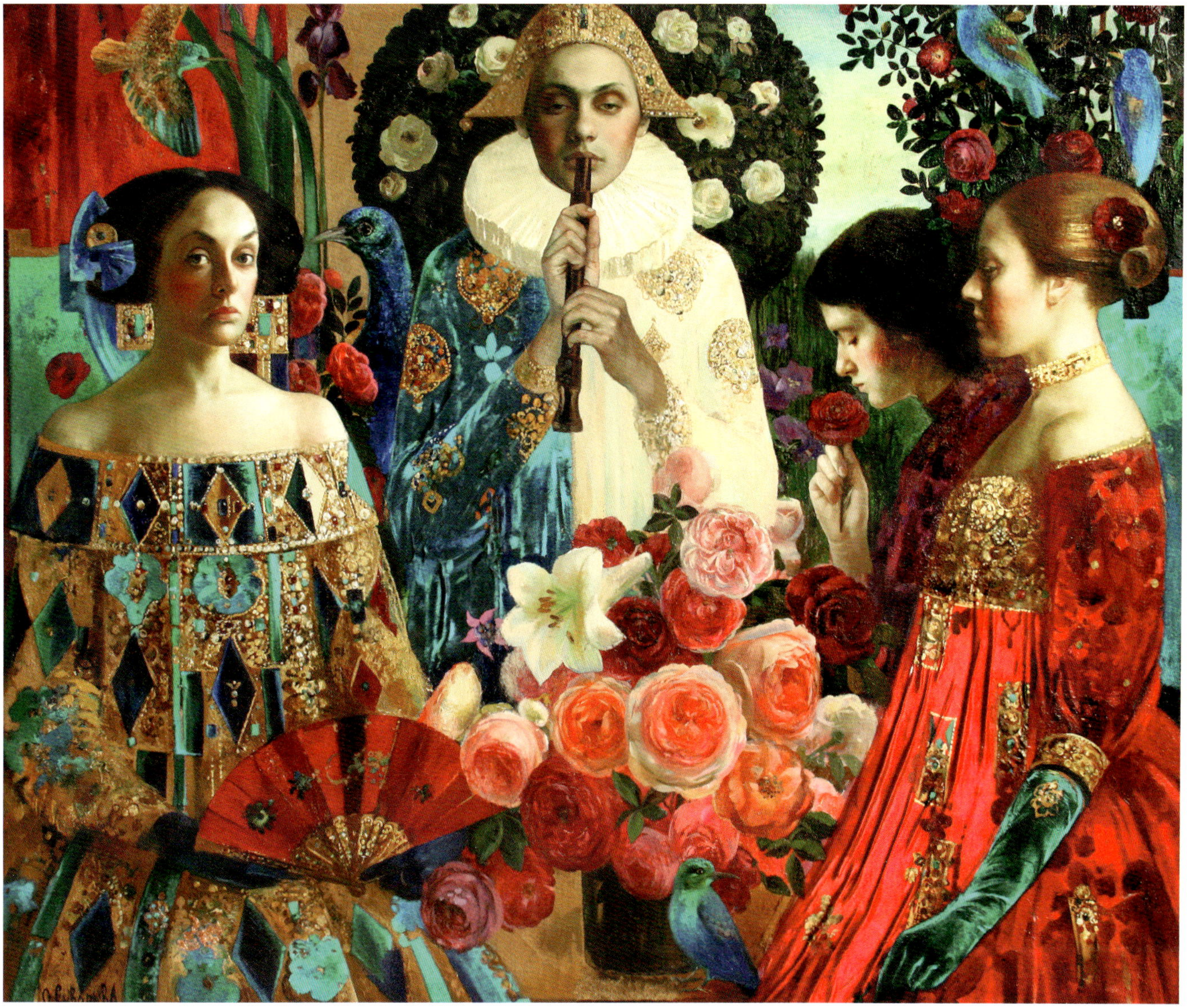

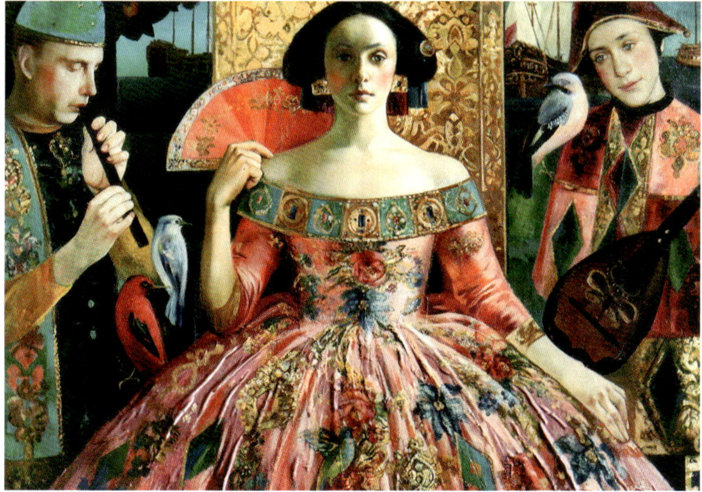

Melody I, by Olga Suvorova, oil on canvas, 111 × 132 cm (2010)

Music I, by Olga Suvorova, oil on canvas, 95 × 140 cm (2005)

OPPOSITE

Minuet, by Olga Suvorova, oil on canvas, 140 × 95 cm (2014)

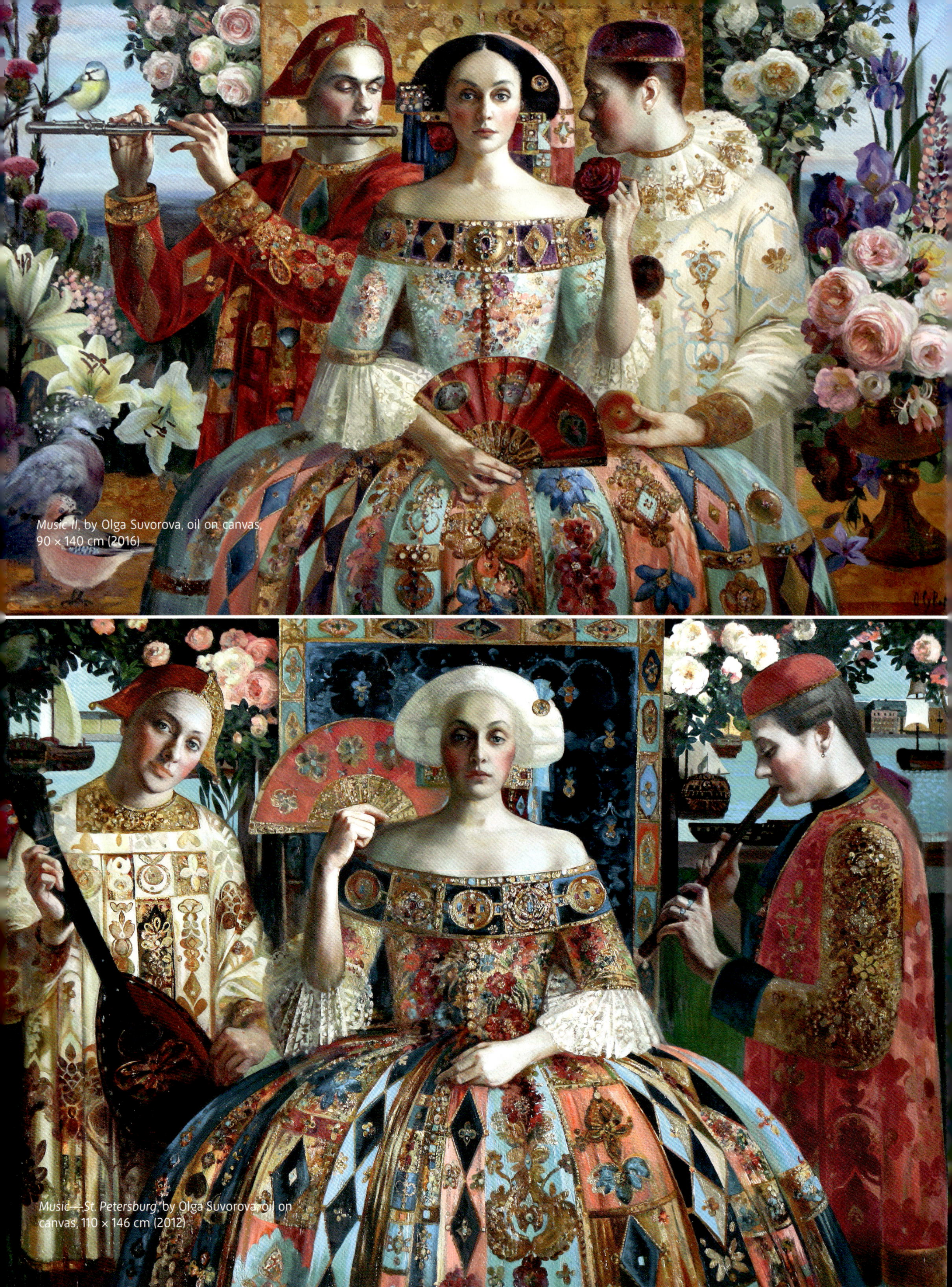

Music II, by Olga Suvorova, oil on canvas, 90 × 140 cm (2016)

Music—St. Petersburg, by Olga Suvorova, oil on canvas, 110 × 146 cm (2012)

Homage Rembrandt

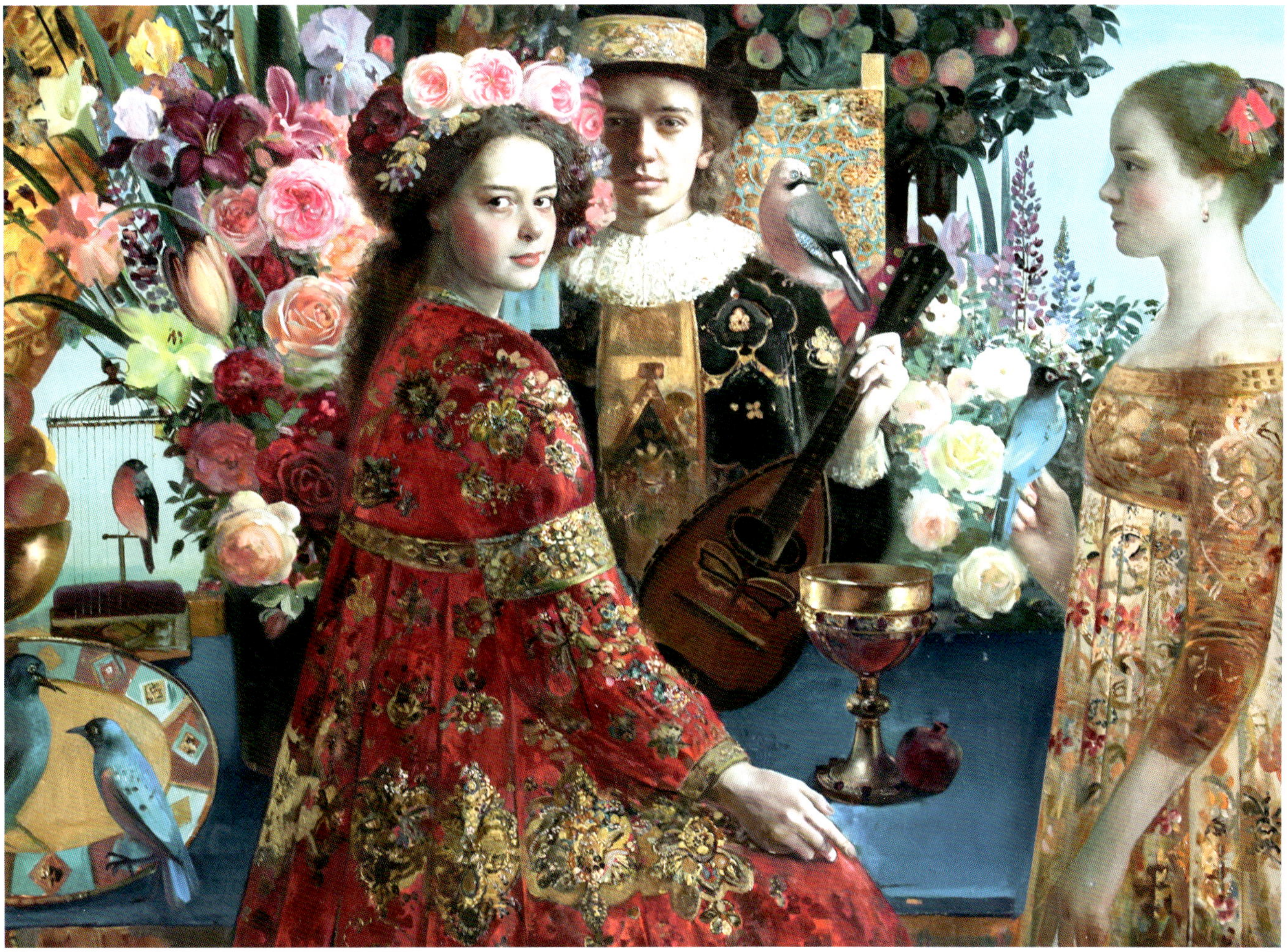

Rembrandt's Memory, by Olga Suvorova, oil on canvas, 95 × 135 cm (2014)

I go back to Rembrandt again and again in my works. He gave and still gives me many new ideas. So I paint one picture after another in his honor.

Changing the composition, supplementing it with new characters and symbols, I create my own unique interpretations of established plots. However, I am mostly interested in color variations. I was inspired to draw a version of the painting in *Rembrandt's Memory*. In this work, the main character, Flora, sits in a bright yellow velvet dress. I enhanced this composition with Harlequin playing the flute and, as I usually do, put some symbolic idea into the picture. In this context, the bird in the cage speaks for the female soul, which is not free in its actions. It is not able to escape from the "magic flute" captivity. The ginger cat is watching the bird and waiting in the wings for a chance to play with his victim. Perhaps this game will be the last for the bird.

The rich background of fruit and luxurious bouquets is just a screen that hides the true intentions of the flutist. This situation is reminiscent of an ancient Indian fakir, whose cobra, under the spell of the magical pipe music, forgets about its strength and venom and obediently moves to the beat of the dreamy melodies.

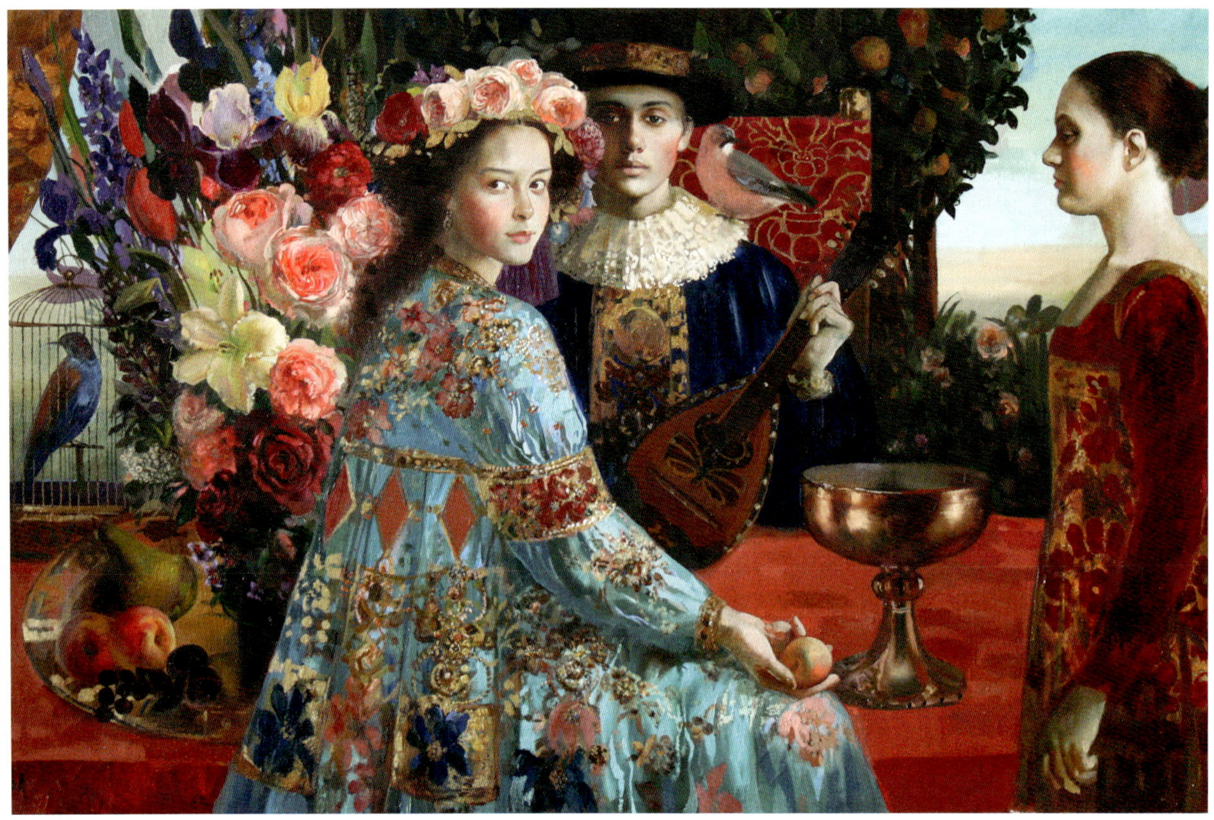

Dedication to Rembrandt, by Olga Suvorova, oil on canvas, 118 × 68 cm (2016)

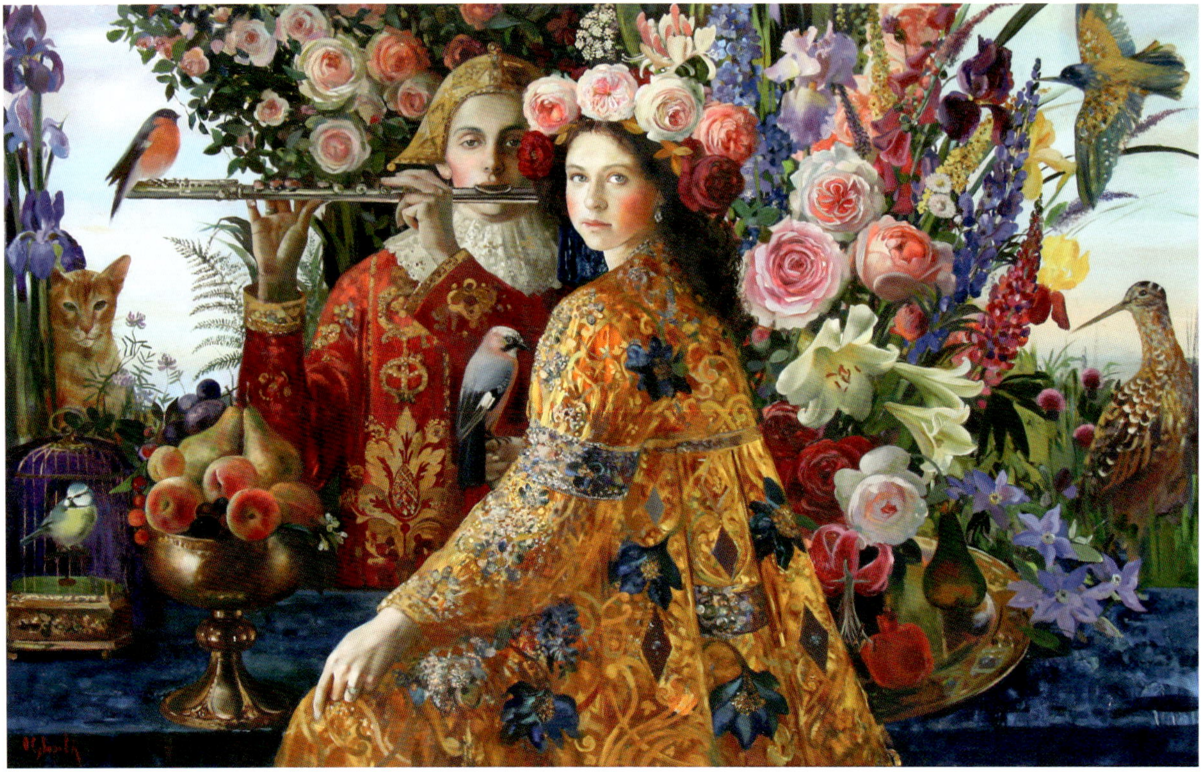

Melody II, by Olga Suvorova, oil on canvas, 90 × 138 cm (2017)

The faces of characters are brooding and aloof, everyone thinks their own thoughts and plans. Only Flora's gaze is directed at the viewer, as if asking: "What decision should I make?" But it's going to end well. She will be free from the magic flute hypnosis. A bird sitting on her hand indicates that.

Commission Works

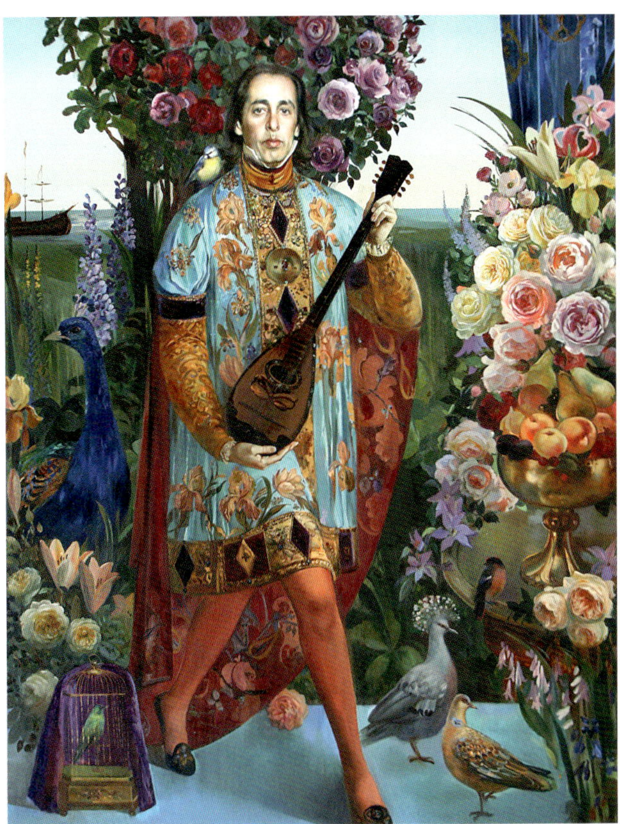

Family from United States Portrait, by Olga Suvorova, diptych, 150 × 110 and 150 × 130 cm (2017)

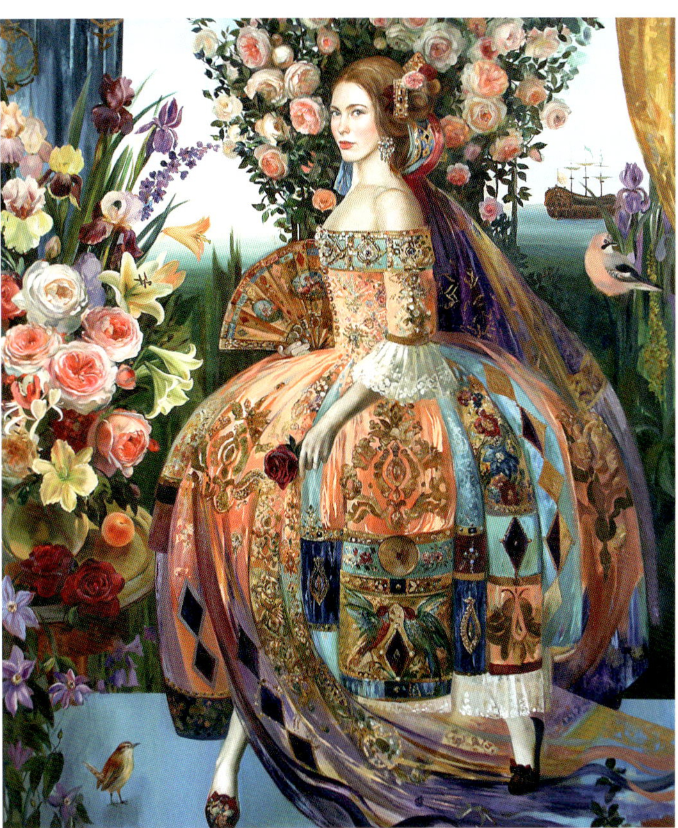

Family from United States Portrait, by Olga Suvorova, diptych

Once I had to complete an extremely difficult commission. The task was to place six characters on a huge canvas. I used my earlier picture called *Annunciation* as the basis of the composition. So, Madonna stands in the center, surrounded by angels on her right and left side. The customer wanted the image of Madonna to depict a mother with five children—four girls and an elder son. I really liked his idea, because the mother image accompanies us throughout life; it fills childhood with meaning and, after separating from her physically, children continue to receive her care and devotion.

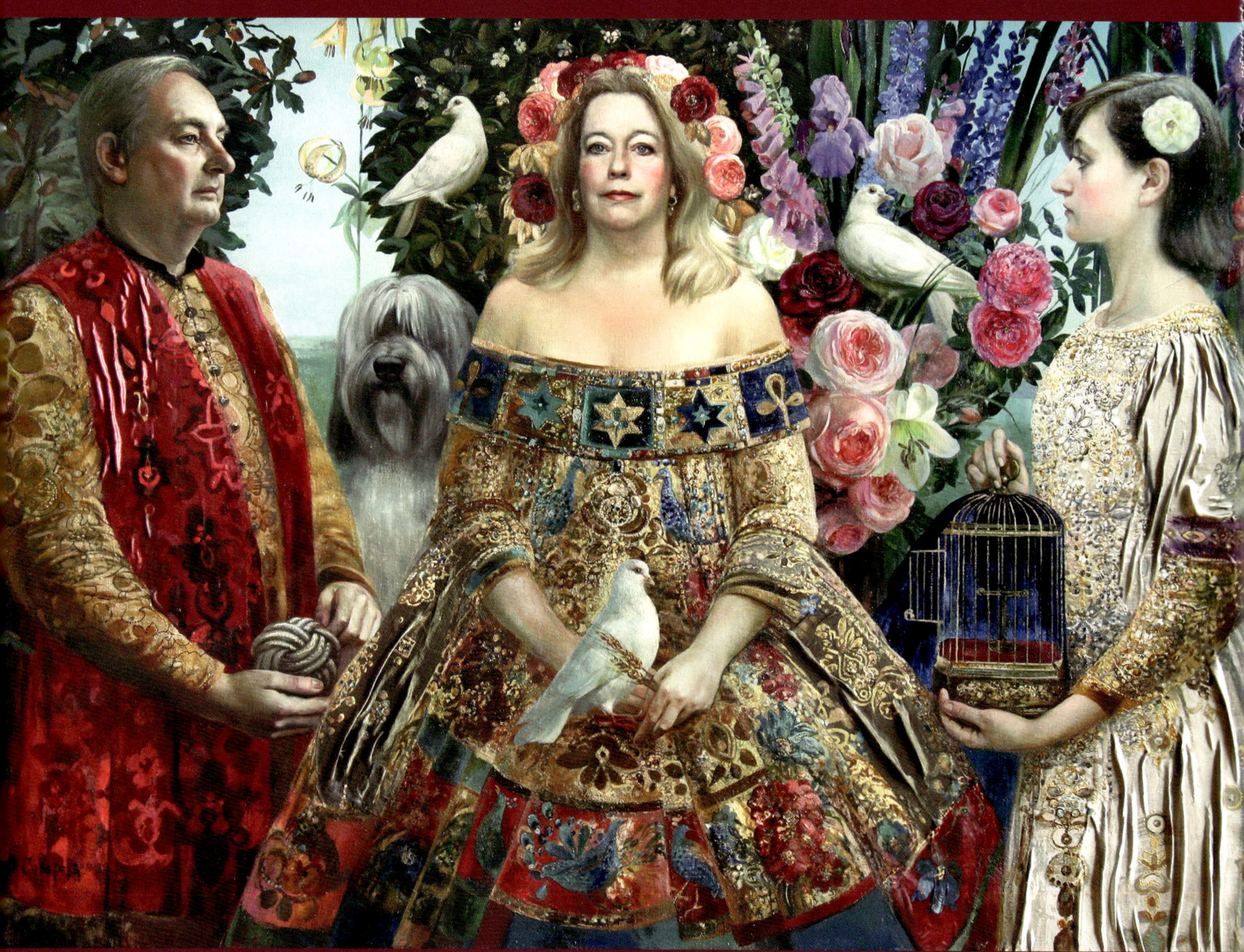

Family from Holland Portrait, by Olga Suvorova, 95 × 145 cm (2011)

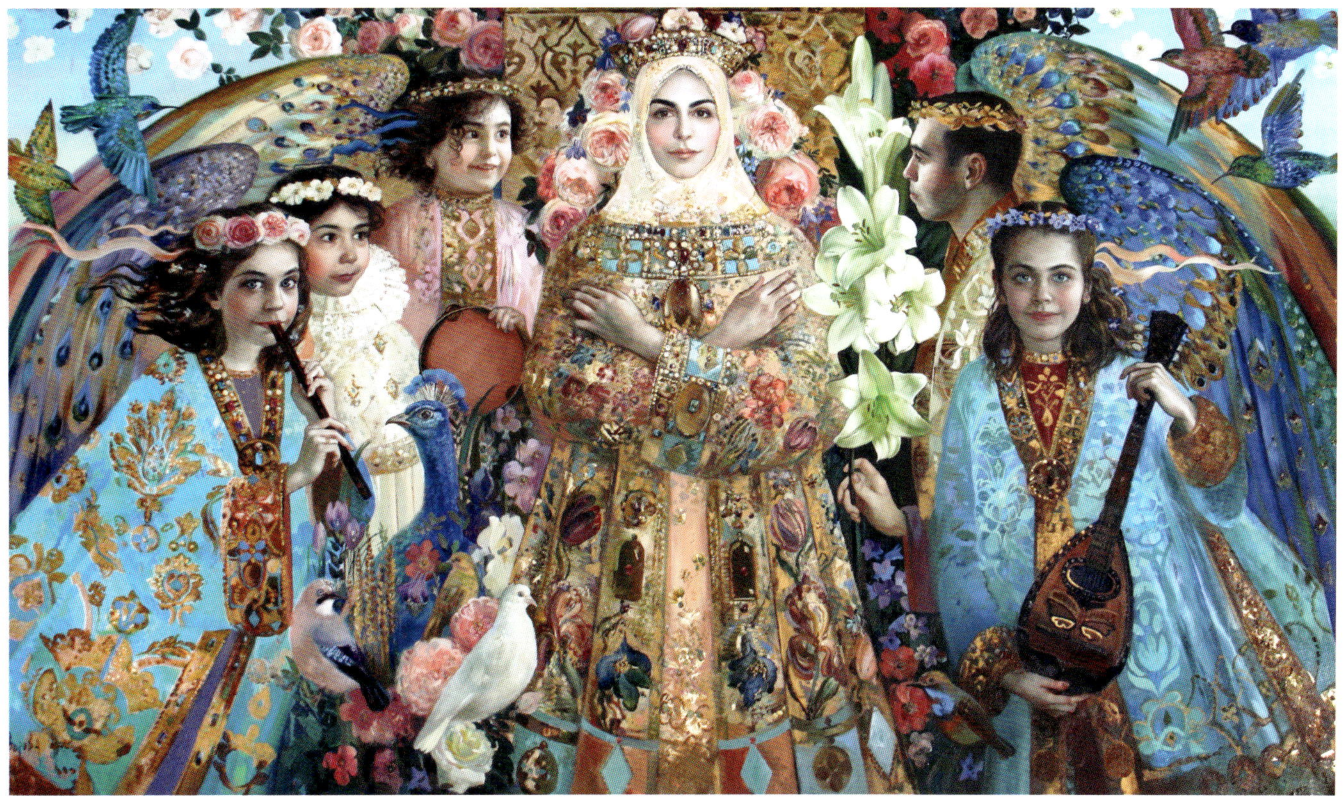

Family from Israel Portrait, by Olga Suvorova, 95 × 175 cm (2016)

I wanted to create an image of the universal mother, the nurse and protector, but also the portrait of a living person. Psychologists connect the mother concept with emotions, instinct, feelings, tenderness, and capriciousness.

I did a lot of sketches, trying to decide which kids were going to become the main characters and which would be secondary. The difficulty was that angels are asexual beings, and children, though similar to angels, are earthly beings. I needed to combine the images of angel and human. At the same time, I wanted it to look as natural and beautiful as possible, and, most importantly, for the children and their mother to be recognizable. I invented a wreath for each girl and directed the figures' movements to the center of the picture, so that all the children were grouped around their mother, a Madonna prototype. That was not easy, given the number of figures and the complexity of the composition and color solutions.

However, the most important thing for me was my customer's approval. This would mean that my hard work had achieved its purpose and I had completed my difficult task successfully. Which I did—this was my small art victory.

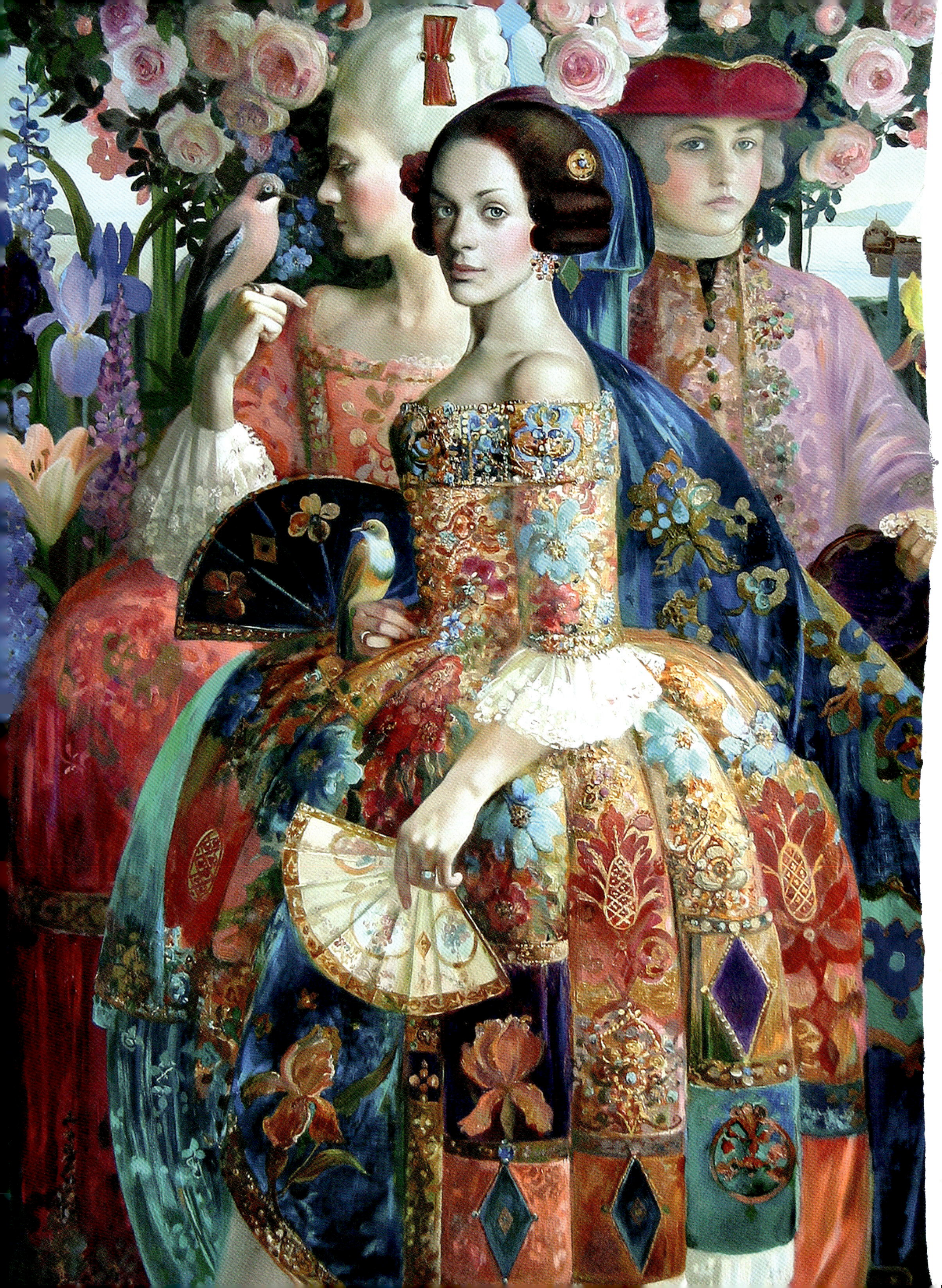

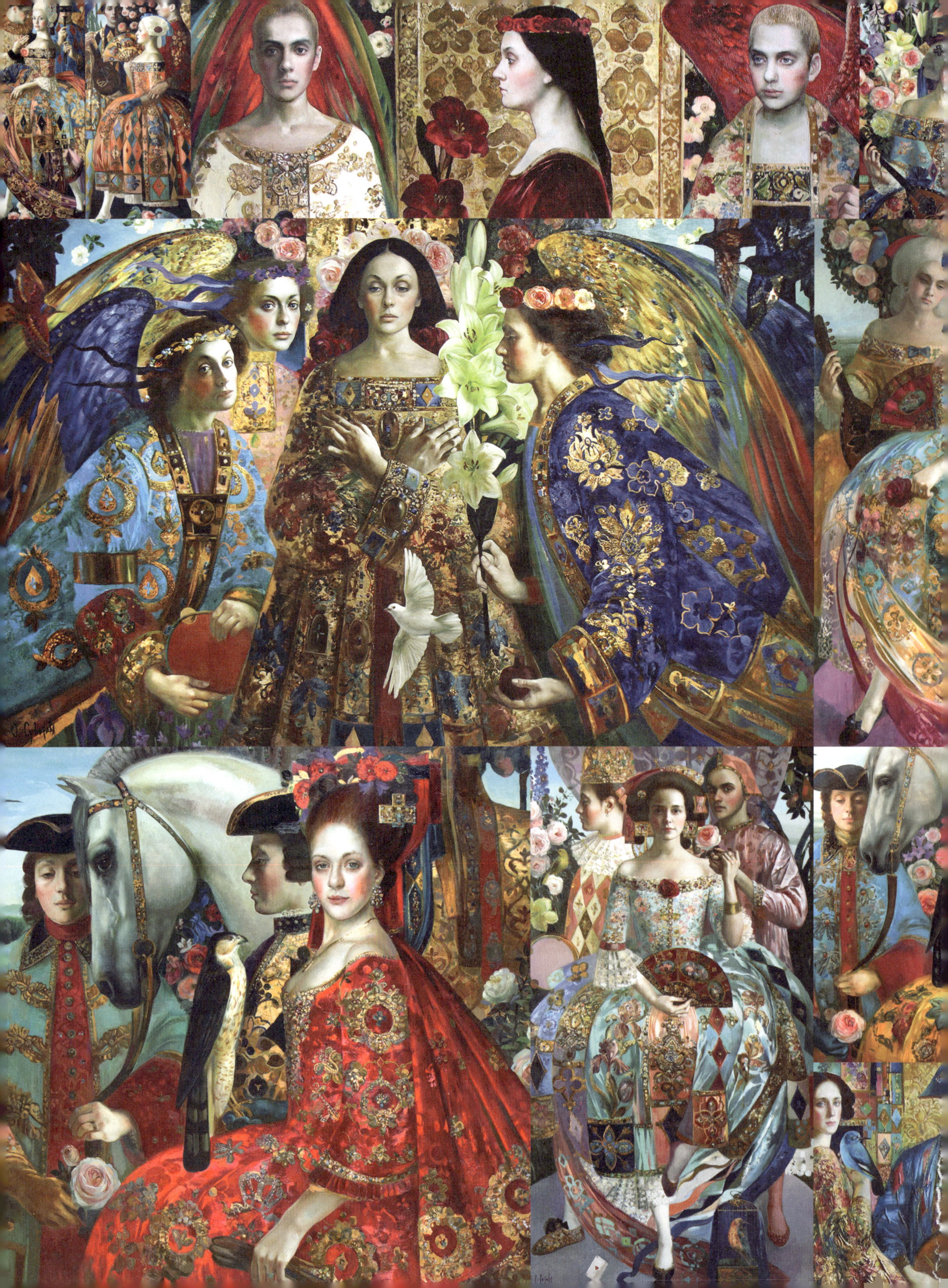